Loɛ

A f
part
ove

—

0
2

26

0

2 2

Once a Brother

An Irish Christian Brother's Story

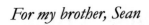

For my brother, Sean

Once a Brother

An Irish Christian Brother's Story

Patrick C. Power

Appletree Press

First published in 2008 by
Appletree Press Ltd
The Old Potato Station
14 Howard Street South
Belfast BT7 1AP

Tel: +44 (028) 90 24 30 74
Fax: +44 (028) 90 24 67 56
Email: reception@appletree.ie
Web: www.appletree.ie

Once A Brother: An Irish Christian Brother's Story

A catalogue record for this book is available from the British Library.

9 8 7 6 5 4 3 2 1

ISBN-13: 978-1-84758-087-0

Desk & Marketing Editor: Jean Brown
Copy-editing: Jim Black
Designer: Stuart Wilkinson
Production Manager: Paul McAvoy

9 8 7 6 5 4 3 2 1

AP3535

CONTENTS

One of Her Sons

And how do I explain why I became a member of the Irish Christian Brothers? First of all, my mother had determined that one of her sons, as least, should be a priest. My background was completely Catholic. In our native town of Dungarvan there were some Protestants but all others were Catholics, and the few Catholics who neglected going to Mass on Sunday were considered very odd.

At about the age of thirteen one day I read carefully what I had seen often over three years. This was an advertisement in *Our Boys*, the Christian Brothers' monthly magazine, asking boys of fourteen and older to join the Irish Christian Brothers. I had read the advertisement but now I decided that I was going to act on it.

That was in the early spring of 1942. I told the Superior of the monastery in Dungarvan, Brother Flatley, that I wished to become a Brother. Years later he told me how surprised he was. 'Postulants', as they called young lads who intended joining the Order, were recruited from the First and Second Year students in the Christian Brothers' Secondary Schools or the Sixth Standard in National Schools, but here was I wishing to join them without any hint as to where I received the idea.

I never said a word about the advertisement in *Our Boys*. I told nobody about how the notion swam into my mind because who was likely to believe me? I heard afterwards that most of the others were recruited by Br Markey, a small bald-headed man who visited the Christian Brothers' schools. He visited National Schools from which boys had joined the Brothers over the decades; schools whose pupils had met some of the Brothers from the area, who came home for a few days' holidays now and then.

The Two Colleges

The train, heavy with passengers and working on the worst of fuel, took ages to go to Dublin from Waterford city on 6th August 1942. There were twelve passengers in the carriage. A man alongside me talked about the war and the women complained about the scarcity of many items. The man took out a piece of yellowish stone.

"That, my boy," he announced, "is a scrap of TNT and it's a powerful explosive."

"What? Why do you have it, if it's so dangerous?"

"It's only dangerous if it's detonated by something else," he explained. A woman blessed herself.

"May the Blessed Trinity save and protect us from all harm!" she prayed. The man asked me where I was going. I was not going to college, he prompted.

"But that's where I'm going," I insisted. "I'm going off to be a monk!" I announced.

"A monk?" queried one of the women. Sure, you're a *gorsoon* from your mother's kitchen. How can you be a monk and you so young?"

I explained it, but he said "Well that beats the band, so it does. They must be hard up when they're taking the children." This surprised me.

The train left Waterford at 10.30am and reached Dublin after 3pm. As I left the train, a dapper Christian Brother with greying hair came to me.

"You must be Patrick," he remarked, "and I'm Brother John."

He was a man in his forties, who chatted with me as if he knew me always. I told him that I had nothing to eat since breakfast, and he smiled as he said, "You must be hungry then."

We took a tram to Amiens Street station and a train from there to Baldoyle. I asked about a few long one-storeyed concrete buildings by the street side.

"What are these houses without windows?"

He seemed to awaken from a reverie.

"They're built to house troublesome monkeys."

I saw a smile just stir and cross his face as he said this but he added, "Patrick, I was joking. These are air raid shelters to give safety in an air raid."

When we reached the college surrounded by a high wall, he left me with a Brother.

"I bet you're hungry!" he said as he gave me a meal of meat, potatoes and vegetables in a refectory where there were ten long tables. The Brother sat nearby. I noticed that he had no cincture around his waist.

"Why don't you wear the cincture?" I asked and he smiled a little.

"I'm a lay-Brother and none of us wears it. We're the labourers elsewhere and the kitchen staff here. Brainy lads like you become teachers, but not us."

After the meal I met the Superior, Joachim Kelly, who seemed to demand and receive obedience. He asked me to hand over the wristwatch and the money I had, and noted the details in a ledger.

Kelly, who wore a black biretta, spoke to me about the college.

"You're an aspirant to our Congregation," he began, "and not just an ordinary student. God has chosen you to serve him in religion." Kelly paused as he held me in his sight through his steel-rimmed spectacles. "Serious disobedience to rules and orders is punished with instant expulsion."

Kelly led me to the study where the boys were reading and he opened the door of a large room, where I saw about eighty boys sitting at desks. Kelly then announced my name in a loud voice.

They all stood up cheering and many rushed from their desks towards me. My hands were wrung; I was clapped on the back and the welcome pleased me very much. Another monk wearing spectacles with dark lenses left his desk and came to me.

"Hello!" said he to me. "You're welcome."

He turned to the boys and snapped, "Back to your desks, boys!" There was silence as everyone slunk away and he turned to me with the words, "Get a book over there on one of these shelves."

When I returned with Rider Haggard's *King Solomon's Mines*, a lad whispered, "Pretend that you're reading or old Black-Eye will have a fit!"

Our supervisor Black-Eye had poor sight but his hearing was keen. When my informant whispered, "Old Black-Eye is as blind..." the supervisor heard him and snapped.

"Listen to me all of you!"

There was a rustling of pages and silence as we sat up and looked at him.

"You're here to read but there is very little reading going on as far as I can see." He paused for a moment. "We must have total silence! I insist on it. We don't want..."

"...*you either*," a whisperer concluded for him.

"Who whispered?" The supervisor shouted in rage. "Stand up!"

No one did.

"Sir, it's time for a walk!" someone said.

Before the supervisor lost his temper, the Superior walked in and we were soon on our way out. I was told we were going for an hour's walk before evening prayer. I was given a college boy's little peaked cap with an emblem above a short visor. From this time onwards I knew the whispering lad as 'Whisperer'. Before teatime we formed two groups and walked as we said the Rosary aloud in the garden; one group said the first part of each prayer while the other one responded as we walked under the apple trees.

We had the evening meal in the refectory, where bread was rationed and each four shared a portion of butter and a loaf of bread. We divided the loaf in four portions and when we left the table nothing remained of it or the butter.

"Where are you from, Patrick?" asked Charley who sat alongside me at table.

"From Dungarvan!"

"My father was robbed in Dungarvan one evening. Did one of you people do it?"

I was embarrassed. Another lad, Fred from Dublin, joined in.

"Don't mind that Charley fellow. He doesn't know where on earth Dungarvan is and must be tormenting someone, and his father isn't a farmer and neither is he."

The fourth of our table group, Dan Doyle from Wexford, smiled across at me.

"If you're sensitive, you'll have everyone like Charley teasing you."

Charley was already a year in St Joseph's, where he was two years studying for the Intermediate Certificate. I finished first year at home, so my term here was just a year.

Shortening study course times was typical of the Christian Brothers, who did not join the National School System until 1926, which was the State system since 1831. The government limited the Intermediate Certificate Course for students in Baldoyle to two years and the Leaving Certificate in Bray to one year.

After tea we had recreation for half an hour in the study sitting around talking, and then night prayers in the chapel before we went to bed at ten o'clock. At that time of year it was daylight as we traipsed off to our beds. Each one slept in one of the small cubicles at both sides of each dormitory and stored his clothes in a tiny wardrobe. Every cubicle had an iron stand for a basin of water, some soap and a towel. Over the bed was a crucifix. Wooden partitions separated the cubicles and an outside heavy curtain gave privacy at night and was pulled back during the day.

When I went to bed that first night, I fell asleep quickly because I was exhausted. It was the first time I slept in a house other than my parents' or my aunt's. Life in Baldoyle was ceaseless activity, so I slept like a log during that and every night.

On the second afternoon during the Rosary I felt alone for the first time. Who were those boys with Rosary beads dangling from their fingers? I wished to jump over the high wall and run home. Why must I be a sacrificial lamb cut off from my kin? The five years before I could visit home again stretched far ahead of me.

Ten boys arrived from Cork and their singsong voices filled the air and the field as they shot the hurling ball through the air. One lad could not accept being parted from home, and Kelly addressed us as we settled down to read later on the second evening.

"One of the ten Cork boys is missing. Does anyone know anything about him?"

There was no response.

"I want the nine Cork boys to come out to my office at once!"

We heard that the boy slipped out through the kitchen and the Gardaí were informed. He bought a ticket for Cork at the station with money which he had kept from Kelly. When he bought the ticket, a Garda saw him, took him aside and he was sent home officially later.

All letters were opened before we received them, because the Superior censored all our correspondence. We wrote to our parents monthly – each letter, which I handed up in an open envelope, might be read. I watched what I wrote: letters to parents were probably not read but who could be sure of that?

Our Lords and Masters

Kelly, a domineering type, introduced Br Denis O'Donnell, who replaced him as Superior. Kelly was a burly fellow but O'Donnell was thoughtful looking. His face developed a black sheen through the day so we knew him as 'Black Jack'.

Our companions played games and spoke incessantly about them, so their highest point of the day was the hour spent on the playing pitch. They togged out in their cubicles and in the boot room where shoes were exchanged for boots and the hurlers collected their sticks. I hated the query, "All boys love games, so why don't you?"

Whisperer loved hurling. Once I saw him trip a lad, who chased him before the referee ordered them into the study. That evening Whisperer was whining *sotto voce*:

"Dear mammy, the bold boy tried to brain me with a hurley!"

Some sniggered but someone whispered angrily, "Give us a breeze, you! You're a pest!"

In St Joseph's no female was employed, and segregation from women except visiting relatives was the rule. Centuries of church experience was used to train us to celibacy, so I never knew how wary of women I was until I left the Brothers years later. No woman worked in the college. The lay Brothers cooked the meals but we did the college housework. Each boy had a daily job to do, which was his 'charge' and I wonder how clean we kept the college, but no woman touched it.

My charge was to sweep the oratory every second morning and dust the seats, and on other days the windowsills. Once a week I changed the flowers on the altar but as I had no flower-arranging skills, I was given another chore after some weeks.

Four times in that year I met my mother's cousin, who visited me alone, but once she brought her niece. I felt secure with the older woman but my other relative, who was rather pretty, embarrassed me. I had a feeling that the older woman disapproved of my career but she never said so. She approved of my decision to leave many years later, but worried lest my mother and aunt felt that she encouraged me to leave and blamed her for it.

The Bullies

Br Denis, our Superior, took it for granted that we were well intentioned but never knew that some were bullies. One fellow tormented my friend Fred, and he tripped him on two occasions on the corridor. After a third attempt, Fred punched him in the face but a Brother came on them and reported Fred's violence, which was a serious matter, as we discovered.

Br Denis reprimanded Fred and after a few days he humiliated him according to the Rules. On Sunday Fred ate his breakfast kneeling at his chair in front of me at table and I realised how very unfair it all was.

That evening we assembled in the chapel. Fred went to the altar and on his knees read an apology, "I admit that I did wrong and caused a scandal and I beg your pardon for what I have done. I promise never to act again in this manner."

Denis seemed upset too.

"You may now return to your seat," he said, "and I hope that this is the last time that I punish any of you in this manner."

I saw a fight between two bullies in the boot room after a match which no one reported. The loser's nose was bleeding, it was said, because he slipped on the floor. Bullying was a part of life in Baldoyle and this was the unhappiest year in my life. Charley and others like him snatched more of the butter and rationed foods than their due, and preyed on the rest of us. My other friend Dan was a cooler fellow, who laughed at the bullies. Fred, Dan and I were close friends. We did not play games and they nicknamed us the Holy Family, hardly a compliment in a male society.

Across the road from St Joseph's was St Patrick's, which was for retired and ill Christian Brothers. We were sent there to have a cut bandaged or if we were sick. I remember Sister Judy the matron, who had heavy black spectacles hanging on the end of her nose. Her face and lips were thin and she was the only woman in St Patrick's, but was no temptation to anyone to escape from the trial of celibacy. When we went for Judy's medical attention she applied iodine, with comments on the patient.

"There you are, boy, wincing at a slight pain. How would it be if you had the pains that some of the old men have?"

None of us answered her jibes – nor was it advisable. Charley's comment was a story that he told under his breath.

"There was a nurse like Judy in a hospital at home, where a man's dislocated shoulder was put back after five days.

'Shame on you for yelling!' she spat at him. 'A woman had twins last night and she never yelled.' As he recovered his breath, said he 'If you try to put the two of them back into her after five days, *then* you'll hear her screaming!'"

One of her charges was the eighty-year-old Br Lysaght. He longed to train a choir even for three half-hours a week, and volunteered to teach us choir singing for Christmas. His first class was most disorderly. Whisperer enjoyed it.

"Does anyone know who Palestrina was?" queried Lysaght.

"No, sir!" some of us chorused in unison.

"Katherina from the Palace!" said the Whisperer helpfully in a stage whisper.

"Who said anything about a palace?" asked Lysaght.

"We went to The Palace to see cowboy films," helped the Whisperer happily.

Waves of laughter greeted this, and then came a remark about Lysaght being like a retired saloonkeeper.

"Look at his red whiskey nose!" we were advised.

Laughter broke out but Br John walked in and laughter froze into silence.

"Here is the Lord Chief Executioner!" muttered Whisperer but our merriment ended.

From disliking Baldoyle, I grew to hate it. I was in 3B Standard, which met in a classroom on the third storey of the college, from where I could see Lambay Island and Howth. One day a German fighter plane swept in and was greeted by anti-aircraft shots from Howth. It swooped over the college and roared back to sea.

The principal difference between St Joseph's and an Irish Secondary School was the absence of corporal punishment because we were becoming Christian Brothers. However, Reverend Cal from West Cork, teacher of Mathematics, physically punished us; for a mistake you got a punch behind a shoulder blade.

"See, you," he often snarled at me, "you don't even know your tables, and you're trying to do the Inter. Cert. Exam [Intermediate Certificate].

We have the fools of the country here nowadays!"

The punches that he threw at Charley did not land on him, because he ducked out of range or dodged under the desk. I thought that I was immune to such punishment because I was joining a religious Order, but how wrongly I had thought!

Cal loved Gaelic football and hurling, and after All Ireland Finals he drank mainly bottled Guinness in a parlour.

"The smell of booze in that room," said Fred, "would nearly smother you!" Of course, O'Donnell, John or Kelly never took any alcoholic drink.

Christmas brought us a respite from classes. We had midnight Mass on Christmas Eve and sang carols and hymns, which Lysaght taught us. One of the Brothers played the organ, which a big lad from County Kildare had to pump manually.

The Superior gave us his Christmas morning talk from the back of the chapel.

"If you were born in a palace, you'd be a rich man but Christ was born in a stable," he said. "Imagine now, if he was born on the roadside, people might say he is nothing but a tinker! That's what people forget about Christmas," he continued. "God became man as a member of the poorest of families!"

Most of us were thinking of the food being prepared for the tables.

I had forgotten how I felt until lately, when I found a letter that I wrote to an aunt near Cappoquin, whose house was a refuge from my father's strict discipline. She sent me apples in November, so I thanked her in a Christmas letter.

'It will be a lonely Christmas because home is the only place to be at that time,' I wrote. I enquired after a boy who had TB. 'I always pray for him and if it is God's will, he will finally recover.' What a different person I was then!

Sausages and black puddings appeared at breakfast, which we had not eaten since August. The bullies took most of the extra food and left scraps of black pudding for the rest of us. Boys who had already spent the previous year there simply said, "They wouldn't do that, if Kelly was the boss! He'd know and deal with them!"

Pious Living

I think over the pious expressions which my mother and women used, but which I never heard a man say before Denis said them. In the churches women formed the majority, though none was deemed fit to be a priest. Piety was feminine but authority in the Catholic Church was in men's hands, as it was always and still is.

The chief piety promoted in the Christian Brothers was devotion to the Virgin Mary, and in her honour we said two Rosaries daily. In all the images of her, that I saw, she was and still is depicted as a woman without a Semitic appearance, although she was a Jewess.

Our chaplains, the Holy Ghost Fathers, promoted devotion to the Virgin Mary, and Revd Fahy published an anti-Semitic news sheet during the war. He seemed to forget that Christ's mother and the first Christians were Jews, and its object seems to have been to promote Christian anti-Semitism. Revd Fahy's news sheet was entitled *Maria Duce*, which means led by Mary. In every issue there were references to the alleged Marxist-Judaic conspiracy, which caused the World War with the support of the USA and the USSR, he said. The newssheet was pro-German and Nazis fought the "Marxist-Judaic conspiracy", as Revd Fahy put it. Even in my naïveté I suspected then that his opinions were odd. The little *Maria Duce* periodical was the only newspaper, magazine or periodical, which we were allowed to read at St Joseph's. As often as I think of it, I still cannot understand why this particular item was ever circulated among us.

Every afternoon we did religious books and lives of the saints which were all fifty years old and more. No one thought of buying modern books. Denis advised us to read the Gospels daily in a Douai version of the New Testament. I had never read hitherto nor even seen a copy of the New Testament. I decided to read Matthew's gospel and was surprised at what I found. I discovered that Christ had brothers, and this set me thinking about his mother whom we called the Virgin Mary. If he had brothers, I thought, she certainly was not a virgin, whatever about Christ's conception by the Holy Ghost. I kept that thought to myself. I read a note in Matthew's gospel, which stated that the word 'brothers' did not mean blood-brothers, but I forget how that was explained so that it agreed with the official Catholic teaching. By the way, there was nobody reading it with us and explaining anything, which surprises me as I look back. They probably thought that we did not have any queries on the Scripture.

About twenty-two of the hundred and twenty in the college had left to go home by the end of November, and two were expelled for some reason or other. By the summer up to thirty had gone and some later joined the RAF or the British Army, pretending that they were older than they were.

With the month of June came the Intermediate Certificate Examinations. I was no longer as homesick as I was at first, although the whistling of the trains going into Dublin made me long sometimes to go home to Dungarvan. During and after the examinations we had peace from the bullies. There were days when we could read or play football or practise for the sporting competitions, which were to be held in the first week of July. Fred, Dan and I had many long chats. One days Fred introduced an important personal matter.

"Why did you join, Patrick?" he asked.

"Oh, it just struck me that I should."

"But that makes no sense to me. You had to have a reason. Are you telling me that no one put it to you that you should join?"

I began to consider the matter a while.

"When I was a child," I answered, "people often said to my mother that I should be a priest. I don't know why they said it, but I wonder was joining the Brothers another way of doing something like that and doing it years earlier? Oh, I don't know what the real reason was!"

No one made any comment and we were silent until I asked Fred, "And why did you join?"

"One day last April a Brother called Markey called to our school. He spoke to us about the good work that the monks did, and said we could join in it. He went on about the fine life we'd have, so I joined. My mother was against me going but my father said, 'He can always come home, if he wants to, and he'll benefit from the education that they'll give him there'."

"And how was it with you, Dan?"

"There's not much to tell. My mother is a pious woman and she said that she thought that I had a vocation for the religious life. She asked me what I thought, so I decided that I might as well go. My father agreed and was well pleased to see me off."

"Why?"

"There were two boys of us at home and I wasn't any use at farm work, so my mother was pleased to see me joining a religious Order."

"She must be a holy woman!"

"Oh, yes! Every night we knelt to say the family Rosary but my father was always absent at the pub playing cards. To tell the truth he did not like praying at all. Sunday Mass was enough for him."

Fred, Dan and I were watched. We had what was described as 'a special friendship' and were suspected of being homosexuals. Years later it seemed funny that we were suspected of a *ménage a trois* when we were just innocent friends.

On 16th July Br Denis came to address us and announced that seventy-five of us were leaving, and that twenty-five of these were going to Booterstown to be novices. All in this group were over sixteen years of age and had a good record, as far as the Superior knew. They left next day and Dan was among the privileged. Denis read out a list of forty who were going to Bray. Eleven were notorious bullies, whom I dreaded, but I was glad that Whisperer and Fred were going with me.

Bray

The July day that we left Baldoyle railway station was sunny, where a horse and cart carried our suitcases in many journeys before we left. This was the first time that we were out of Baldoyle and I felt happy as the college receded behind us.

We went into the city and the train went on southwards. As we went southwards from the city the sight of Bray Head and the Sugar Loaf Mountains took my breath away, as the train came out of the long railway slip at Killiney Bay. It was so beautiful compared to Baldoyle, where on foggy nights we heard the moaning of foghorns.

When we alighted from the train at Bray, a tall Christian Brother awaited us. The big man spoke to us after a noisy throat-clearing and much heaving of his Adam's apple.

"Well, boys, I am Brother Hubert your Superior, and I welcome you to St Kieran's College in Bray. The college is about two miles away and I'll lead the way to it."

We walked in threes up the Quinsboro Road. Sellers of vegetables were on the paths and street and we wove our way through the crowds. I was with Charley and Fred well back in the file and we noticed a blackboard ahead of us, which tumbled down suddenly.

"That will be Whisperer," said Charley. "I bet he's walked into it!"

We laughed. Whisperer knocked it, and the owner who wrote the prices of vegetables on the board was fuming when we went past.

"Bloody *laa-dee-daas* of college-boy pups, God damn them!" he spluttered. "Couldn't they pass a poor man's property without knocking it over?"

Whisperer, I heard, laughed like a hyena and hurried off but Hubert was leading the column and he never knew about what happened behind his back.

St Kieran's College, where we spent the following year, was built for a Protestant Archbishop of Dublin, Plunkett, whose stately house faced south in the midst of elegant parkland. When our Ireland became independent after 1922, religious Orders bought such houses to use as colleges. The real outcome of national independence was a huge growth in religious foreign missions led by Irish men and women. In the 1930s and 1940s the Christian Brothers rented the house and grounds; they bought it after World War II with the walled garden near it and a double line of trees, which formed the Beech Walk. It was ironic that the only people whom these mansions suited were the modern Catholic religious Orders, because very few Irish people at that time had the means to maintain them. While we were studying there, the owner served in World War II as a British officer.

There was a spacious nineteenth-century front hall at the main entrance with a stairway sweeping upwards. The rooms downstairs were classrooms or dormitories and one was the oratory. Upstairs the rooms were used as dormitories but Hubert slept in the master bedroom, while the other Brothers slept in smaller ones and some boys in sub-divided rooms. The refectory and kitchens were in the cellars of the house. The Brothers added to the mansion an incongruous one-storeyed timber shack with a galvanised roof as a study and boot room. It was a grotesque addition, as I saw it later but then I noticed nothing odd about it.

There were two entrances with gate lodges to the college grounds. A widow lived in each. Both were Protestants but one become a Catholic and attended Sunday Mass in our oratory. She was the only woman we saw in the college except for visiting relatives. As Whisperer said, "Yonder withered crone doth warn us away from the ladies!"

Two lads stayed from the former year's group. One never spoke to anyone but the other said plenty.

"So you've never met Pop before!" he began. "Oh, that's the boss. He's all right but if you annoy him, he'll never forget. That's why I was not sent to the Novitiate, because he wants to have me here another year to torment me."

"And what did you do?" I asked.

"That's my business to know and yours to find out," he replied tartly.

Our informant left us when Pop Lawlor came over to the four of us. He asked us our names, and I was amazed, because in Baldoyle no Brother chatted to me or my friends.

I began to like Pop. He was bony as well as tall, walked with a slight swagger but seemed gentle and looked a leader. I was content for the first time since I left home. That evening he assembled us in the study and enquired about the games we played.

"There's a playing pitch for hurling and another for Gaelic football," he told us. He then added, "I think it important that everyone plays some game, but there must be a few of you who don't like games. Who are they?"

The hands went up hesitantly.

"Eight, I see, Very well. You can go to a little field at the side of the house and kick a ball around. Just have fun and be occupied."

I was delighted and so was Fred. The game enthusiasts named this field the Cripples' Acre, where we played a kind of football. I loved it under the lime trees, where we enjoyed exercise in the fresh air and could leave the books behind us. Of course, hurling and Gaelic football were the only games that were played at the college and never soccer or rugby. They were foreign games, which a true Irishman never plays, as Pop told us, because the British Army and their Irish allies played them.

On our third morning in Bray rumours were bruited about some of the bullies and I noticed that they were quiet at breakfast. Fred whispered to me in the main corridor.

"Charley and three of his heroes were caught last night." He sped off until later, when we had a chance to talk.

"Did you know that Pop patrols the corridors every night? You didn't? Well, he does. Last night he heard a laugh in a cubicle where Charley was entertaining three mates. Pop pulled across the curtain and ordered them all to his office in their pyjamas and grilled them for an hour. He threatened to expel them all if this happened again."

It was the best thing that could have happened and was expressed in what someone quoted, 'When a strong man keeps his house, in peace are they who dwell therein'. Charley, whom I liked, became less lively than in Baldoyle and grew morose.

The Christian Brothers drew their members in Ireland mainly from the working classes and the lower-middle class of small shopkeepers and farmers. The Juniorates also were among the very few colleges in Ireland where students came from almost every county on the island. I remember one thing about those from the Six Counties compared to those from the rest of Ireland. They could turn their hands to practical skills such as carpentry but the rest of us could not, and some of us could not drive a nail or saw timber.

The Belfast boys were pleasant. I remember one telling me in gales of laughter about the Luftwaffe bombing the city, and he gave me a description of a paint factory ablaze after incendiary bombs hit it. I cannot recall any pleasant boy from Derry: maybe there was one whom I do not remember. None of the boys in college were natural entertainers as the Dubliners, who were unique in this.

I remember John, a farmer's son from South Armagh. He was a big burly man, honest and friendly until he saw me using my left foot to dig with a spade.

"Look at that now!" he blurted out. "You're digging like a Prod!"

I never heard until then that Protestants dug with their left feet but I had never done much digging in my life. The country lads from Derry, Tyrone and Armagh suspected me for quite a while afterwards as a converted Protestant, an untrustworthy turncoat.

I remember that there was no one there from Donegal. Later someone asked Markey, the recruiting Brother.

"Don't you know," he replied, "that Donegal people have a tradition of leaving home for one season in the year, when they work to send money home!"

He added that they never stayed long away from home, and pointed out that the wealthy farmers' and well-off shopkeepers' families in Donegal, who provided the priests everywhere else in Ireland, never joined the Brothers.

The boys from Clare were interesting characters, such as Maurice from the Burren, a mighty hurler, a great worker with the shovel and as tough as the Burren rocks. We regarded the Clare men as crafty and secretive and loath to let anything be known about themselves or their families.

One lad, Paul, came from Limerick at the end of August and two more arrived from the Midlands. That made fifty-five but the taciturn fellow, who had not been sent to the Novitiate, was so bitter and resentful that he left and went home to Carrick-on-Suir. He went to England, where he later became a Spitfire pilot in the RAF.

We did all the housework as we had in Baldoyle. My job, or charge as we called it, was to go the walled garden each morning to collect apples. Fruit trees and vegetables were there in abundance, and apples were heaped on plates on the tables.

Above the door at the entrance was the Latin inscription *Festina Lente*, which means 'Make haste slowly', or as we might translate the words liberally, 'No fussing here!'

Our Spiritual and Educational Welfare

Reverend Michael, a priest of the Holy Ghost Fathers and trained for the African missions, served our spiritual needs at St Kieran's College. He celebrated Mass for us every morning, and on Thursday afternoons heard Confessions in the house conservatory, which was part of the sacristy. He usually had a short chat with each of us, knew most of us and heard of all that happened in the college.

In the late autumn a boy called Shanahan left. He had completed the Leaving Certificate at home but was repeating the year's study to prepare for the Novitiate. Pop had a great regard for Shanahan and openly expressed regret in the oratory at his departure the night before he left, which was never done before this occasion or later.

One day Guerin said, "Patrick, do you know why Shanahan left?" I did not. "One of the lads," said he, "heard from Shanahan that he was leaving to join the Holy Ghost Fathers. He's going to their Novitiate to study for the priesthood."

I did not believe a word of it. Then one Thursday evening Revd Michael talking to me after Confession as usual, motioned me to a chair and began.

"Are you happy here, Patrick?"

"Well I'm happier than I was in Baldoyle anyway."

"That was a badly run college, let me tell you! People like you should be treated better!"

Aha! So he had heard about all that, I thought to myself, but who told him?

"You're talented and you should be going on for the priesthood."

I was surprised at this. Talented? No one ever told me that. The priesthood? I as a priest? I had never thought of that for ages, since I was at home over two years ago. We fell silent and I looked at him for a while.

"Patrick," said he slowly. "You can be a priest, if you wish to!"

"But how?"

"Just remain here until you complete your Leaving Certificate in June; leave after the examinations and write to me at once. I'll be meeting you every Thursday. Above all, don't ever tell anyone here what I've said to you."

"I'll think of it," I said quietly to him, "and I'll have an answer when I see you on Thursday."

What an interesting development that might be, if I became a priest and could see my parents and family when I went home from this college. What a delight it could be for my mother, if I were a priest! Then it struck me – could I join an Order that provided us with a chaplain who was as treacherous as he was?

I never told anyone what he said, but let him know that I was not interested. It struck me also that Shanahan might have been poached but I never heard the truth of that. Some months afterwards this priest ceased to be college chaplain, and one from another Order replaced him unannounced. Did Pop hear of other attempts at poaching? It had to be something like that but we lived within a wall of secrecy.

The new priest was from the Marist Order, whom we nicknamed Micky, and was pudgy and well nourished. As I knelt in front of him on the first day at Confession, he put a hand on my left shoulder, which I felt moving down from shoulder to waist. As it moved down further, I pulled back and he stopped. I shivered within myself and thought, 'No man of any kind did that to me before.' He must have acted that way to others in the college – or did he?

Brother Brendan

My favourite teacher was Br Brendan Donovan. He was a lively fair-headed man, middle-sized and quite a teacher. He was the only monk of his group rejected for final vows at the age of twenty-five, who went home but returned after an appeal to the Superior-General. When Brendan Donovan was at home for a few days after rejection, he wrote to Revd Tom Counihan, a Jesuit who became well known to all young Brothers. Counihan knew him well and made a plea to have him re-admitted. Brendan was invited to Marino and after a lengthy interview, was re-admitted and took his vows eventually. All applicants for final vows had to undergo a secret scrutiny. The senior Brothers, wherever an applicant lived during the three years before he applied for final vows, were queried about him. If someone made a serious case against him, he was rejected.

On Saturday evenings we assembled after games in the hall, which was used for recreation, as a study and for classes. We took out our Irish poetry books and Br Brendan led us into singing some of the poems. I never realised that nearly all the Irish poems that we were learning were ballads. He accompanied us on the piano as we yelled out the songs. I remember a ballad, *Preab san Ól* (The Drink-Up), which in English begins:

It's many a way that some folk have
To make some money which they can save;
Who seldom think how short their lives are
And that they'll end beneath the clay.

Whether you're landlord, duke or monarch,
Not a coin at death will stay with you,
So for every reason there's nothing gladder
Than always passing around the booze.

I remember Revd Kelly in Baldoyle reading that poem and concluding with "Oh, now, now, that's not a Christian way to order your life. May God forgive him! Amen."

Brendan was different. Here we all enjoyed the rollicking song. He trained us for the chapel services, where the Congregation was the choir and the music was generally Plain Chant. His singing sessions were a great release of emotion, and the music varied from plain chant and hymns to songs like that above.

I still can see in my mind's eye: Brendan in the afternoons togged out in a green-and-white Limerick jersey playing hurling with the students as Pop did. Both must have been in their early forties. I met this extraordinary man in 1995 for the last time, when he looked fit and well, a few years before he died when he was over ninety.

He taught us Scripture and chose Luke's gospel, which was the first and last time in my life that I attended Scripture classes. He enjoyed reading the gospel and especially the parables and stories of Christ's miracles, which never raised any specific Catholic doctrine. There did not seem to be any controversial subjects in St Luke's gospel, such as I saw in Matthew's and as the sailors say, it was all plain sailing.

For the first time I read *The Imitation of Christ*, which is a little book written by a Dutch monk, Thomas à Kempis. A page of it was read aloud publicly every day. He never mentions Christ's mother, Mary, but I read his remarks about women: 'Be not an intimate of any woman but commend all good women in general to God'. His words on death reflected for me the Middle Ages, when he wrote: 'One man died at table, another falling from on high broke his neck, another died by the sword. Thus death is the end of all.' Thomas à Kempis made many interesting remarks, such as, 'He that is seeking to be more free and unrestrained will always be in trouble, for one thing or other will ever disgust him'.

We recited aloud each weekend the Little Office of the Blessed Virgin in Latin. Part of it was recited on Saturday evening, more of it after breakfast on Sunday morning and the remainder in the late afternoon. At the end of the evening recitation for much of the year we sang the plain chant *Salve Regina*, 'Hail Holy Queen'. It is a beautiful hymn and it is sung at the burial of a Christian Brother to this day.

One former colleague, still a Brother, said to me in 1994 that he hoped that there might still some of his companions alive to sing it at his funeral. He need not have worried. He died in his sleep in 1995 and there were forty Brothers there to sing it.

This was part of the Liturgy, which was the official prayer of the Church. It was years before I realised that the English reformers' 'Common Prayer' was an English form for the Latin word, which expresses the notion of 'liturgy'. It was never the Irish people's prayer, and the Divine Office was confined to priests, nuns and Brothers.

When the Christmas vacation was over, we had the 'Retreat', six days of silence, prayer and meditation, which a Jesuit priest directed. He was a young man who taught in Belvedere, whom Pop thought might suit us. I remember that he wore a simple university gown, as he spoke to us three times a day. His Roman collar was wider than what most priests wore and he had a sense of humour, but had also what I later knew as an air of learned distinction. I liked this.

The retreat began at 9pm on Sunday night. I forget what the Jesuit said then or in the days afterwards but he was not a religious bully, who threatened you with heavenly thunderbolts. We went to bed after prayers at the usual time about 10pm. These six days were the first time that I found myself alone for more than a few days in the company of others. The boys kept the rule of total silence well, I think, but I did hear Whisperer muttering to someone with a stifled laugh that Pop's Lord Jesus was not to be found in silence, but in the wildness of thirty hurlers. When Whisperer saw me, he did his best not to titter.

"The tongue of the dumb shall sing!" he whispered.

The Jesuit spoke much of the founder of the Society of Jesus, Ignatius of Loyola, who had written notes for the conduct of a thirty-day retreat, and treated us as if we were Jesuit novices. Six days are bad enough, I thought, but what is the thirty-day Jesuit retreat like, when every unwelcome thought reverberates through your mind like a whiplash!

From the third night onwards I awoke to the chattering of my companions talking in their sleep. I suppose I did the same, which sounded so weird in the darkness. One night I awoke in terror, as I found myself going up the stairs from the entrance hall in my sleep, when the chiming of the clock on the wall at 4am awakened me and I rushed back to my bed in terror.

On Saturday night the end of silence came when grace before meals was said. An excited burst of talking followed, which was a release from six days of trapped emotions. In the din Whisperer's high-pitched cackle, chattering in relief, rose above all other voices. Then on Monday we returned to the classrooms.

The Springtime

Great storms of wind and rain came during March 1944, which hurled loads of seaweed on to the beaches and one Saturday the strongest fellows were sent at low tide to collect what they could of it. It was used as a fertiliser for potatoes, along with the farmyard manure which was available, but many did not appreciate. There was no artificial fertiliser available because of the war but this was a blessing, I thought.

Pop came into the study the next Saturday and interrupted one of Brendan's singing sessions. He sat at a table on the stage, clasped his hands tensely and noisily cleared his throat.

"Boys," he began, "the war is worsening and may soon reach us. I'm just warning you of what may happen, if the worst happens."

A few, who were shuffling their feet, now sat still and stared at Pop as the tone of his voice suggested that something serious was afoot.

"Our country is neutral but the English and American upholders of democracy may be planning to invade us from the Six Counties. If they do it, we'll be swallowed up in two days or less."

It struck me that this could be fun compared to our unexciting life in the college, but little did I know what war was really like!

"If we have early notice of an invasion," Pop continued, "we intend to send you home as quickly as possible, which may be difficult." He went on about this matter and told us not to worry about invasion because it might not happen but, as he said, "It's a fool who does not prepare for the future and I'm responsible for you to your parents."

"Yes," as I said to someone later, "he's in our parents' place alright but we do not have the basic freedom of home here, though it's better than Baldoyle."

I tried to conceal my delight at being shipped off home! How marvellous, I thought, if the Yanks and British free me! And then I wondered did this mean that I wished to have a holiday at home, or else to leave for good? I kept my thoughts to myself; but did others feel that way too? I never discovered and never asked them. Oh, yes! Silence is golden, but is continual silence a breeding ground for mental canker in a community? Is this not also what they also call 'reserve'?

There was no invasion and we all stayed as we were. I remember a newspaper advertisement in the 1950s about the sale in Belfast of wartime army surplus goods. Some thousands of Irish tricolour pennants were sold, which were designed to be hung on tanks and armoured cars. It made me think.

Pop was a reasonable man but he spoke that springtime about what they called 'self-abuse'.

"I'm not speaking of self-abuse by alcohol, but of masturbation," he said.

He differentiated between what happened during sleep and deliberate acts, which he described as a sin. He spoke of this a few times later and seemed a little embarrassed, shrugging his shoulders and turning his head as if to avoid our gaze.

The Church's attitude to sexuality is well illustrated in Augustine of Hippo's crude statement, translated as follows: 'We are born between the urine and the faeces'. Augustine had much experience of sex until age cooled it and made abstinence easy. I laughed when I read that he called his son, born out of wedlock, Adeodatus ('given by God'). It struck me that this man, whose statements never appealed to me, was suggesting that God presided over his parents' illicit sexual encounters.

This teaching on masturbation succeeded in creating a great sense of sin in us innocents, where there was little or no evil. The good Pop had 'convinced us of sin', as the Scripture says. The thinking behind this morality was an assault on innocence.

Approaching the Term End

From some time after Christmas our group had become smaller when fifteen left, with the bullies among them. They went singly as did Charley, who was the first to go, but we never knew who went voluntarily or who were advised to leave. For two days before he left, Charley was unusually quiet and one day he was absent from breakfast.

He was preparing for his journey home, and was having breakfast alone before he was escorted to the train. He disappeared and no one could bid him farewell. In about three weeks others left us one-by-one, and every morning I looked around the tables to see who was missing. Paul had told me that he was thinking of going.

"What am I doing here?" he queried to my surprise. "And what is there to live for?"

"Tell me, Paul," I said. "Why did you join?"

He winced as he said, "I listened to that fellow, Markey, telling us about the fine life we'd have."

Here was the work of the trickster again, I thought, who fooled boys into joining, hoping that enough stayed to justify his lies. It was an odd basis for the self-sacrificing life that we lived. At last I suggested that Paul must have some other reason for joining. I wondered what he was keeping secret.

"And I suppose you never thought of doing what Pop called 'the Lord's work', did you?"

He admitted that he might have.

"Of course," I added, "is there is some girl friend at home?"

He did not answer. Paul, however, stayed on until we both left in 1953.

After prayers one night Pop addressed us from the back of the oratory. He reminded us that fifteen had gone and said, "You should settle down now and prepare for the examinations. Enough have gone and I'm asking the rest of you to stay."

I wondered had Pop decided to advise all the bullies and their friends to go. No one left after that, a week after he told us about a possible invasion by the Allies.

The Leaving Certificate Examination started on 4th June. The last day that we studied was Sunday 2nd and on the Monday we went out for a day on the beach. If we were not prepared for the examination then, said Pop, "Cramming can't do you any good, because you can't fatten a pig on the day of the fair!"

It was a very warm sunny day as we walked to Bray railway station and travelled to Killiney on the cliff face overlooking the beach. We brought food in baskets with us and we were the only ones there. I recall clearly that day in early June, when the world was under the clouds of war but we enjoyed ourselves on the beach not knowing what was happening outside of our country and our little world.

When we began the Leaving Certificate examination, there was no tension or 'nerves' bothering anyone, because we were concentrating on the work ahead and had no distractions, not even normal family life. Above all, we did not have newspapers discussing the examination *ad nauseam*, as they do now, creating tension and worry.

On Thursday evening after tea before the wash-up, Pop made an announcement.

"You might as well know," he began, "that the English and the Americans invaded France on the eastern coast of the Normandy peninsula this morning. I'm in the dark and have no details. I heard about it from someone who phoned me on business and I'll ring Dublin today. I'll let you know what the news is as soon as I can."

I should explain that there was no radio or wireless in the house, so all news was passed on to the college by newspapers and telephone, or by a few friends who had a radio. We young fellows were forbidden to read newspapers as the novices and young Brothers were. It was forbidden to have a radio in a monastery and monks were forbidden to listen to it anywhere.

On Friday before the examination was held, newspaper cuttings on the Normandy invasion were pinned on a notice board. I had not seen a newspaper or a press cutting since 5th August two years before. One piece on the board was unforgettable, which showed machine gun-fire in the night, where rounds of tracers lighted their path upward in the blackness of the sky. As I looked at it, I shivered.

Brendan told a group of us about the various landing areas on the beaches, and the task of transporting huge numbers of men and masses of equipment across the English Channel to confront the finest army in the world. The Germans after all, he reminded us, had conquered most of Europe and almost defeated the Russians but now their western enemies had landed in France to form a second front. It was four years since the British fled across the Channel from the German armies, when the French surrendered after a short fight.

One night shortly after D-Day I was awakened by a thunderstorm and rain lashing on the windows. I heard people scurrying about the place and talking excitedly. The rain poured into a dormitory upstairs when the wind tore a hole in the roof and the occupants were transferred to cubicles left vacant since the fifteen had left us.

It happened that only those affected by the storm dared to break silence. Discipline was so strict that I and others did not leave our cubicles or speak a word and only in the morning did we hear about the night's happenings.

In one year we filled our heads with what we could cram to cover a two-year course for an examination. We were about sixteen years of age and were too immature to comprehend much of what we drummed into our heads so hastily, which had been designed for a two-year study, which in our case was reduced to a year.

The National Teachers of Ireland spent five years doing these courses and were chosen for teacher training if they attained distinction in some Honours papers. We were guaranteed entrance to the profession as Christian Brothers and had only to win one Honour mark, which was in Irish. Thus we had a rather sketchy education, an odd way to train members of the oldest male teaching Order in Ireland. This policy reflected our Superiors' attitude to knowledge, which was an acquisition of facts without regard to content, implying the unimportance of thought. It was simple rote memory. As one Brother said to me, "If I've to learn Chinese to pass an exam without understanding a word, I'll do it!"

We were taught that knowledge was a commodity for examination marks – without any consideration of its content – which offered nothing to the minds, but that attitude suited our Superiors. I remember hearing that a person remarked: "Oh that fellow thinks too much and asks questions. I'm telling you he'll be a dangerous man to deal with yet."

In the last few weeks we went to the seaside for a swim on fine days or played games. On one side of the Cripple's Acre, there was a row of flowering lime trees, which filled the air with fragrance. I loved it and could not have enough of its delights.

The Beech Walk near the walled garden, where we strolled during breaks on rainy days, was in its glory of bright serrated leaves on the elegant trees. When next the beeches will wear the beauty of autumn colours, we shall not be here, I thought, but in the Novitiate. That was our next and unavoidable step.

I knew all the beautiful areas near the college where we went on long Sunday walks. We often made short trips seeking wild flowers and their habitats during most of the year. Brendan taught us botany and I can remember practically all that he taught us. This opened a new aspect of life to me that I did not even surmise had existed before I studied it for this first time. I was leaving all that now to live in the city.

Whistler with a wry grin on his face nodded one sunny evening towards the college buildings as he said "We'll be going soon to taste the delights of Booterstown. There won't be many laughs there, I'm telling you my dearest friend!"

"We didn't join up for laughs," I countered.

"Bad and all as Pop is, we'll have worse to contend with in Booterstown, so we will", said he.

The Novitiate

At Booterstown railway station a Brother with spectacles on his snub nose met us. He introduced himself as the Socius, the Assistant Novicemaster, and squeakily ordered us to form threes. A younger Brother, John Kelly, went with the first three of us to lead the way to Stillorgan Road, while the older man walked behind us alone.

I was with Fred and Whisperer, who muttered "Cometh the day, cometh the snub-nosed four-eyes."

There was an air of menace about the little man. The tall and gangling Whisperer misquoted the prayer, which we said daily to our saintly protector against fever, St Rock, as he muttered, "Save us, oh holy St Rock, from the little germ of disease with the snub nose that crawls behind us today!"

As we trudged along, we saw few cars or lorries. There was no petrol for private motorists since 1942, but some was given to those who used their vehicles for essential services. Northwards of the station Fred caught a glimpse in the distance of a white building by the shore of the bay.

"Do you see that, Patrick?" asked Fred quietly as he pointed towards it. "Wake up, Whisperer! Do you see the laundry, you daydreamer?"

"And so we go on the rocky road to Bootingdown," intoned the Whistler to himself.

"What are you on about, Fred?" I asked.

"About the laundry over there!"

I looked and saw in large letters: 'The Bell and Swastika Laundry'. Whisperer awoke and muttered. "Let the bell ring for us all if we come under the tumbled cross. Amen!"

Fred and I did not laugh; it was no day for that. We spoke little on that walk from the station.

The Novitiate was at St Helen's, where the Provincial of the Irish Province lived with his four Consultors. When we passed through the tall iron gates, I was struck by the magnificence of the Georgian house (which was built in 1750, as I heard later), whose entrance hall had marble floor and pillars and it was called it the Marble Hall.

The Novitiate was housed in the stable area, where our dormitories and an assembly hall were built in three timber hutments with galvanised roofs. I later realised that they looked tasteless alongside the eighteenth-century mansion. Irish Christian Brothers bought this landlord's mansion in the 1930s to train an increasing number of new members. It was the finest of what was bought then and the Christian Brothers have sold it since their decline.

We went into the old stable yard, where we saw fifty silent novices dressed in soutanes and narrow Roman collars, who looked subdued. The snub-nosed Socius eventually addressed us.

"You're all welcome, boys," he sniffed and then continued. "First of all, I'll read out the name of the novice assigned to each newcomer to advise about the rules, regulations and customs of the Novitiate."

I was assigned to Dan Doyle who as Br Vincent was my 'guardian angel'. Dan Doyle from Wexford town once had sweets smuggled to him at Baldoyle farm, but was a tame fellow now. Said he to me, "It is a serious matter for all of us to keep the rules strictly," but in Baldoyle Dan did not care tuppence about any of the rules.

Later on I met Fred for a moment, when Dan was not haunting me with his piety. Fred reminded me that Dan, who was my 'guardian angel', was one of the tumblers of young girls in the Baldoyle barn. We never knew why he was sent here instead of Bray, because he loved the good things of life that he could eat or embrace.

"What has happened to all of them?"

"How do I know? Anyway, the spirit is gone out of them, isn't it?" I shivered.

"By the way, who's the man who met us at the railway station?"

"As we know, he's called the Socius, the Assistant Novicemaster. The Novicemaster is retiring on 16th August. I suppose he'll be given the job."

John Kelly, the younger Brother who led us from the train, was recovering from illness. I saw nothing odd then about a Novitiate as a convalescent home for him, but later I understood that something as bizarre as that could happen. Kelly refereed matches and went with us on walks. We went in threes and he was like one of us, but he seemed to smile, unlike us. He was a normal person. When the Socius was present Kelly addressed us as 'Brothers' but otherwise he began, "Look here now, lads! Will ye cheer up and do this for me?"

The Novicemaster, Br Berchmans, was over six feet tall and walked with a limp. He met us as we sat in the assembly hall. Whisperer muttered, "Enter the baldy Bilbo!" His 'guardian angel' novice heard him and wagged a warning finger at him.

"Dear Brother Novices," intoned Berchmans, "we all welcome the Novices-to-be who came today. May the Lord in his goodness bless them all!" They all chorused a soulful "Amen" to that. He spoke with a deep solemn voice. I heard a mild titter from the Whisperer, who resisted a desire to make a comment. The Novicemaster added: "Good novices-to-be, you are to prepare yourselves for your clothing in the habit of our Congregation of the Christian Schools of Ireland on 15th August. I hear from the Brother Socius," Berchmans went on "that when young people come from St Joseph's, Baldoyle tomorrow, we shall have fifty-five novices. May the Lord direct every one of us to do His will at all times!" To this the novices chorused "Amen". He then said, "Live Jesus in our hearts!" and we said, "Forever!"

I had never met anyone like Berchmans. He was institutionalised after thirty years as a Novicemaster, more than a quarter-century away from life, in his cell of silence.

The Baldoyle fellows completed our group and we all looked the boys we were. Even going to the toilets after breakfast was regulated. A toilet was assigned to each six and was locked at all times. We went there according to age, and each received the key, attached to a piece of wood, from their immediate senior. As Whisperer put it, "We'll be shown how to sleep at night, judging by all this!" We were shown how to close a door silently. You pushed the door with one hand on the handle and put the palm of the other hand above it to make no noise. I thought that it was fine training for a house thief.

The dining room was in the stable area. We sat at long tables and the Novicemaster with the Socius and John Kelly sat at a table on a platform. At breakfast and dinner we ate in silence, while during dinner someone read aloud a biography of a saint. On the second day the Novicemaster called on the reader to halt.

"Will that young man at the end of Table 5 repeat please what was last read?" It was Whisperer, who stumbled to his feet and spluttered through food in his mouth.

"Sir, the saint was saying lots of prayers when the Holy Ghost descended on him."

The Novicemaster replied, "Young man, resume your seat and please attend to the reading!"

As Whisperer muttered to me later, "Old Bilbo lives in a holy cage. How can I listen to that stuff, when I have the nosebag on to consume basic comestibles?" Certain lads read during meals. I remember one lad reading "There were cannibals living on the archipelago" as "There were canny balls living in the arsey-pull-haygo" – I heard a smothered laugh. The Novicemaster tapped on the table and declared, "Please restrain yourselves, young men! Such levity does not befit any serious religious man!"

We were allowed one visit by a relative, but nobody visited me in that year of silence, when petty rules shackled us – such as not to swing your arms or put your hands in your pockets when walking. Inside this cone of regulations we were 'formed'; that is, the Novicemaster and the Socius brainwashed us.

Reverend Berchmans was determined that we should eat plenty. His ancestral memory of the Great Famine made him determined to feed us well.

"You must never forget, Brother Novices and Novices-to-be," he began, "that you eat to live and require plenty food. You're growing men, who need nourishment. Teaching is very arduous, and you must eat regularly to keep you healthy."

I was surprised at this common sense, which I did not expect.

Dressed in Black

We had a silent eight-day Retreat from 6th to 13th August. The Novicemaster told us to write our impressions of what we heard after each lecture. On 15th August we had the reception of the habit. In former years the boys from Bray and Baldoyle were at this ceremony but not in 1944, when train services were few because of the scarcity of coal. The novices, the Novicemaster, the Socius and John Kelly were the only spectators. No parents or relatives were invited and to me it all expressed the attitude, 'What business of theirs is this?' We were cutting ourselves off from home and belonged to the Congregation of the Christian Schools of Ireland. At ten o'clock in the morning fifty-five of us stood in the oratory outside the altar rails and each went into the sanctuary. When my turn came, I took off my jacket and handed it to John Kelly saying: "I put off the world and its vanities and put on the Lord Jesus Christ!"

The Novicemaster pinned a Roman collar around my neck, which was joined to a square of black cloth. He put the black soutane on me and I said: "I put on the Lord Jesus Christ!" The black cincture was put around my waist, with a pendant of the same material hanging from it at the left side. The cincture was the symbol of chastity. Berchmans limped from one to the other giving a card to each with his new religious name as a Christian Brother on it. I found that they re-named me as a Brother. We had no choice in the new name just as we had none in our baptismal names.

"When you were christened, you were given a name, but your new family renames you to-day!" John Kelly congratulated each but the Socius remained aloof.

We went out on the lawn. Fred was Br Wilfrid and Whisperer received the name of de Sales.

"Patrick," said he, "oh sorry, it is Br Luke or something! Isn't my name wonderful? Going to the de Sales or the sales, am I?!"

Afterwards we who came from Bray received the results of our Leaving Certificate examination. I had secured Honours in Irish, Botany and Geography. The other papers were at the Pass standard because we could not cram a full Honours course in ten months. The Botany course was short, while Geography was supposed to be easy.

On the following day the older novices set out for Marino, the chief house of studies where the Superior-General lived with his councillors. After they departed, we came together in the assembly hall.

"The new Novicemaster, who has been appointed, will meet you in a moment," the Socius announced. He rambled on and spoke about our need to exercise "self-control" and not to be boisterous. We took it seriously and did not smile as he twittered on, because if we did not take him seriously, we felt we might be returned to our parents rapidly. The door opened at that stage and in walked Br Denis, our former Superior in Baldoyle.

The Socius stood down from the dais and said, "This, Brother Novices, is your new Novicemaster!"

I was astounded and saw that Whisperer was shaken.

"Black Jack!" he whispered. "Oh, light of the Holy Ghost and damnable fires of Hell!"

Brother Denis walked to the dais and the Socius left the hall. As I looked at his dark-hued skin and jet-black hair, he was quite a contrast to his predecessor. Instead of the solemn speech of the old man, Denis spoke rapidly and fiddled nervously with a pen, tapping the desktop as he spoke. It never struck anyone to clap or to greet him. We were his subjects. He spoke of perfection, which was, as we noticed, a form of sublimity but remained an obscure concept, and was a puzzle to me while I was there and later.

"We cannot be perfect," Denis continued, "but can only aspire to it in all our actions."

We listened and although none of us knew what he meant, we had not the temerity to inquire. Whisperer contributed asides in a whisper to what he saw as a divine farce and a spiritual cloud-cuckoo land.

"Perfection and Correction," I barely heard him mutter. "That is the way we go, my friends!"

"In practice, my dear Brothers," said Revd Denis, "perfection can be attained by obedience to all rules, regulations and commands of the Brother Superior. We must regard discipline as the basis of religious life and the key to all virtue."

We heard that the virtue of perfection was the highest virtue of all. We heard an interesting viewpoint on the subject of discipline from John Kelly.

"You see," Kelly began, "the boys that our founder taught in the early nineteenth century were little better than savages. You had to be a tough man to control them."

"Why, sir?" asked someone.

"After the 1798 troubles there was little order anywhere, and in the monasteries the Brothers had to have tough discipline among themselves."

"Why was that?" I asked him.

He smiled as he said, "Only in that way could their work be effective among the pupils. Pupils must pay attention and must be forced to do so."

"Sir," remarked one novice, "was that when they first used the strap in school?"

"The strap, my dear Brother, was humane compared to what the schoolmasters used. It was the same everywhere. The Yanks said, '*Reading, writing and 'rithmetic, / Sung to the tune of a hickory stick!*' Some think that we should abolish the use of the leather."

The Socius nosed in at the door and ended a worthwhile conversation. We should have had such discussions at all times as part of our Novitiate but we never did. The Christian Brothers, like all teachers in the nineteenth century, were sticklers for discipline over their members. This gave the Christian Brothers cohesion and I think that when it was relaxed in the 1960s, it heralded final collapse. Discipline and not prayer seemed to be the basis of a religious Order in Ireland in the nineteenth century. As Whisperer saw it, "No wonder they quote, 'Feed my lambs, feed my sheep'! We're a flock of sheep, herded wherever the shepherd orders us. We'll be lucky not to be sent to a heavenly slaughterhouse yet!"

We had games about four o'clock every day on the two pitches, where we played Gaelic football. Hurling was played years ago in the Novitiate until the Novicemaster banned it, when a hurley injured someone on the field. In the Novitiate I enjoyed games for the first time. I rushed about after the ball and if I did not kick it, I collided with others. We loved going to the field where we ran about and acted as boys.

Our Daily Routine

And what did we do each day? At 5.45am when the bell tolled, we tumbled out to shave, although I had only a human form of a cat's whiskers on my face. I cut myself with the razor in Bray, so discovered that I had to be careful. We 'slopped out' and went into the assembly hall for morning prayers. As we sat in our seats we said the prayers and then had meditation, which lasted until seven o'clock. We were told to meditate on excerpts from the Scripture or on a religious subject, which was read. We completed the meditation walking between the buildings, but on wet mornings we walked the corridors.

Towards 7am we made our way through the cellars of the mansion and climbed a spiral stairs to enter the oratory for Mass. Our chaplains were Jesuits. Denis knelt at the back of the oratory where he fidgeted, unlike the old man. The pews in the oratory were chairs lashed together and we knelt on timber kneelers. A gallery high up on one wall housed an organ, whose keys were golden we heard. Kelly played the instrument, but he dodged questions about what the keys were made of.

Breakfast was at eight o'clock, when we enjoyed porridge and there was silence during the meal except on feast days. A saint's life was read to us, such as Evelyn Waugh's *Edmund Campion: A Life*. This saint was hanged, drawn and quartered at Tyburn. After breakfast some washed up and others had a charge. Mine was in the mansion's walled garden, where I helped an old Brother, but I knew nothing about gardening. He was absent for much of the time, so I was alone unlike the others.

At half past nine we assembled in the hall, where Denis instructed us as Christian Brothers.

"The spirit of this Congregation is a spirit of faith," he said.

I repeated this as a mantra, but never understood it until I left the Christian Brothers later. When I no longer needed it, I knew fully what the Novicemaster meant by the spirit of faith. We had 'spiritual reading' at eleven o'clock. A book by a Jesuit, Rodriguez, entitled *Christian Perfection and Counsels for Youth* translated from Spanish was used, and we spent nine months going through it. I forget all his odd stories of the saints with which he illustrated his text, which was written in the sixteenth or seventeenth century.

At half past twelve we had a cup of tea, or whatever passed for it in 1944. Instead of spreading butter on bread we used grease, which we called "tar". During that snack one day in October I looked at the others. Whisperer had lost his sense of fun, and I saw him tugging at his collar as if he wished to tear it from his neck, which was becoming thinner inside it.

After the midday snack we visited the oratory and then went to the yard, where we were allowed to talk for a quarter of an hour for the first time in the day. We spoke so loudly at first that the Socius ordered, "Exercise self-control! Don't be boisterous!" On that day Whisperer was nearby and he confided in me while the others were quietly talking.

"Is Black Jack away in his mind, or who's the boss here? Didn't he say that God gave us our voices to talk? I'm asking myself was the Socius ever young?"

He fell silent and looked straight ahead. I felt depressed and never answered.

After this we dressed in overalls and went working on the farm or in the garden. One day, we followed a mechanical digger lifting the potatoes, while we collected them from the damp earth in baskets. Before the digger began, we rolled back a carpet of chickweed which covered the field, and deposited the rising wave of greenery at the end of the field like a low ridge. I wondered later what the driver of the potato digger thought of the fifty boys working silently in that field. We were all mobilised that day to do that special work.

After we had completed whatever work we were doing, we had dinner at three and then a wonderful hour or more playing games, when there was no need for much restraint, as long as you did not assault someone.

That Retreat

About twelve days before Christmas we wrote our letters home, the second of three letters that year that each of us wrote to his parents. Two days later the eight-day Retreat began, directed by Revd John Duggan, a Redemptorist. Duggan was quite corpulent. His talks for the first two days were not very interesting, and it was difficult to stay awake as he droned on. On the third day he seemed to come alive when he spilled forth an eloquent cataract of words on what seemed to be his favourite subject. None of us ever forgot it.

"My dear young men," he began, "you're taking a vow of chastity next Christmas twelve months. What you must never forget is that the vow of chastity reaches beyond the Sixth Commandment, which binds you. You are protected from sins of the flesh here but sin against the Sixth Commandment includes sinning with your own flesh." He stopped for a moment, stared at us steadily and continued. "The spiritual man has three enemies: the World, the Flesh and the Devil." He stopped for effect and then continued. "The World around you opposes God of itself; the Devil is the essence of evil; the Flesh is your own search for sinful pleasure." There was a shuffling of feet. "This is self-abuse, a serious sin. Your bodies are violated, which are the temples of the Holy Ghost. If you sin by self-abuse and die in your sin, let me warn you that you will be cast into the fires of Hell for all eternity."

Up to this point I listened with disinterested attention and at least with boredom, but this was something personal and aroused my interest. You could almost feel a feather flutter to the ground in the oratory.

"If you consent to what happens in your sleep as you wake up, that is a mortal sin. It is an act that you know is serious, and you consent to committing it. And young men, just imagine the extra mortal sin, if you go to Holy Communion next morning in this state. It is a sacrilege against the Lord God!"

Now I was frightened. I asked myself in alarm, is an eternity in Hell a fair penalty for what happens in sleep, if you happen to awaken or act on half-sleepy purpose? I shivered within myself as he went on. Next morning about twelve novices did not go to Communion but I went reluctantly, because I felt that I might have committed a sacrilegious unknowingly, but that was not a sin – or was it? As I recall this episode in my life, I feel I am exaggerating but I know otherwise. We were trapped in a place where we were vulnerable to every vibration in the silent air.

Duggan returned to this subject each day until the second last morning of the retreat when the communicants dwindled to a few. On the last morning it included everyone, because the previous evening he mildly retracted what he said, telling us that we were innocent if we begged forgiveness in Confession. He spent days making devils of us and then suddenly restored us as angels.

"That was a spiritual massacre of the innocents," someone recalled many years later, when we were no longer Brothers. "That Duggan blighted the lives of many and he fouled the wells of our living!"

I recalled this when I read in Paul's epistle: '*He convinced us of sin*'. None of us felt innocent again.

"Do you think," my friend suggested, "that he caused some of us to reject the Catholic Church later?" We both agreed that it was quite possible. I had.

This was my second and memorable introduction to the subject of masturbation, which Duggan described as "self-pollution" and "self-abuse". As someone said to me later, "He should have minded his own business, instead of preying on us at an impressionable time of our life!" This condemnatory attitude, as I realised later, equated private masturbation and illicit lovemaking as acts of immorality. As someone said years later, "Why not chose lovemaking? Isn't it better to have complete enjoyment of your sin?"

I often wondered what the Novicemaster thought of Duggan. He was a gentle person compared to the priest, who was a product of a moral theology, which disapproves of love. Yet is it not strange that his Church forbids a castrated man to be ordained a priest? For some years afterwards Duggan directed retreats for teenagers in Christian Brothers' schools, where he preached his version of the gospel. He seemed popular with our ruling class, who must have known what he said, so they passed him around to spread this ethical teaching and immersed their students and us in his moral bilge. I never heard Duggan discussed at that time and only once afterwards while I was a Brother. His poison niggled at us until some of us freed themselves from the Church.

Christmas and Afterwards

I wondered how we might spend Christmas Day and expected the usual rigour. When grace was said at breakfast, the Novicemaster gave us permission to speak with the words "Live Jesus in our hearts!" to which we responded in disbelief, "Forever!"

Then talk came tumbling out as floodwaters through a breached dyke. We were given Christmas letters from our parents, which we read in silence and then began to converse.

"Oh Lord," joked Whisperer, "isn't it shocking that conversation pollutes the religious life! We need penances for this!"

Nobody except our parents was allowed to write to us. Each of us was cut off from his family because we had not received letters since September. I read my mother's letter and tried to distance myself from how I felt. My father had joined the army and she was alone with her other six children.

Whisperer was smiling to himself, when he read his letter.

"Well, what's funny?" I asked.

He put it in his pocket.

"It's not just what's in the letter," he said, "but what it brings to mind. Our neighbour Tom Neddy is dead since November, my mother says. He was the best card player in the village and his little house was a card school, which the old Biddies called a den of sin. One night at Christmas I went up on the low thatched roof and put a wet bag on the chimney and filled his kitchen with smoke. Tom came out shouting, 'Oh Lord above, protect me! My guardian angel is sending smoke from Hell to stop us playing cards. I'll never play them again, so I won't!'"

Whisperer smiled.

"You see, he didn't play for a while after that, but it was the case of 'when the Devil is sick, the Devil a saint will be, but when the Devil is well, the Devil a saint is he'. The card school assembled there again. Whenever I'll go home, won't I miss Tom Neddy?"

We had two periods of football and walks around the grounds before teatime, and then we said the Rosary in a yard near the dormitories. After a few minutes everyone stopped saying the prayers and we heard gales of laughter. The Novicemaster waited until the laughter ceased.

"Brothers, you're excused from the evening Rosary."

As I stood there, I felt relief, as the tension aroused by Duggan was dissipated just a little. I breathed with relief.

On Christmas night Alban O'Donoghue came to talk to us. He was the good-natured treasurer of the Irish Province of the Brothers.

"Probably none of you know that we once had a mission in China. Am I right?"

"Yessir!" chanted a few.

"Well, we had one in the 1920s and I was one of those who went there."

Years later I heard that the Superior-General was asked to send some men to China, and he passed on the request to the Irish Provincial. It was 1920 and the Provincial chose all the young men known to be Republicans, who might be in danger from British Forces. They were sent to Australia first and they had an Australian Superior in China called Harty, who was a martinet.

"We went to China," our speaker told us, "and two Jesuits accompanied us on one of the great rivers upstream to a city near two others. One of our men almost tripped over a Chinese man on the ferryboat, who apologised profusely. 'How polite he is,' said our man to a Jesuit, who replied 'I must tell you that this man said to his friend, 'Look at the unmannerly foreign dog!' Remember, Brother, you never offered an apology to him as you should have done!'"

The Jesuits knew the Chinese language and heard what he said, but our men did not and never learned a word of Chinese.

"And you may ask how did we get do there. First of all, we were not prepared for China." He launched into a long story ending with "Our Superior General considered that China was like India, where we taught the whites and ignored the natives. It is hard to believe that our Order had no concept of a foreign country with its own culture, and that we followed the British flag using the English language except in China." He could have added, '...and that's how we are still!' but he was talking to Novices and said nothing further about that. I knew that the Brothers disliked native pupils in their Indian and South African schools, as I heard later from those serving there.

"Well, here's how it ended. A warlord with a huge army approached from the north. Many of the Europeans fled. Our Superior decided that it was dangerous to stay and we left for the nearest city on the coast that was safe."

I heard later on that Harty, the martinet panicked, and together with his men was among the first of a few priests and religious to flee at the approach of danger. He telegraphed the Superior-General.

'*Where do we go?*'

He received this reply:

'*Go to Hong Kong!*'

In other words, 'Go to the British!' or as the cynics put it, 'Go to Hell!'

After we had night prayers, we went to bed happy on that Christmas Night, which was an oasis in our desert. I heard Whisperer muttering as he patted his belly happily.

"They ate, drank and played and then lay down to sleep!"

Those Vows

As monks we were due to take vows of poverty, chastity, obedience, and perseverance in the Order, and a fifth to teach the poor 'without fee or reward from them or their parents'. Obedience, the third one, we were told, could comprise the other four. One day Denis began talking to us on the subject of 'blind obedience'.

"You must obey all your Superior's orders without questioning any of them in intention or action. They represent God's will."

He told us about the novelist, Gerald Griffin, who joined the Christian Brothers some time after his book *The Collegians* was published.

"He was instructed that a Brother must act at once, when an order was given by word or the sound of the bell. After his sudden death in 1840 in Cork at the age of thirty-seven, it was found that he had stopped writing in the centre of a sentence to answer the call of the house bell."

I must say that Denis did hasten to qualify what he said.

"If your Superior orders you to do wrong, which is unlikely to happen, you must not do it."

I wondered how was I to know whether a Superior was right or wrong but did not ask how was I to know. We never discussed anything with him that he told us. It was a practical experience of the saying: 'Rome has spoken; the case is closed'. For us he was 'Rome'; he was in the right and there was no question of discussing anything.

One day Denis stated that the only serious sin was that of 'formal contempt'. I was surprised. Was it really the only real sin, although I thought there were ten according to Moses? And what did 'formal contempt' mean? It was "the formal rejection of God," he told us. This seemed crazy and I wondered could anyone commit a sin. To reject God, you must acknowledge a God, it seemed to me, and if you believed that, how could you reject Him formally? Let me admit that I was naïve.

As the days went by, it occurred to me that a person's health, pressure by others, a person's temperament and so on could cause a person to 'sin'. I wondered after a few weeks was there any such thing as a real sin? What was guilt then; had it any basis in itself, or was it an emotion without moral substance? I never asked the Novicemaster about it. He might think I was a heretic.

How did Duggan's statements on sin stand in the light of this? I wondered whether there was such a thing as a real sin for us, as I began checking the basis of the ethics of religious living. I decided to speak to our chaplain, who seemed bored until I blurted this opinion out.

"Where did you hear all this?"

"I thought of it myself."

"What a strange young fellow you are!" said he more to himself than to me. "You must put away these ideas. Do you hear me? If you go on thinking like this, you'll be either an atheist or an agnostic. Hold on to your faith."

Thus he dismissed my ideas, and I put them out of my mind gradually for some years. The dictionary, as I discovered, stated that an agnostic was one who doubted anything that was not of the material world, unless it was proved true from Nature. I understood later what Lord Attlee, the former British Prime Minister said, when replying to a query about whether he was an agnostic, "I do not know!"

That I could not speak to the Novicemaster about any difficulty was a serious defect in our training. The monks, who had adopted the Lancastrian system of group- or class teaching, seemed to think that it could be used to train novices. We were being mass-produced in a spiritual Lancastrian system. The nearest to individual attention was the 'private conference', an interview three times a year when each one met the Novicemaster. Three matters were discussed. First, there were our shortcomings or faults, which were paraded before us. Secondly, the question was asked "Is there anything troubling you?" The answer was a polite "No, sir!" Why incriminate yourself? The question, "Is there anything you wish to tell me?" must also elicit a firm "No, sir!" As members of a teaching Order you never told the teacher anything more than you thought it was prudent to reveal.

At one such interview I was given a hint that some of our companions were not very angelic.

"Have you ever heard stories," Denis began, "which are not suitable for a novice?" I was surprised at this and considered the question a moment.

"Just one story, sir!" I answered. "I forget who told it to me," I hastily added. He looked sharply at me and said almost casually, "I think you'd better tell me."

I drew a deep breath and told him one of Whisperer's yarns:

46

"One day a man gave a stranger a belt on the cheek and knocked him off his feet. He stood up, rubbed his face but did not retaliate, as the gospel advised. Then he struck him on the other cheek and the stranger fell again. When he stood up again, the stranger belted the other fellow on the face and knocked him down. The man complained: 'Christ said that you must show the other cheek when you're struck.' 'Yes' said the stranger, 'but he never said anything about what to do after the second blow.'"

Denis looked closely at me and he seemed to be trying not to laugh outright.

"Oh, go on off, young man," said he, "and God bless you!"

I wondered years later about these stories. I heard later that there was a story being told about the huge size of Revd Duggan's penis. Was that what Denis had heard? I was an innocent who was not yet interested in anything that was practically sexual at that time. However, I went to great lengths to acquire simple knowledge of sexual matters from the dictionary. For example, I discovered in the dictionary what a penis was. I also learned about circumcision and thought 'Christ's Circumcision' was an odd name for a feast day. When I was puzzled at the statement in the Old Testament that a warrior took his dead enemies' 'prepuces', I discovered what they were. Words such as 'vagina' and 'clitoris' were unknown to me because I never saw the words, so I did not know their meaning for some years afterwards.

The Ascetic Life

Who has ever heard of the Chapter of Faults? I did and I learned about it in the Novitiate and while I was a Christian Brother. We had Confession to deal with sin, when a priest shrove us, but the Chapter of Faults in the Christian Brothers dealt with non-Confessional matters, such as a public confession of breach of rules. We novices held our Chapter of Faults in the assembly hall. You knelt down and said this, for example:

"My very dear Brothers, I accuse myself of the following faults and beg your forgiveness if I gave bad example to anyone. I broke the silence three times; I was angry on the football field twice and rushed through the dormitory corridor once." After this the Novicemaster said something like, "Act better in the future, Brother. Say three Hail Marys. You may now return to your seat."

Whisperer, our Br de Sales, once surpassed himself. He was serious because his sense of fun was blunted, and he was embarrassed at what he said. He coughed a little as he began, "I broke three cups and one window pane in the kitchen. I drew a kick on the dog at the kitchen door because he annoyed me. I…"

"Br de Sales, will you please be serious?" the Novicemaster said. "This is not a glee club; this is a serious matter. Br de Sales, you will eat breakfast on your knees for the next three mornings because of your mockery of the Chapter of Faults!"

Whisperer had actually broken the cups and awkwardly threw something towards a windowpane shattering the glass. The wretched dog also felt the novice's boot, so Whisperer was innocent of mockery. After this Whisperer seldom spoke much for some time, but stood listening to the rest of us as we were talking. We were told often that we must accept punishment silently, but I could not understand in any way how the Novicemaster treated Whisperer.

When Lent came, the Novicemaster told us that because we were under-age, we were not obliged to fast, but the snub-nosed Socius had another opinion. He put it to us like this one day after Ash Wednesday: "You are all members of a religious Congregation and must mortify yourselves for the forty days of Lent. I must admit, however, that there is not as much boisterous conduct anymore among you as there was formerly."

Yes, I thought, you have hounded us on that often enough.

"You should now abstain as much as possible from the pleasures of the table."

These pleasures, let me say, consisted of eating some bread, porridge, potatoes, meat, eggs and vegetables. These items were simple food cooked roughly in large quantities, and not toothsome snacks or luxuries from a delicatessen.

"You must offer up your abstention from overeating to the good God, my dear young Brothers, in this holy season of Lent…"

Yes! I know that thousands of boys like us were on the verge of starvation, but they were victims of the war and without a choice. We young lads were told in God's name to deprive ourselves of nourishment as a virtuous act. I believe that the Novicemaster never knew what his assistant was doing. During that year all the well-built fellows were becoming thin. The cinctures became loose and the clips were drawn in further to accommodate the wasp-like waists which some developed. I also lost much weight as the others did, and my cincture was so loose that I used a pin to hold it up.

Whisperer, who was tall and gangly, now became frail and wispy, and another fellow's fat neck became scraggy and thin. Fred was lightly built and looked like a spectre because he ate little, and was no longer like the lad who had been with me since 1942. One day at midday tea he became agitated, jumped up and started screaming. The Novicemaster and John Kelly came and linked him out of the refectory. We heard no more of him. Later on, his cubicle was empty, his clothes were gone and so was he. I did not even have the opportunity of bidding him farewell. I heard long afterwards that he suffered a nervous breakdown, and six years later died of tuberculosis.

During that Lent we were introduced to a penance, which I can scarcely believe I experienced, but I certainly did. In this the Novicemaster was concerned and not the Socius, when a week after Ash Wednesday he spoke of penance before his morning instruction. More of the same, I thought! However, what he said was something new.

"My dear Brothers," he began, "we must mortify the flesh to obtain forgiveness for our sins and the sins of the world. Fasting is not for you because of your youth…" Did this man know at all, I wondered, what the Socius was urging us to do? "…but the saints mortified their flesh also by the use of the discipline."

'The discipline'? Was that control over people or what on earth was it? He took out of his pocket an object of five leathern thongs forty centimetres each in length, tied together and with three knots on each. I could hardly believe what I saw.

"This is the discipline, and with this you punish your body on certain nights after prayers before you go to bed. You must lash your back over each shoulder in turn." I heard a quiet sound from Whisperer; was it a bare laugh or suppressed despair? "My dear Brothers, you're not bound by rule or order to use this. If you decide to do so, the Socius will give one of these to you tomorrow or on later days."

I should have guessed that this man had to be in it somewhere! Thus we were introduced to this penance. Everything that arose during the Novitiate had been signalled somehow beforehand, but not the Socius' penitential regime and certainly not this 'discipline'. We read that this was the penitential fare of the saints.

On Friday nights we heard the slap of leathern thongs on bare skin as everyone did penance. I hated it and could not justify its use, so I gave myself minimum pain once or twice and never used it again. I did not have a taste for masochism, neither then nor at any time of my life.

Whisperer acted differently. He stood with his back to the open wardrobe door and the door took the punishment. One night the screen was pulled aside and the Socius stood there. Whisperer ate a breakfast on his knees for this and his leathern discipline was confiscated. I kept mine as a memento until before I left the Brothers and then I burned it, but I should have kept it as a relic of my days as a religious. I hated what it represented.

Easter Sunday was bright and suited our mood. We were free of the Socius' Lenten discourses, which he had indoctrinated into us. There were no Easter eggs or the like because, as the Socius announced, such fripperies were pagan practices. Revd Whisperer de Sales was cheerful. He spoke quietly when we were on a walk that day by the seaside to Blackrock.

"I must say that paganism must be fun, but what fun is in Christianity? Isn't it better to have pagan fun than to sink into holy misery?" He half-laughed and looked nervously around him in case he was heard. "The ears of the holy Socius are everywhere! Am I going raving mad like poor Fred did?"

We must have looked quite a spectacle on these walks. Each was dressed in black clothes with a Roman collar and with a hat on our heads. We were dressed like Victorian gentlemen but we were pale, and our emaciated young bodies were as sedate as middle-aged people after listening to the Socius and doing his bidding. However, we were only sixteen- or seventeen-year-olds, which must have made the contrast between our faces and our clerical clothes bizarre. A few times I saw some people stare at us. We probably looked like walking caricatures of youth. One time I heard a woman say, "Will yez look at the baby priests and they only out of the cradle, will yez? Do their mothers know they're out?"

Strange Ideas

I have an odd memento from these days, which is a notebook. I made it with scraps of paper from many sources pinned together with a clip, to keep notes on church history. I could not obtain a small copybook and many of the paper scraps are used envelopes. Other scraps were paper wrappers containing toilet paper with the name 'Toilet Paper Beacon' and an inscription which declared it 'safe soluble and sanitary'. A few are old typed examination papers cut to smaller sizes.

During the last four weeks of that Lent I read all I could find on the English Martyrs, priests trained in continental seminaries in Elizabethan times and hanged when they were arrested in England. The description of their deaths left nothing to the imagination. The priest was hanged, then cut down while still alive. The hangman disembowelled him and showed his heart to the spectators. The priest was then beheaded and his body quartered. This was not for the ears of the squeamish.

After months of this unwholesome fare I came to a decision about the status of non-Catholics. The Catholic faith was the true, faith so all must be forced into compliance with it, I decided. For refusing to do so, the penalty must be a merciless death. I find it hard now to believe that I came to this conclusion.

"Did you ever know any Protestants at home?" I asked Whisperer.

"I did!"

"Be serious now! Did you like them?"

"They never tried to knife me or burn our house or anything like that, and they did not grow horns or walk on hooves. Why are you asking such a daft question?"

"They have no right to do wrong!"

"What wrong? Cycling on the right-hand side of the road or eating meat on Friday?"

"They must believe in the True Faith!" I trumpeted. Whisperer stared at me as I continued: "Oh, yes! They must be jailed and even put to death if they profess heresy."

Whisperer did not smile.

"Oh, the Socius and his talk!" he murmured sadly with mock solemnity, "What harm, dear Brother, hath these heretics done to thee or others that thou art meditating murder because of zeal for the Lord God Almighty?"

So now at the latter part of my Novitiate year I was becoming a fanatic, although no one preached such dreadful notions to us and I never heard sectarian talk. My intense year of religiosity was bearing nasty fruit, but it left me when I left the Novitiate as foul stenches from a room when fresh air is allowed to blow through it.

Meanwhile the instruction on the vows went ahead. When we were taught about the vow of poverty, each of us received a document stating that we renounced all claims on money earned while we were Irish Christian Brothers. I signed the paper but no one witnessed it, and we signed another document stating that we agreed not to "enjoy the use and usufruct" of property given to us. In plain language we were not forbidden by the vow of poverty to own property or money but dared not use it or the income derived from it for personal use or to administer it. That was our religious vow of poverty in practice.

"It's great fun," said Whisperer to me, "that we're making wills, when we haven't a penny piece to rattle on a tombstone. We're living in some cloud-cuckoo land with the Socius, and also with our dear Brother Novicemaster. Weird."

I had not handled one penny since August 1942. In the Novitiate we submitted a written request for what we needed, such as stockings, toothpaste, shoes or a shirt. The Novicemaster could not be bothered with such trivia so the Socius handled this. When you sought something, you were summoned to the little man's presence.

"Yes," he said to me once, "and I see you want some toothpaste. Has it come to this that novices must have luxuries? Can't you scrub your teeth with a toothbrush? Do you have one? I suppose you'll be replacing that brush soon also!" He continued the monologue to wear the petitioner down. You were usually ordered "to come to me tomorrow and we'll see". Once when he went away for a week, John Kelly took his place and everyone received what was needed without being badgered.

If you had a headache or a cold or felt unwell, you also went to the same good Socius. Once after three days of severe headaches I asked him for an aspirin.

"You should offer up all pain for your sins, Brother!" he began. "What do you need an aspirin for? In my Novitiate days I never asked for such a thing. It is a luxury and not suited to the penitential life that we must lead." He looked closely at my head. "No wonder you have a headache," said he in triumph, "Your hair is full of dandruff. Comb that from your hair and you'll have no further headaches!"

Years later on I heard a barber told me that worry and tension increase the volume of dandruff in the hair. However, I learned from the little Socius how to cultivate a certain stoicism in the face of pain and discomfort, which served me well, although once it nearly cost me my life.

We received little instruction on the vow of chastity. Denis simply said, "You are renouncing marriage by taking this vow, but remember that the ordinary demands of the sixth and ninth commandments are more binding on you all than on others. I think that you all understand the facts of life." The truth was that I hardly knew the minimum.

We were advised to have no contact with any woman and we were to practise 'the guard of eyes'.

"You must learn how to appear to look straight at a woman's face, when you're just looking at her forehead," he told us.

Thus, we must not be ensnared by a woman's wiles or tempted by her to commit sins of the flesh, which were very serious, it appeared. No one ever gave us a good reason for celibacy. The vow of chastity, as I see it now, was based on negativity and while obedience and poverty make some sense for a religious person, chastity does not. Women were seen as temptresses to those serving God, as if the Devil created sexuality. I learned later on that in bygone years some Christian theologians thought that women did not even have immortal souls.

Concluding the Noviceship

While we were in religious isolation, the world outside us was collapsing but I had heard little about the World War except when prayers were said for peace. One day late in April Br Victor, manager of the kitchen, whispered to me to go to the backdoor, where I met Br Flatley, who taught me in Dungarvan. I had not met nor spoken to anyone outside the Novitiate in over ten months, because the Rules forbade us to do so but this was different, as I told myself. We shook hands and he told me how my family at home fared.

"It's hard on people to keep food on the table," he said, "and warmth in the house. There are shortages of everything."

As we shook hands, when we was about to go, I asked about the war and he whispered in Irish, "Poor Hitler is finished!"

We then bade goodbye to each another and I scuttled back to the kitchen. I never mentioned this major breach of rules in the Chapter of Faults.

Brother Victor was low-sized, burly and built like an ox. He could lift and move anything and he tended the heater in the kitchen, which looked like a small blast furnace. When the little door was open, it reminded me of hellfire, which Revd Duggan had told us was the punishment for any "sins of self-abuse". Whisperer, whose charge was to help in the kitchen, told me stories of Victor.

"He hates rats, did you know that?"

"Does he?"

"He has a cage trap, which catches rats alive and he kills them, when he has time."

"How?" Even though Whisperer was never boring, I felt that he was tedious now. I was startled when he went on to say:

"He pours boiling water over them in the cage trap and they die screaming. This scares all the rats in the neighbourhood, he says. Good old Br Victor! Hell has no heat like Victor's scalding water poured over trapped rats who're still alive!"

I shivered.

"One day he caught hold of a rat in the trap with a tongs, lifted him out and held him in the flames until he was ashes. Happy is he who escapes hellfire, reverend sir!" Oh, the cruelty of a good-natured, tolerant man, so kind to the youngest novice!

"Isn't that needlessly cruel?" I asked.

Whisperer smiled. "But you can't be nice to rats. They're dangerous things to have around the place!"

"Has he any cat around the kitchen area at all?"

"Not a single furry creature. Anyway, the mother cats produce kittens twice yearly and you must drown all these little so-and-sos. As to tomcats, they go off hunting tabbies and are absent too long, and they often die during their woman-hunts."

"I never thought of this before but isn't there cruelty everywhere?"

Whisperer did not reply but laughed quietly. He no longer indulged in wild laughs, which were boisterous and, as the Socius regarded them, scandalous.

On the morning of 10th May the Novicemaster paused after the short prayer in the study, which we said before he gave us daily instruction. He began to speak slowly.

"You might as well know that the war in Europe ended ere yesterday. The Germans are defeated, their country in ruins and a while ago Hitler committed suicide in the ruins of Berlin. So now Brothers, he that takes the sword, shall die by the sword, and Hitler died as a hardened sinner by his own hand."

In Whisperer's words, "Adolf Hitler has gone to his reward, whatever that may be!" So the war was over!

Many people and neighbours at home thought that Hitler was a great man, one who could put the British in their place. We wished the German armies well in France and in the invasion of Russia, although there were many Irishmen in the British Army and some from Dungarvan. It sometimes confused me.

"The worst of it all, Brothers," said the Novicemaster, "is that the atheistic Russian communists are now in the centre of Europe. We'll all be in danger and many of us may die as martyrs if they sweep westwards. Let's pray for all in danger from atheists who do not believe in God and who hate those who serve Him."

The good man never told us about what happened to the Ashkenazi Jews at Auschwitz, Treblinka, Birkenau and elsewhere. He probably never read the newspapers, and he depended on what he heard from the Provincial and his staff. I began to wonder was the good man becoming as isolated as the former Novicemaster was.

That May, as I recall it, was a beautiful month. I heard a blackbird whistle in a bush one day, when I was lining a pathway with stones. I tried to discover what notes he was singing, but he was a virtuoso performer and sang an *obbligato* after each tune and both were irrecordable. Each tune led him into a further ecstasy of music. I loved it and revelled in it, as if I had never listened to a bird singing before.

When it was decided that we were to spend a day on Killiney beach in June, I could hardly imagine that we were allowed into the sinful world! We were actually about to taste a little freedom from the binding routine of a novice's life. The previous night people rushing about in the dormitory awakened me, and I heard toilets flushing. Finally, I rushed out with cramping pains. It was eleven o'clock the next day when the sorties to the toilets ended. We simply could not travel to the beach.

"I know what happened," said the Whisperer, "Victor dumped Glauber's salts in the tea urn last evening and we all got the runs."

"How do you know?"

"He's like that. Someone had to do it and it might as well be Victor, the ratkiller." Victor provided Whisperer with relief from boredom and isolation.

When we did go to Killiney a few days later, it was fun and we enjoyed the hours on the beach as lads of our age should. As I saw them swimming, I noticed many were skinny and worn. We wore football togs because our genitals could not to be seen bulging through them, as in the swimming togs that we had since we were in Baldoyle and Bray. These were left in our clothes closets.

That afternoon, when we returned, there was ice cream, which was a luxury in the Novitiate but we did not have it even in Bray and Baldoyle. The Socius must have thought that our religious life was becoming lax, because the Novicemaster was breaking a Victorian tradition, unlike his predecessor and the Socius.

We must have heard more news of what was happening in mainland Europe. On 12th July I mentioned in a letter to my mother that "I hear that nothing will stop a famine on the continent next winter." However, we had other concerns at that time, which did not include further lectures from the Socius, who went on holidays out of our sight. Our successors as Novices were coming from Bray and Baldoyle, and we prepared sixty places for them. We spent hours cleaning and waxing. We were also on the farm turning hay, the cows' winter fodder, and most of us used sticks to turn it because there were not enough hayforks. The tension was lessening a little now.

We walked down to the seaside by the railway station for a swim most days, and then crossed the rails to the sea wall and undressed on the beach. It was wonderful not to be cooped in. We enjoyed swims in Dublin Bay, then unpolluted, where we saw ships moving in and out in the silence of journeys on water.

I recall seeing a priest from the USA in his shirtsleeves with a pretty girl, who laughed at everything he said. As Whisperer put it, "Ah, she is no doubt his sister, safeguarding him from the works of the Devil. She'll save his virtue from other women, who await him with temptations to commit jolly sins." Really? Whisperer must have been joking!

In the middle of July the new lads came to Booterstown. We stood silently in the yard with hands in sleeves awaiting them, until they chattered their way into the yard. As they arrived, the talking ceased.

I thought Whisperer muttered: "All hope abandon, ye who march in here."

I was always imagining how he might comment on something but he was very wary during the past year. He was sure to have breakfast on his knees, if he commented on all that grated on his sense of the ridiculous. The Socius never welcomed the newcomers. As Whisperer in other days might put it, "He didn't say a word, or 'ye're welcome'! 'Kiss me arse'! or 'a ha'porth'!'"

I was to be the 'guardian angel' of Joe Walsh from Co. Galway. He was quiet, said little and seemed most unexcitable. I felt that if I asked him to fetch me the moon or collect a star, he might say, "Yes! Brother!" A few novices were not appointed as 'guardian angels', such as Whisperer. I felt that the Socius barely tolerated him and might have dismissed him, if he had the power to do so, but only the Novicemaster had that.

Those who were being dismissed or voluntarily leaving the Novitiate slept the night beforehand in a room far from our quarters, which we called 'the White Man's Grave', where the doomed one spent his last hours with the Brothers. We never knew when anyone was leaving, and never had the opportunity of bidding good-bye. I think about five left us but am not sure. The Novicemaster and the Socius declared that a vocation to the religious life was a special grace. The latter added that anyone who rejected this grace and left the Order was eternally damned. I believed it and prayed for lifelong perseverance. I wondered at the eternal fate of those who left us, all doomed to Hell, or so it seemed.

One time Whisperer dropped his voice as he remarked, "Maybe the Socius wishes to send me to Hell via the White Man's Grave." He lightened my days for many years afterwards, as he slowly regained his sense of humour and could laugh safely at the oddities of our life, when we left that place.

On 5th August our last silent eight-day retreat in the Novitiate began, which ended on the night of the 13th. We had a Jesuit this time, called Mallin, whose father was executed after Easter Week 1916, and who was not emotionally deranged as Duggan was. He spoke in a light-hearted manner. I was relieved that he did not add to the tension that hung in the air. I know that some of us felt at the end of our tether, but the Jesuit had a sense of humour and we laughed gladly when he gave us the opportunity.

One morning during the eight-day retreat he said, "Young men, you'll be interested to hear that two days ago the United States Air force dropped a new kind of bomb on Hiroshima in Japan. It is a fearful weapon, which melted a town when it exploded."

He speculated about it and I heard the words "atomic bomb" for the first time. We heard more about this from him, and also what had happened in the European war. Then he told us also some days later about the bombing of Nagasaki and added tit-bits of news, which he garnered from the newspapers.

The Novicemaster called me aside and asked what I thought of the 'secular material' in the priest's talks, and I heard later that he questioned others also. I told him that I liked knowing what was happening in the world.

The good man looked sharply at me and said "Very well! Go along then!"

In his last 'private conference' with me he told me that he had high regard for me but he added, "There is something else, which is very important for me to bring to your notice and serious for your future with us, but I just cannot put it in so many words. I wish that I could but at any rate I wish you all the best."

With that inconclusive and vague statement I left his office, where we seemed to have met in some form of mutual misunderstanding. He was a kind but inexperienced Novicemaster, who was learning the skills of directing novices. We were supposed to be instructed as a group of disparate people to cultivate what was to be an individual spirituality, but were trained spiritually like recruits in the barracks in a system that made us disciplined members of a lay religious Order.

On 15th August the new Novices were officially received. We were no longer Novices but we were not professed Brothers until we took our vows on Christmas Day. When we left Booterstown, the Novicemaster seemed moved as he bade us goodbye. We were his first charges, whom he tried to make good religious men, hoping that we were now feathered enough to bear ourselves aloft in the rarefied religious air.

Before we left, when the Novicemaster had wished us future happiness, the Socius nodded to us as we marched out to the railway station. I wished our successors well but doubted if they could benefit from mere wishes. They had to deal with the Socius, who embodied a form of mental violence towards simple human beings.

The Novicemaster's last words to us were: "Go now to serve the Lord and your reward will be great in Heaven. Remember the words of Scripture, 'They, who will do and teach, shall shine like stars for all eternity'. May the Lord bless you all! Amen!"

A decent man uttered these good words, but the future has its own plans ready for me, I thought. What these were, I could not and did not try to guess.

In Marino

We were never so much alone as in the Novitiate at Booterstown and we did not have visitors. When we were leaving it on 16th August 1944, we left solitude behind us and what was solitary, and faced once more into part of the real world in Marino, where we learned to teach and take some part in 'real life'. It was the gateway to the world for us but it was a hindered gateway, because we had renounced the world. We had become religious men at the age of seventeen, which was rather early in our lives for such a wide ranging decision, but each of us took his vows intending them to be for the whole term of his life.

When we left Booterstown on 16th August to go to St Mary's, Marino, we were thin seventeen-year-old lads, who never smiled and our black hats shaded our faces. We acquiesced in all that happened and any show of independence meant dismissal; each of us learned to keep his own counsel. The monastery in Marino, built of granite in the early twentieth century, overlooked Dublin City and was the most prominent building in the area. It was built for £30,000, which was collected in a funding campaign throughout Ireland. Behind St Mary's stood the separate college of St Joseph, which was built without a front door – I was told – as 'an extension' of the older building to avoid payment of rates.

Besides the student Brothers, the Superior-General of the Irish Christian Brothers lived in St Mary's with his four assistants and bursar. Some called the area near Marino monastery 'the Holy Land'. Here was St Patrick's monastery for those teaching in St Patrick's Primary School, as well as the nuns' Primary School for girls. There was the O'Brien's Institute, an orphanage, and near it the Casino, a neo-classical building from 1762. When I asked what it was used for, I was told, "That thing? It's a pagan temple and should be flattened!" It is there still.

In the Great Monastery

We were all relieved to go to the teachers' training college at St Mary's,

Marino, which we entered by the back entrance where there were flowerbeds in a yard. We were led into a large study, where the Superior introduced himself. He smiled as he spoke, and the tilt of his head showed determination to see all things through to their conclusion.

"I am Brother Dermot, the Superior here," he began, "whose duty is to look after you all." Whisperer tittered for the first time since last autumn. "You've a year's study ahead of you," Dermot said, smiling, "and you'll be taking first vows at Christmas. If anyone is troubled about anything, he should come to me and we can talk." As an afterthought he added, "You'll be studying to prepare for your teaching work, so eat well, because you seem to need lots of food to study and teach effectively."

He talked for about ten minutes. Then about thirty young Brothers came in whom we knew already, and they showed us around the monastery with much laughter and talk.

One of the Superior General's staff remarked, "These boys need nourishment. What happened them in Booterstown?" Another said to Dermot O'Brien, "You must feed these young men; what on earth is the new Novicemaster doing?" Dermot often examined the plates after meals, to discover if everyone was eating sufficiently.

As Whisperer put it, "We had holy hunger in Booterstown and the Socius told us not to eat to satiety, but now we know that it was semi-starvation!"

The monastery was three storeys high and E-shaped. The whole building faced towards the south. The oratory was in the centre shaft with storerooms underneath and a central heating furnace below them. The offices of the Superior-General were on the ground floor in front. The college staff slept in the top storey, and we were in the rooms above the study and classrooms. There was a large farm attached to the monastery, which supplied it with vegetables, potatoes and milk. In 1945 some of the new Dublin housing settlements were gradually enveloping this Holy Land of Marino.

There were bedrooms in the eastern two top storeys of the huge house, where fifty-two men about twenty-three or twenty-four years of age lodged. They studied for the final year of the teacher training course after some years' teaching. They had done the first year's training course and were sent out to teach at the age of eighteen, when about half of the Primary School Brothers teaching in the Twenty-Six Counties were half-trained. We were not allowed to speak to the Second Year students, the largest group that returned to Marino. They were used to life outside Marino and resented their confinement there. The fifty-two men called themselves "the pack of cards" and resented being treated like Novices. Two of them went to Dermot to complain that their letters were opened, but he told them that he was acting within the rules and that they had made a vow of obedience. It struck me that Dermot, who was kind to us, had reason to speak to them abruptly. They were all teachers, who were used to giving orders. They formed a choir and each night we heard the resonance of choruses from their quarters. It seems to me that they released in song their frustration at being confined almost like us.

I remember one night when I looked from a large stairway at the lights twinkling in the darkness in the city, which was as inaccessible to me as the Milky Way.

"What are the people there thinking of, and what are they doing?" I thought. "Are they sleeping, dancing or having fun? Will I ever be able to walk under these lights?"

Professor of Education

Our Professor of Education was Jan Martin, a florid-faced man from Cork City. I can see him with his left hand clasped behind his back, even when writing something on the blackboard.

"Use the visual sense in teaching," said he, "as well as your voice. For effective teaching all five senses should be used.

"Ah," he said the first day, "the prestige of the monks as teachers is high among Irish parents – but who're their children's teachers? You'll be foisted on the youth of Ireland as half-baked teachers with one year's training." He formed chubby cheeks and lips into a fleshy smile. "You'll be teaching children as half-trained teachers, and others of the same type will follow you!"

He reminded us that about ten young men also were sent teaching every year without any training. Some failed the Leaving Certificate examination in Bray, repeated it in Marino and were inflicted on the pupils as teachers without any training. It was clear that those leading the Order considered teacher training unimportant. This was how the oldest male teaching Irish religious Order prepared their teachers.

"Don't ever forget," said Jan, "that the Brothers had their own teacher-training before 1926 and their own schoolbooks, especially the English reading books." I recalled the Third Standard book that we used in Fourth Standard at home, because the standard of English fell after the Brothers joined the National School system in 1926. "They had their own School Inspectors," said he, "who trained the young Brothers. When you're teaching, you'll deal with the State's School Inspectors, who daren't bully you because you're monks. However, they bully other young teachers, especially the young women." I later discovered that the women were the most dedicated teachers of all, and that there was not even a good excuse for this bullying.

So we enjoyed hearing the Professor of Education criticising the Irish Province and the Department of Education, when we had been trained in the Novitiate never to criticise anybody in authority. Most twentieth-century Irish governments contained ex-pupils of the Christian Brothers, including many Taoiseachs. The schools supplied the British colonies with officials, whose parents could not afford the college fees.

Half-trained teachers taught in the Southern Irish State but in the Six Counties of Northern Ireland all teachers were fully trained under the British system. From our group three lads were sent to Strawberry Hill teachers' training college in England, to be fully trained for schools in the Six Counties. I found it very odd that the Brothers ignored the authority of Dublin Department of Education successfully but that its English counterpart was obeyed.

Very many of those who left the Order in the south did so in their early years, so tuition money was saved. The good Brothers had no intention of training young men fully as teachers in Dublin, when three-quarters of them of that age group left or were dismissed. This led to all Brothers teaching half-trained or untrained in their first five years of service. The Irish Department of Education agreed with this for decades.

Jan often spoke of the early Christian Brothers.

"This monastery was built at the beginning of the twentieth century," he said, "a century after our founder, Edmund Rice, began teaching the boys from the streets of Waterford City. He was a widower and a very successful Catholic merchant who traded in the late-eighteenth century. Even though he had a comfortable life in Waterford, he dedicated the rest of it to teaching the city roughnecks. He taught free of charge those who were never considered worth teaching before that. His motto was 'They that will do and teach, shall shine as stars for all eternity'. Let that be yours also." Jan went on. "He had a mentally retarded daughter. The Brothers pestered him in his old age to give them the money settled on her, because they thought it wasted on a girl who was simple, as they put it. Oh, yes!" added Jan reflectively, "Don't think that our founder was just a zealous teacher. He taught children in Waterford religion to prevent Protestant proselytism."

Rice and his friends had neither Novitiate nor teacher training, he told us, but were amateurs who worked in fever-infested cities and towns. When Marino monastery was built after 1900, it reflected the emergence of the Christian Brothers from poverty to minimum comfort.

"Do you young gentlemen know that the Brothers in the Primary Schools never received salaries from 1804 until 1926?" Jan asked one day. "A yearly collection was taken for the local monastery to supply their needs for twelve months. They lived very frugally and could be ranked among the poor of the land. If they had to depend on the yearly collections, their poverty was permanent because they refused to join in the National School system and receive salaries."

"Why did they refuse to join the National Schools, sir?" somebody asked. Jan turned his rotund form away and then came back to face us with dramatic effect.

"The National Board of Education forbade prayers and religious symbols in the classroom except during religious teaching. The monks dared not say the hourly 'Hail Mary' or have a statue displayed in the classroom under these regulations."

However, the Brothers sometimes had rich friends, who gave them money, and in small towns they had farms to grow food. We murmured our interest and I saw Whisperer steal looks at a novel on his lap, which he read for his artistic benefit, as he put it. He could shove it under the desk, if need be.

Jan continued talking between his impressive throat clearings.

"The first time in the history of the Christian Brothers that our men earned money from teaching was from the 1870s onward, when the Brothers used the Secondary Education system, an examination board. They were paid on the results of preparing pupils for the Junior, Intermediate and Leaving Certificate examinations. To do this they had to teach themselves Mathematics, Science, English, French and Latin, and never attended a university because there was none that Catholics could attend. I think that was an odd form of education for both the teachers and the taught!"

As he concluded with this remark, he smiled. Whisperer shoved in his book as Jan looked at us, tasting his own words and preparing to leave us.

Student Teaching

One Friday morning we heard that we were going to have teaching practice in schools for three weeks. On the following Monday morning, 15th October 1945 ten of us went to St Patrick's School nearby and I was sent to 5B standard, where the not-so-bright children were. The night beforehand I received school books which reminded me of the year that I spent in Fifth Standard in Dungarvan with Br Rogers, when we used at least two of these.

At 10 o'clock when I arrived in the classroom, the Brother motioned me to a desk at the back of the room where I witnessed a quarter of an hour's teaching. He held a black strap in hand as he set about drilling his pupils in multiplication. It went thus:

"Five nines?"

"Fifty!" The child's hand is extended and a great smack cuts across his palm.

"You!"

"Forty-five!"

"Nine sevens?"

"Sixty-two, sir!" Another hefty slap.

It went on until eighteen of the forty boys were nursing their hands with tears running down their cheeks. I remembered what Jan said:

"No one is allowed to punish a pupil physically for failure in lessons. Only the principal teacher may punish corporally but he delegates this to each teacher!"

On that first day as student teacher, I saw in a school how it could really be.

I took two classes that day; one in English reading and the other in Geography. I loved teaching and I spent all the time I could with the boys, teaching them that week while the teacher sat at his desk. I wondered did he like children at all. Every morning before we went to school, we were inspected in the study hall before we went to teach. Dermot went from one to the other to see had we trimmed our nails and shaved properly, and he inspected our clothes.

The second week some of us were sent to Lawrence O'Toole's School in a poor quarter of the city. We walked there every morning and as we passed near a jam factory in Ballybough, I remember the sweet smell of cooking fruit. I was posted to Sixth Standard, whose teacher was Br Philip Slattery.

"Did you have a good breakfast?" he asked.

I told him how well I had eaten.

"Good," he remarked, "but remember many of these boys in front of us here never eat a decent bit. When we teach them, they haven't much energy to take in knowledge."

He set to work as I watched. He was strict and intense but never slapped a boy or said more than, "Won't you listen a moment?"

The boys were mostly dressed in hand-me-down clothes, mottled with patches and some of them were in rags. They liked Philip and although he was lenient with them, he exercised firm discipline. The words "great respect" occur to me when I think now of him and them.

That evening Jan met me and asked how I liked teaching.

"I arranged for you to be with Br Philip." I muttered something about how good he was. "As a teacher, is it? I bet you didn't guess that he's a regular weekend visitor to Mountjoy Gaol as well, where the fathers, big brothers or relatives of some of his pupils are or were." Philip was the only Brother that I knew who visited Mountjoy.

One day after Religious Instruction, Philip wondered about the boys.

"Why do you say that?" I queried.

He was tidying books on his desk.

"There's at least one boy of twelve years here, who's the father of a child, I hear. He's said to have fathered a child to be born soon, I'm told."

"What?" I exclaimed. I was shocked at this. In the 1980s and afterwards this was never kept secret, but when it happened in the 1940s, very few knew it. I was more shocked when Philip said that the pregnant girl was the boy's sister.

"In crowded tenements it's strange that incest isn't more common." he added.

"Why?" I asked.

He shrugged his shoulders as he said, "In one bedroom you have boys and girls together with their parents, who become familiar with one another. It is a short step from seeing to doing when they come to puberty. It's a blessing when families are moved into the new houses, where boys can be separated from girls and parents from children at night."

As I thought of this, the phrase "eye-opening" describes how I felt about it.

The Principal of the school, Br Magrath, was a 'walking Principal' and never taught. He was boss and record-keeper of "Larrier's", as they called the school. Magrath wore a biretta and the staff nicknamed him 'Father Magrath'. His office was at the front door and only teachers, pupils and Inspectors were allowed to enter the school. Above all, no one was allowed to go to a classroom door.

When angry mothers called to Larrier's "he put manners on them", a teacher told me. "On a Monday morning we often had brawling mothers at the school doors until he came here." When Philip called Magrath "our good reverend headmaster", he smiled gently.

I spent my last week teaching at St Patrick's with a teacher who was a Brother and a student at University College, where he went to lectures at night to secure a degree. When he graduated, he then qualified as a Secondary Teacher by gaining the Higher Diploma in Education. Some Brothers attended university full time, but not he.

In this the Christian Brothers were the antithesis of the Jesuits. The teacher-Brother must know at least the elements of literacy, numeracy and other basics, in order to transmit it all to unwilling youngsters and insist on strict order. They worked among the urban poor in the nineteenth century and learned that education did not fill stomachs. To instruct the ignorant, they learned, they need not be highly educated, which might be a liability. What good are knowledge and thought, if your only object is to fill minds with facts to pass an examination? I heard a Brother describe the university degrees and the Higher Diploma in Education as "excrement for increment!"

I enjoyed my time with the pupils of another teacher who studied as I taught, and was experiencing again as an adult how it felt to be taught and to learn. He stopped reading sometimes to make a remark such as, "Will you listen to the man who's teaching you, Peter, down there? Get out of your feathery dreamland, boy!"

On All Hallows' E'en in that year of 1945, when I arrived for dinner a little late from school, I saw oranges on the table, the first since 1939. The war was now really over.

From Day to Day in Marino

I seldom played games in Marino, so I joined the firewood gang instead. Fuel was scarce, the belly of the heating furnace had a huge appetite and trees were felled to feed the monster which kept our damp Irish weather at bay. The leader of the fuel gang was the Professor of Mathematics, Br Adrian Mulholland. We all spoke Irish but he spoke a weird form, which was often a massacre of its vocabulary, idiom and syntax. He translated the mathematical term "simplify", for example, by words which meant "Make it let to be simplified".

I can picture Adrian armed with an axe splitting great rounds of sawn timber, but I forget what work I did; not much probably. One Saturday afternoon I remember the felling of a magnificent oak about two centuries old that had been prepared to die. He and some strong farmers' sons sawed into the tree to undermine its stability. They tied a long rope to the upper branches and forty of us pulled it as in a great tug-of-war. We heaved and pulled until we heard a loud *crack*. The oak split loudly as it died and fell slowly, rocking on its great spreading branches. It took about two months to reduce it all to fuel for the furnace after its two centuries of life. I can picture Mulholland dressed in under-vest, pants and boots on the cold winter days, wielding his axe and dealing mighty strokes.

We were all inured to cold. Each of us had a heavy black cloak with a cape, which reached almost to the ground and within it we found shelter as in a house of heavy cloth. Brass fittings fastened it at the neck and it was very comfortable. I recalled the words of an English sixteenth-century poet Spenser describing the Gaelic Irish cloak as "a fit house for an outlaw, a meet bed for a rebel, and an apt cloak for a thief".

"Did you know that some guns smuggled into Howth in 1914 were hidden in that tree?" Jan remarked. "Oh, let me tell you that these Mauser rifles from Germany used in Easter Week 1916 were cast-offs of the German Army, after they armed their troops with modern Mauser rifles instead."

My charge each morning that year was the bedroom of Revd Gregory Hogan, who was Assistant to the Superior-General, a man from Tipperary, who walked with a stoop and was, we heard, an ardent enforcer of the rule prohibiting smoking. He carried out the Assistant-General's duty, when he visited Brothers' houses throughout the world to interview Brothers, to ensure that rules were observed. Gregory was once sent on an official visitation in China, where the community smoked amid the odours of the packed city. When he was brought on a walk through a foetid area, Gregory exclaimed, "Oh, my God! This is a putrid place! Give me a cool smoke of a pipe!" They said that he seemed to be experienced, when he grasped the pipe between his teeth.

I stayed longer in Gregory's room each morning than I should have done, as I read the books that were on his shelves. I was surprised to see a translation of Hitler's *Mein Kampf* that was much thumbed, and I read parts of it that I had heard discussed so much. One thing struck me about significant books, which are discussed widely, is that few people bother to read them through, although that does not hinder their critical comments as happened in the case of *Mein Kampf*.

There was a silly apocryphal story about Gregory that was whispered in the college. It described how he was going by car, when there was a collision with a cow, which scattered its milk teats on the road. Gregory was stunned but his companion, a city man, was uninjured. He saw one of the teats and wailed, "What will poor Gregory do now?" Only the cow lost it and Gregory's masculinity, as we heard, remained intact.

Our Professor of Science was Augustine Malone, whose hair was scanty and whose rimless spectacles seemed to emphasise his sensitive features. Malone was a fanatic about the Irish language and never spoke a word of English, if he could. When he mentioned English, he never said *Béarla* for English, but *Sacsbhéarla* ('Saxon tongue), which he spat out but yet we knew him as a very gentle soul. He taught us about general hygiene and the cleanliness of wash basins in bedrooms, because Brothers cared for their own rooms. Our fellow-Brothers were notorious, he said, for having untidy bedrooms and ill-kept basins.

He advised us, "Shave your face every morning and brush your hair. You must never present yourself before children with a hairy face and an unkempt appearance!"

Malone was the only Brother to rail against excessive corporal punishment.

"We've a reputation for being rough on our pupils. I ask you never to do that, as I did when I was young. Sometimes I see a former pupil in Dublin, who walks off when he sees me. Learn from me and don't have to learn from what you've done to your pupils."

He spoke about a Christian Brother indulging in alcoholic drinks.

"If you're offered a drink, be careful," he said. "Drinking whiskey is the sign of a hard man; a porter drinker shows he's a steady toper, but taking a glass of wine is what you may do if you're offered a drink." He insisted that it was better that we should not take any of these. "All these drinks can destroy you if you're not careful," he said often.

Years afterwards I met a nephew of his.

"Did you know that Uncle Gus's father," said he, "was an alcoholic? He disrupted family life, beat his wife and ill-treated his children." No wonder, I thought, that Malone detested alcoholic drink.

Malone was a competent hurler, who went out most days with the students and shared in the game. I was impressed when I saw him on the field. Above all, Malone spoke about caring for small injuries that school children might suffer at school. We must care for our pupils' well-being as well as instructing them.

Brother Francis Dowling, younger brother of the Socius, was Professor of English. Francis seemed to have no feeling for literature, and he bored us pleasantly during the week. He stood with a text in one hand and the other in his pocket, never raised his voice but smiled to prove he was alive or seemed so. He was not a fanatic like his brother in the Novitiate, never hurt anyone or gave offence; he liked an easy life and enjoyed a few discreet drinks, I heard. Frank was not an inspiring teacher but was a good man, who was tolerant towards everyone.

As he did not seem to have a great interest in English literature, we made our own of the poetry in his class, which I grew to love. He read each poem and asked, "Well, what you think of that?" This elicited odd replies but Frank seemed to swill his tongue about his mouth as he said, "Well, make the poem your own and enjoy it!" Whisperer thought it comical.

"What a wise frank statement, my dear reverend sir!"

It was a new experience for any of us, when we formed our own ideas on the poems. I had detested Shakespearean plays, because they were taught intensively, but here I enjoyed *Twelfth Night*. Out of Frank's neutrality towards English literature, his ignorance of it and his lack of interest in it, I appreciated at last a Shakespearean play.

Christmas and its Aftermath

As Christmas drew near, we practised hymns for Midnight Mass. The chapel had a high ceiling with an organ loft, under which at the rear knelt the Superior-General and his Assistants and our staff. Dermot led all the prayers from there.

We, who were called the "garks" (after the Irish *gearrcaigh* for nestlings) sat on the right-hand side of the chapel, the men's side in Ireland, and on the left side were the Second Year students. There were over one hundred and forty people of all ages there kneeling in the body of that little chapel.

The organist was Br Farrell, Professor of Music, of which he knew little – and Professor of History, of which he knew almost nothing. He derided those students he disliked, of whom I was one but you could not defend yourself because he was assured he was never wrong. Farrell had the musical taste of an inferior bandmaster. He knew as much history as Frank did English literature, but Frank allowed us to discover English for ourselves: Farrell combined his sophisticated airs with arrogance.

Before Christmas the eight-day retreat took place. A few days beforehand Dermot asked me to his office, where I found Kevin.

"We want you to come with us to the city," Dermot explained. Why? I asked myself. On the tram Kevin said that he was going to see an optician.

"I'm going blind; did you know that?" he asked.

When we were returning to Marino, Dermot sat in another part of the tram and left me with Kevin, who was upset and confused.

"What were you told about your eyes?" I began.

"Oh, they're so weak that I'm unfit for teaching, so I'm not taking vows."

Tears ran down his face as he told me that he could be profoundly blind in a few years. Two women near us looked at him and one of them spoke about the poor *priesteen* (little priest) being upset, and I felt I was suspected of causing his tears. It was clear that I was brought to support Kevin. Three or four days later he left us. Unlike other departures, I spent time with him the night before he went, and bade him farewell before Dermot O'Brien saw him to the train in the morning.

I discovered that he became a successful auctioneer. When I met him forty years later, his sight had slowly improved. If Kevin had taken vows, they dared not dismiss him from the Brothers, but he was compelled to go because he was unprofessed.

Christmas

I forget who directed the Christmas retreat and what he said but I suppose he spoke about the vows we were taking. They were to be renewed annually for five years or until the age of twenty-five, when final vows were taken. I expected to renew them for seven or eight years because I was seventeen years of age.

On Christmas morning before breakfast we sang a Plain Chant piece in the chapel, *Veni creator spiritus*, "Come, creator spirit", which Farrell tolerated because it was required for this occasion. Some senior men took final vows and the Superior-General signed their papers, while others renewed vows afterwards. Our turn came next. It was a solemn moment and the culmination of three-and-a-half years of idealism, training and brain-washing. I knew nothing of life, had no worldly wisdom, no sexual feelings and was not street-wise but a naïve innocent fellow. We were the products of a formation machine, whose object was to promote the interests of a religious Order and designed to bypass a person's normal course of life. I believed that I was a Christian Brother for life but as Thomas à Kempis put it, "Man proposes and God disposes". I had one object but fate decreed that I take a different course, when I no longer believed in the religious life of monk or Brother.

Some days afterwards Whisperer said casually, "Dear Brother, as a professed member of the Congregation, do you feel like one of the angels?"

I laughed as I said, "Not while you're there to laugh it out of me!"

It was an enjoyable Christmas. We had plenty of food compared to what was available on mainland Europe, where many were starving at that time in 1945. Dermot and the others wore paper caps and Whisperer was in manic good humour.

"I remember one Christmas our postman stayed for the day," he said.

"Is that so?" I commented casually.

Whisperer was chuckling as he went on, "He fell down drunk at our door on Christmas Eve, so we put him in the barn for the night."

This aroused my interest.

"In the hay?" I asked.

"That was the very place," he replied, "where he slept with the hens. The postmaster in town sent out someone to find him, who stayed 'til midnight drinking poteen until he was canned too!"

"I don't believe a word of what that fellow is saying," someone said. "Was he tippling the altar wine this morning or what?"

We had a concert that night where we heard the older students singing what they had been rehearsing since November. Farrell had produced the play, whose name I forget and in which the women were portrayed by our companions, such as Paul and Whisperer. I surprised him and Paul embracing in the corridor. Whisperer kissed him and the other exclaimed, "Oh beautiful Holy Ghost!" I thought it funny but years later knew that it had a significance beyond light-hearted fun.

On Stephen's Day the Novicemaster visited us and gave us congratulation cards on our religious Profession.

"Doesn't Black Jack look frail?" Whisperer remarked afterwards. "The Socius is sucking his blood! The poor man will never hear another cuckoo."

Those who played games had a fixed period for them every day during the holidays but we also went on long walks. When I think of where we went, I realise that Dublin has changed. For example, we could go to Fairview by Philipsburg Avenue where there were fields on both sides of the road in front of the college. We returned to classes after New Year's Day, when a 'flu epidemic broke out. At first there were five lads very ill.

After two days, Dermot arrived in the study hall to ask, "Who will act as volunteers to nurse the sick? We need to help ourselves."

I was one of the volunteer nurses, which suited me fine because I was free to go and come as I wished. We gave each sick fellow a small glass of liquid cascara, a purgative, with a large glass of hot milk after it. What the two items did to the patient can be imagined, and what we nurselings did to care for them was rough and ready.

Eventually more than half our group became ill and the 'flu hit me. Dermot came to administer the cascara, which I swallowed. I had no mind to drink it but did as I ordered others to do. Then he pulled a bottle of lemonade from his pocket.

"And now the nurse must have a luxury!" he remarked.

Years afterwards I discovered that a purgative and boiled milk were given to patients in Irish fever hospitals in the nineteenth century. We gave the ill ones the same treatment as fever patients received in the fever of 1831 and the Great Famine years, but they were given calomel instead of cascara with the hot milk.

Just when I became ill, two nursing nuns took over our duties. I was too ill to recall them or whether they came to visit me. At night I felt great flames drenched in water roasting me in my fever-land of fire and water. When we recovered, we were so weak that few went to play games. Those that I nursed spent relaxing days sitting about reading books and playing games of cards with neither study nor classes. We 'nurses', on the other hand, recovered just in time to resume the routine of prayers, study and classes and had no convalescence.

I heard that Mulholland spoke of what epidemics do.

"When a great fever came to Europe, religious rules were relaxed," as he put it to his timbermen. "Look at the days after the 'flu! When that went on, not a rule was kept in the house!"

Mary Mother of Christ

The name of the college was St Mary's and we were told to cultivate "devotion to the Blessed Virgin Mary", which Catholics legitimise as good religious practice but which Protestants regard as idolatry.

The Novicemaster reminded us, "Let me tell you, that our perseverance as religious until death will depend on the intensity of our devotion to Mary. Never must anyone of us forget that!"

As I said earlier, two Rosaries a day were said in honour of Mary and we had a prayer, which begins, "*Remember, oh most pious Virgin Mary…*". In the Novitiate we studied a book from medieval times, *True Devotion to the Blessed Virgin*, by Grignion de Montfort, which to me seemed to be mariolatry (Mary-worship), an opinion that I kept to myself. There were statues and pictures of the Blessed Virgin in Marino and in Brothers' houses, based on the image of "Our Lady of Lourdes". The lady was very beautiful and I recall a lad in Bray who had a picture of her where she looked like a lover. I wonder was 'marianism' (devotion to Mary) an attempt to sublimate a man's need for a woman? I remember these images, which suited the populist Catholic piety of the twentieth century. There was a picture of 'Our Lady of Perpetual Succour' in every monastery, a Byzantine *ikon* without the emotion of the Lourdes images. Its severe ornate form reflected a non-populist attitude different from that promoted among Irish Catholics in our time.

In the middle of the nineteenth century the Irish bishops decided to forbid the Irish Christian Brothers to wear clerical garb in public because they were not clerics. The matter was appealed in Rome and someone advised the Brothers to avert damage by devotion to Our Lady of Perpetual Succour. Devotion to the Virgin Mary was the only recognition that the Catholic Church gave to women. The church does not consider its women fit to be priests, yet women continue as the vast majority at church services. Ruling the church was a man's domain, something that was never challenged.

One day I was walking with Whisperer, when he suddenly declared, "Do you know, that this devotion to the Blessed Virgin provides us with a goddess, that we can love instead of a real woman. But isn't all love fired by the imagination?"

What was this? "You're a heretic!" I said.

"Who told you that?" he laughed, saying, "I'm only joking! That's all!"

Easter Week and Afterwards

That year in Marino the men in Second Year staged a rebellion, which threatened the "religious obedience", the bond that united the Brothers. The college staff tried to treat the older men like Juniors, which they resented because they were teachers and did not like being treated like naughty pupils. By Easter their resentment reached breaking point, when Malone nagged at them about breaches of rule, such as chatting after night prayers. He did not like contacts between them and the students of St Joseph's across the road from us, who were destined for schools in England, the Commonwealth countries and the United States.

Malone provoked the Second Years to rebellion. They did not have a leader, but looked up to Tom Reilly.

"Suffer the little children to come to me and do my bidding, though they're all over twenty-one," he sneered at Revd A. S. Malone.

A hurling match was arranged by Malone for Easter Monday between the Second Year men and a Dublin GAA club, but a game of soccer was arranged with the Brothers in St Joseph's. Malone heard about it and rushed to the playing field. He was ignored, when he shouted at the Second Years in Irish and some jeered at him in English. He was fuming at the remarks, which to him constituted serious indiscipline.

This was Easter Monday, as he reminded all, the anniversary of the Easter Rising 1916, and the men under his care had dishonoured themselves that day by playing a British game. They ignored his orders to leave the field, as he complained bitterly. That evening he spoke sternly to them about their national treachery. Some coughed and others smiled.

Tom Malley stood up and asked a question in English.

"May I inquire, sir, are we allowed to play a game with our Brothers in religion, or are we a nationalist organisation?"

Malone retorted that he did not understand English too well. Malone was enraged and went to speak to Dermot. He complained about the older men's breaches of rule, but Dermot asked him to be patient. When Malone went to visit the Provincial in Booterstown with his complaints, a widespread interrogation of each of the Brothers individually was ordered to be conducted. When the central role of the soccer game in the disruption was discovered, the Provincial decided to close the case and left Malone high and dry. This was the first time that a group of monks successfully defied college discipline.

The central issue was never addressed, that is, how Malone should impose discipline. He fought on ground that he did not choose and depended on an ally and a superior, Dermot, who did not support him. We Juniors never heard about this business until we left Marino in August because secrecy was at the centre of our lives. An incident in one wing of a building could be kept secret from those in the other. We, unlike our elders, respected Malone. The dispute over the games was a symptom of something stirring in young monks. It did not show itself fully for nearly a quarter of a century later, but fifty-two men never again formed a group in St Mary's, because smaller numbers are more easily controlled.

During the Easter vacation, we young fellows listened to talks about the history of the Christian Brothers instead of having formal classes. We were told that Edmund Rice played a part in the Catholic/Protestant conflict over the education of Irish children. We heard about the priests' incompetence in religious instruction in the Diocese of Waterford and Lismore in Rice's times. When a bishop ordered that a sermon lasting a quarter-hour should be given each Sunday, one priest repeated *ad nauseam*, "Ye must say yer prayers or ye'll all go to Hell!" When he wearied of this, he shouted to the sacristan, "Is the quarter of an hour up yet, Maggie?"

We spent three weeks of supervised teaching that spring. I was in St Joseph's in Fairview with Rory O'Driscoll, a teacher who as a member of the IRA was interned from 1940 until 1945 in a concentration camp at the Curragh. O'Driscoll spoke Irish to his pupils, except when teaching English. A raw egg in milk was delivered to him twice a day because of his poor health, the result of a hunger strike. Malone remarked that he was an honour to the nation.

As someone said to me years later, "Malone is an IRA man, so he is!" He added, "Of course he did not have to rear a family and earn a living, and had the black clothes and the Roman collar to protect him. The IRA lads were treated like dirt. They faced beatings from the Special Branch and they endured hardships at the Curragh, where they bickered among themselves until their morale sank very low."

During the weeks of teaching practice we saw briefly the reality of life, which it was impossible to understand while we were in college. We were in seclusion from reality and yet were sent to teach children, the most impressionable members of any society.

Residential Schools

Once during that year we went on a visit to Artane, which was an Industrial School, prison, detention centre and orphanage. Paul, Whisperer and I walked there together to visit it on the Howth Road from Marino.

"Anyhow, my dear friends in Christ," said Whisperer solemnly, "we go to Artane prison to view the little convicts there, which God forbid, we may be teaching one day yet."

Paul seemed to shiver as he commented, "It's the last place I want to go! I hate the very thought of whipping urchins into place and being with them from morning and throughout the day and into night."

"Holy young sir," Whisperer laughed, "you took a vow to teach the poor, didn't you?"

"Oh did I?" Paul retorted wearily. "Oh, sometime in the future we'll see all about that, if it becomes inconvenient."

We trudged on silently to Artane and as we glimpsed it, Whisperer hissed, "Oh Christ! What a god-awful place it looks!" The sight of hundreds of boys under fourteen years of age in the playground dressed in the same type of shoes, shirts and rough pants, made me uneasy. There was a stale whiff of maleness about this place, which I did not like.

The headmaster was Br Kelly, the Superior in Baldoyle when I came. He wore a biretta and resembled an Irish bishop, that is, an infallible popelet, the first of his calibre to be Superior in a place like Artane. Americans compared the "industrial schools" unfavourably with Revd Flanagan's

Boystown in the US – a better place than Artane, because it was American, as many said with some asperity.

We assembled in the Brothers' dining room for a cup of tea, while Kelly addressed us unctuously. I can recall part of what he said.

"One time this was a sinful place but it has changed since I arrived. Every boy goes to daily Holy Communion and they've all changed for the better."

He touched on Flanagan's saying that 'there is no such thing as a bad boy'.

"Some say there are no bad boys but we believe in original sin, which means, we're all born in sin, which is the Church's teaching and the other is heresy. We train boys to goodness here."

We were being shown around the dormitories and the classrooms.

"A crowd of males with only males to civilise them is not good," said Paul, "because men will use the stick liberally." He continued, "They need women but where are they?"

"Don't you know why there are no women at all here?" I retorted. "They might tempt the Brothers to sin."

We talked to one of the Brothers, who told us about Artane in the early twentieth century. Brother Mulhall was appointed Superior and was the 'Chief High Executioner'. There was a big lad there, a rebel who never escaped a thrashing any day and when Mulhall came, he determined to dethrone him as the wretches' hero. When the boys were playing during recreation time after Mulhall arrived, he sent for the leader, ignored him for a while in his office and then spoke to him in a kindly way. The lad stammered at Mulhall's kindness, especially when Mulhall gave him sweets to confuse him.

"Now, go out and take two apples with you," he said, "and may God bless you, my son!"

A crowd of admirers, who found the boy's pockets bulging with sweets and the two apples, asked him why he was not thrashed.

"You skinned on us!" someone shouted. "Why did you get these things?"

He denied betraying them. Mulhall brought in one who had been reported to him, thrashed him and then others. After this the boys blamed the hero, beat him and thus ended his leadership. When we were returning back to the college, we walked in silence.

Then Paul blurted out, "I don't want to be a gaoler or a flogger."

We also went on a visit to the Institution for the Blind in Cabra. This residential school was a great contrast to Artane, where practically all the pupils were profoundly deaf but a few had a little hearing. It was so weird to perceive two hundred boys going about in silence except for their footsteps. I often wondered why no one publicised the work that was done here, where there was goodness in peace.

Counsels for Life Outside

Dermot O'Brien gave us talks about life in the various monasteries we were to be sent to that August, and what to expect when we went there.

"When you go out on the mission," as he put it, "you'll notice that there's no radio in any house, which according to the rules is banned." He went on to speak of more prohibitions. "Only the fully professed men are allowed to read secular newspapers. The only newspapers you're allowed to read are *The Irish Catholic*, the *Catholic Tribune* and *The Catholic Herald*."

We listened with equanimity because we had been told since we left home that all these prohibitions enabled us to lead a better spiritual life. He then spoke on other subjects.

"Above all," he warned us, "no Brother whatever, junior or senior, even a Superior is ever allowed to smoke cigarettes or tobacco. You're also forbidden to have or to ride a bicycle or visit a cinema or a theatre. All these can be described as 'worldly', and lay activity and laicism is destructive of the truly religious life."

The prohibition of visits to the cinema recalled my childhood in the 1930s and 1940s, when my parents forbade us to go to the cinema and condemned the films as "Hollywood filth", which corrupted young people. The films of those days, let me say, were innocuous compared to what has appeared on the screen since then.

Dermot concluded, "Above all I advise you strongly to play games, which is a safe pastime for a young religious man."

We were forbidden to visit private houses, in case, as I thought afterwards, we enjoyed a little normal domestic life. Dermot described this by the Irish word *bothánaíocht*, 'cabin hunting', as he spoke about it. We were certain to meet at close quarters there the supreme temptation – women – where they could not be avoided. Dermot explained to us that we were obliged to obey the *Acts and Decrees of the Statutes of Maynooth*, which were drawn up for priests at a synod in Maynooth in 1927. The lay Orders had no say in the framing of these but since we dressed like clerics, we were subject to the rules in case we gave scandal to the laity. According to these Statutes we were forbidden to attend concerts and horse- or dog races, but permission to attend theatre and opera could be given on occasions. It was forbidden to attend circuses or to ride to hounds without a bishop's permission. This did not affect the Brothers, whose members were not of the foxhunting classes. I never read these Statutes in full until nearly fifty-five years later.

Afterwards Whisperer smiled grimly.

"Thou shalt not enjoy thyself but must live behind a thorny hedge of 'Don'ts'," he said in a singsong voice. "Keep a sour puss on thy face and never crease it with laughs, my truly forbidden brethren!"

It strikes me that the prohibitions created a social ghetto for us, and cut us off from the recreations of daily life. We were forbidden to enjoy life, so we lived in a life of prohibition as teachers of the youth in twentieth-century Ireland. You lived in negativism, even if you circumvented the prohibitions or because you did. Unknown to us at that time the 'worker-priest movement' had begun in France, when some priests left their sacristies and lived and worked among people. This experiment failed but in the Irish Catholic Church nothing like it was even considered.

I remember that in summer 1946 John Charles McQuaid, Archbishop of Dublin, sent a circular to the Superiors of male religious Orders. He condemned bold-faced and hatless young religious men walking the streets of our capital city. Dermot O'Brien read out the circular without comment but with the hint of a smile.

Whisperer commented, "When we're swimming, why should we, good children in Christ, wear togs if we crown our heads with hats to shade our impudent faces?"

Yes! It was quite a sight to see us seventeen- to nineteen-year-olds going about on warm days wearing black hats.

I realise now that the Christian Brothers tried to find a compromise between the enclosed monks' life and the active life of 'pious laymen'.

We could not be enclosed as real monks because we had to work in the schools close to people. To keep us from normal life they hedged us with anti-social rules, which could not be enforced fully, as I discovered later. The only recreations we were allowed, and which distinguished us from staid Victorian gentlemen, were field games. I neither played games nor had I any desire to attend them.

Men from India

In June we took the First Year teachers' training examination. I remember that Farrell handed us a list of thirty History questions to prepare answers to them. He informed us that eight of these were on the History paper, which he had submitted to the Department of Education. I considered this dishonest, but it was quite a shrewd move. The questions covered the whole course and we revised all of it, preparing the answers to them. Following the examinations he went on his summer vacation. I was pleased to 'see the back of him' and I never saw or met that man again.

The Second Year students left for various monasteries after the examinations. Even though we had no contact with them, we felt their absence, because the chapel was only half full during prayers. We spent our time working on the land, helping to make hay and doing general farm work. Having taken the First Year teacher's examination, we were due to be sent out to the various schools to teach after 15th August, "going on the mission". We looked forward to leaving Marino, although it was not an unpleasant place, when I compare it to the Novitiate, but I was a little bored and it was time for a change.

One morning in July when the senior men went to receive Communion, we noticed nine men, all cadaverous except for one plump fellow. When Mass was over, Dermot addressed us from the back of the chapel.

"Brothers," he began, "you'll have noticed the newcomers, who were in India and now are home after twenty years." He continued talking about the difficulties of the Indian mission. "We have a very comfortable life compared to what these men have in India."

After breakfast rumours went around. Twelve had come back dressed in white clothes, it was said, and were ordered to spend a few days in

Marino to be clothed in black clerical garb. Three of them went home dressed as they were. Whisperer had the best yarn.

"Our dear Brothers in Christ from the sub-continent of India couldn't book a ship to return home. One has a brother in the British navy, who arranged a lift home on a British destroyer for them."

The truth about their mission to India was sad. No one wished to be sent to India, so all who failed examinations in Ireland in the 1920s and 1930s were stationed there. As a result the Brothers' houses in India were punishment stations for some young men. The others in India, who were over their forties, left the hard work to the newcomers. These men spent their lives teaching in expensive boarding schools for Europeans and members of Indian noble families. None of the Brothers spoke Urdu or any Indian native tongue, and never considered that they should. They acted as the British did. Their status of being half-educated and rejected in Ireland caused them to live in a state of unrest. They smoked cigarettes and brought wirelesses to their bedrooms, which the Superiors had to tolerate during the war. They resented being in India, which denied them a visit home, so religious discipline snapped.

Dermot arranged for one skeletal visitor to speak to us. He spoke for about an hour especially about the climate of India.

Someone asked, "Will you be glad to go back there?"

The visitor hesitated, then spoke abruptly.

"No! I never want to see that place again!"

Dermot coughed a little and interrupted.

"You see, Brothers, our speaker's health was indifferent and he needs a milder climate."

A smile flickered across his face to cover up. Dermot enjoyed an ironical situation.

The visitor spoke of the filthy smells in the streets and the lack of hygiene. When monks left their houses, we understood that they were welcome in the British messes and private houses. I wondered how many men quit the Order there. I had not heard if any did, but then I was naïve and innocent in these days. The next day some of us discussed the matter. We spoke honestly because there was no reserve on discussion as in Novitiate days.

"So that is what our foreign missions are!" said one. "You go to India to teach white children and ignore the natives!"

Our colleagues from India were not missionaries. I began to notice that this was always the case when our men went to a mission country. Whisperer summed it up neatly.

"We joined this lot to teach the poor, but some of us don't want to deal with the poor in a place like Artane. That's right, isn't it? And now we're disgusted with what we see in the Indian mission, where our Brothers teach the white bosses' sons. Are we uncertain about our religious vocation or what is it?"

Of these nine men, one died of cardiac failure, the only healthy looking man among them. The others returned to India and spent the rest of their lives there, which included the man who said he never wished to return. He may have loved India but needed a rest from it. When he went to teach in England, he saw it all differently.

This man had said to someone, "The Raj will be replaced by a free India and we'll all lose the good life. We'll have only the rice bowl and live like Indians!"

From this point only Brothers with university degrees were sent from St Joseph's College to India. It was no longer a punishment station: properly educated men went there and not the rejects of the Irish system. When the first Christian Brothers went to India, they took over the schools of an Order of teaching Brothers in Goa, who were Anglo-Indians. This was the origin of the Indian Province but no Indian or one of mixed race ever joined the Christian Brothers while the Raj lasted. After the British left, the Brothers went back to what they should have been in the beginning.

At the End

Every fine afternoon in July and August, we went for a swim at the Bull Wall facing the city. The water here was fit for swimming, unlike what I saw in 1964. In 1945-46 I could barely swim but lay on my back flailing my arms using the backwards-stroke. I liked the sea. As Whisperer never tired of saying, some wondered why I could not swim properly, when I was reared by the sea and enjoyed the salt water.

On many occasions during that summer there was no one in the monastery when we went swimming, but someone had to answer the telephone and the door bell. Once I volunteered to stay in and do this. No telephone call came, but I found the emptiness around me unsettling when I was alone for the first time since 1942. The hall door bell rang once. I was glad to answer it, and found a young man and woman on the doorstep. Of all people they were Whisperer's brother and sister. I had not spoken to a woman for years, and she fascinated me by her beauty and how like Whisperer she was. They left, when they heard that their brother was out but called later. I was so backward socially that I could not speak normally to them. Above all, I did not know how to speak to a woman, especially to Whisperer's sister. When the others returned, I told Whisperer about the visitors and blurted out to him, "I felt lonely there and was trying to read a book but could not concentrate."

He thought it amusing.

"Well, dear Brother in Christ!" concluded Whisperer. "It's obvious that we weren't trained to solitude, and the saintly Socius didn't teach us to be hermits but to live the common life with saints like me."

When his relatives returned, Whisperer spent two hours with them. He was upset after meeting them. He told me next day that his brother, six years older than he, emigrated to the USA in 1939 and was in the invasion of France on D-Day.

"He's jumpy and nervous," said Whisperer. "He was wounded in Normandy and again in Germany in April. A slight noise in the corridor made him jump, and he wouldn't talk about the war. He almost shouted at me, 'What do you know about life? What do you know about death? You're spoiled with good times here!' I didn't know what to think."

Then Whisperer brightened up.

"Isn't she gorgeous? I forgot what a fine woman she was, because I never appreciated her at home when we fought like cat and dog. Do you like her?"

I shrugged off the question.

One day in the beginning of August, when Jan returned from holidays, he entered the study.

"Not one of you knows how to handle chalk," he said, "and you must be shown how to use the blackboard."

We assembled in the large Art Room, which had blackboards on all the walls, where we practised blackboard-writing and our efforts were assessed. We were shown the Cremer system of handwriting, where there were four basic letters, *i, f, o* and *j*. I heard that my father was pleased to see the improved handwriting in my letters, because he scorned my sloppy handwriting compared to his own disciplined hand.

I began thinking over our first days in Baldoyle, where we studied copies of a book entitled *Christian Politeness and Counsels for Youth*. A few times a week someone read passages from it aloud. It was used to teach us to be gentlemen. We were to treat others that we dealt with in a respectful manner. We were instructed that when finishing a plate of soup, it must be sloped away from us, and while stirring tea you must use the spoon anti-clockwise. I wondered whether this rule had anything to do with Christian opponents of sun worship. When I think of these last days of August 1946 in Marino, I remember them as sunny, but statistics state that the summer was damp and cloudy.

On Monday 15th August the first four who were chosen "to go on the mission" were named before night prayers and left the following morning. Someone persuaded me that evening to play in a hurling game and gave me the loan of a stick. I played awkwardly, when suddenly a lad knocked me with a trip. As I arose, I saw him shaking with laughter. I lunged at him with my hurley. I tried to hit him on the head, as he ran like a deer and I chased him until some of the lads held me. Malone was the referee and ordered me off the pitch.

I realised later that I wished to smash his skull. I felt frightened. Malone called me aside.

"Do you realise what you almost did? You could have injured him seriously. You had better learn to curb your temper, because you're going to teach children soon."

I was so shocked that I never played hurling or any game again. For this I should have been punished with breakfast on my knees, but I escaped because I was going the following morning to Greystones in Co. Wicklow. On my last morning in Marino there was the one and only 'breakfast-on-your-knees' punishment of that year. Of course, it was Whisperer. I do not have the faintest idea why he was punished, but I knew that Dermot disapproved of him. He was "very flippant and filled with a levity of spirit", and he lacked "much of that seriousness of mind and demeanour, which befits a good religious man", as the good books stated.

I was eighteen years of age then, and yet had much of the mentality of a boy. I was now going to face an aspect of life which I had yet to know, and from which we had been guarded and isolated. My adult days were beginning.

Greystones

Before night prayers on 18th August I heard that I was going to Greystones on the following morning to replace one of the four Brothers, called Perry. Greystones appealed to me, because it was near Bray and we went there on walks from the college. It was one of the few villages in southern Ireland with a significant Protestant population, which included retired British Army officers and working class people.

I was travelling alone for the first time since August 1942, when I set off from Westland Row, now Pearse Station. I knew the route to Bray already and enjoyed the short distance to Greystones in and out of little tunnels in the cliffs of Bray Head. A tall bespectacled monk was waiting for me, whom I later knew as Richard Lanigan, the Superior. He was one of a large number of Co. Tipperary men in the Christian Brothers, and looked older to me than his forty-five years. Lanigan was a man of few words. When we reached the monastery, I was surprised to see that it was a terrace house of two storeys alongside the International Hotel, named 'Rosaria' and tiny compared to any monastery that I knew. There were four bedrooms upstairs besides the oratory, and mine was over the hallway.

When I left the baggage in my bedroom, I expected the Superior to go to the oratory to say a prayer, as we were told to do when we returned to a monastery.

"That's the oratory!" He nodded to it. "It'll be your job to keep the sanctuary lamp lighting there!"

We had a cup of tea, which a small plain lady served us with biscuits.

"This is our new Brother, Mary," said Lanigan. "He's replacing Br Perry."

She smiled and welcomed me to Greystones.

"Our cook, Mary," remarked Lanigan with a semi-sniffling smile when she left, "is quite good, I must say, and knows her place, which is very important for us."

Well, well, I thought, so here am I now in a house where a woman lives, and whose bedroom I have heard was at the rear of the building. Lanigan smiled archly.

"Nobody will be seduced by Mary's charms. She's in her fifties and past the Cape of Good Hope!"

I was naïve enough then to think that his remark was both indecent and bordering on the scandalous, as he spoke with a pretended archness.

I remembered the rule on female employees, which stated: 'When women servants are about to be employed, the Superior shall take care that they are of mature age and irreproachable character.' It added: 'Except where unavoidable, they shall not be given sleeping accommodation in the house.'

After drinking the tea I made my way to the school. As I went out, I saw to my right the little pier, which embraced an area of seawater where small boats rose and fell with the gentle movements of the shore-waters that day. When I reached the school, I saw that it was a one-storeyed primitive building with walls of yellow clay mortar. It had been built in 1845, as I heard later. Here I met the three other Brothers.

When I entered the classroom where Perry taught, he asked me to take over at once.

"I'm off this evening to Marino, as you know, and must pack my things! I'm glad you've come."

He gathered his books and gave me a leather strap before he made for the door.

"Take this," said he, "and give them plenty of it! You'll never go wrong if you use it often."

He nodded good-bye to the children as he went. It was obvious that he kept a distance between himself and the pupils, which he maintained strictly, as I heard later.

When he closed the door behind him, there was a profound silence in the room as thirty pairs of eyes assessed me. After I threw the leather strap into the teacher's desk, I gradually detected a murmur in the room. Some pupils seemed to be whispering, but who were they? I looked around and saw no sign of anyone conversing. I spent an hour enveloped in this background noise before the close of the school day. Did I try to teach? I forget. I felt frustrated, trying to concentrate while I competed with that low murmur from nowhere. At three o'clock they all stood up and we recited the 'Hail Holy Queen'. I then opened the door and the pupils filed out to return home.

Three of us walked back the one kilometre to the house. The eldest was

Declan Murphy, who was about forty-five years of age, an ex-Superior, and the other was Fergus Buckley, who was about thirty-three. The two men chatted easily, relieved that the day's work was done and a leisurely weekend beginning. Lanigan, Fergus and Perry were founders of the Greystones School in 1941.

Community Life

Before we ate dinner at 4pm, grace was said and I read aloud a small page about some saint, as was the custom. We never ate in silence as we did in the colleges and Novitiate and there was no reading aloud during any meal. The three men never quarrelled or spoke badly of anyone, as I noticed later. That weekend I experienced for the first time a Christian Brother's life in a small house. We said prayers at the usual times. After dinner the three of them went into Lanigan's bedroom and I thought that I smelled cigarettes. That evening after tea we went into the sitting room, where Fergus and Lanigan pulled out packets of cigarettes and began smoking. Declan sat back in his chair smoking a pipe, the picture of contentment as he listened to the others and occasionally smiled. I was shocked to see them flagrantly breaking the rule, which we had been warned to observe strictly. It occurred to me later that those who trained us seemed to consider the vow of chastity and the avoidance of smoking as of equal importance, according to their remarks on both.

On Sunday night after tea, when we went to the sitting room, Lanigan opened a press and revealed a radio. Night prayers were postponed while we listened to a play on Radio Éireann, which the three of them enjoyed. Good Lord! Here is another strict rule flagrantly broken, I thought! They lived quietly together and disregarded petty rules. Later on I met Superiors who were minded otherwise and bound everyone with petty rules, which aroused bad feeling. My companions in Greystones sought peace. They did not show the mildest religious zeal but a tolerance at variance with much of what I had been taught.

On that first Saturday evening I felt lonely. I had not lived among less than fifty people since August 1942 and now was the youngest of four in a small house. It was a form of homesickness that I had not anticipated. I longed – but only briefly – on that Saturday in Greystones, for the regulated existence I had led in Marino and elsewhere since 1942. On Sunday the mood passed.

I was sacristan and the Blessed Sacrament, as it was called, was reserved in the oratory. It had been a bedroom and there were five chairs and prie-dieus or kneelers there. The altar was small with a sanctuary lamp hanging from the ceiling on the right. My duty was to keep the sanctuary lamp burning twenty-four hours a day.

"If you allow the light to be quenched for twenty-four hours, it's a mortal sin!" Fergus told me.

Declan took his pipe from his mouth to announce: "Twenty-three hours fifty-nine minutes and fifty-nine seconds is a venial sin and scorching in Purgatory; twenty-four hours or more earns Hell for all eternity." He smiled benignly and puffed his pipe.

Apparently he regarded these rules as matters to be handled with quiet humour. The Catholic Church in Ireland had chosen a very puritanic attitude to guilt and divine retribution. It may have acquired this from the Low Church attitudes of the Irish Established Church and the Dissenter Protestants, when Irish Catholics adopted the English language, which had puritanical undertones in Ireland.

Colza oil was used on the lamp, which, I heard was inferior to the oil of the pre-war era. I often re-lighted the lamp five times daily to avoid spiritual punishment. One evening in the community room, Fergus blurted out, "You're run ragged with that sanctuary lamp!"

"Well now, he must obey Canon Law!" Dick Lanigan answered.

Fergus tipped the ashes from his cigarette.

"Isn't it hard enough to practise Christianity instead of having the ice-cream sellers creating extra sins for us?"

"Fergus," I asked. "Did you say 'ice-cream sellers'?"

Dick started tittering.

"Young man," Fergus began, "the ice-cream sellers are Roman Cardinals who enforce Canon Law." He lifted his cigarette up in a gesture of emphasis. "If I took them seriously, I doubt if I could remain a Christian. It's the same with the stupid rule against smoking but our dear Brother Top-Men, friends of the ice-cream sellers, arranged that particular commandment as an added sin!"

"Now, now," chided Dick, "don't be scandalising the young man. None of us is perfect. Isn't that right, young man?"

"Yes sir!" I agreed automatically.

I decided that I was not taking chances about my abode in the next life, so I never smoked but listened eagerly to the radio. I had no other choice, as I told myself, had I? I avidly garnered the news because I never read the newspapers, which a young monk was forbidden to read. I began to resent the fact that during the last three years of World War II I lived ignorant of it, because I was in a cul-de-sac of unreality, where I still remained for a while in Greystones, while I did not read newspapers.

One afternoon as Fergus and I went for a walk, he decided to follow a route through the village which we had not yet taken. As we went around a corner, we saw Dick enter a house. Fergus chuckled and muttered, "There you are! Enjoy Maria's company!"

"What?"

"Oh, I'm only joking!"

"Who's Maria anyway?"

"Oh! She's just a music teacher who helped out with choirs and things."

"And is he is going in to ask her to train a choir now?"

"Will you *whisht* now? He's only gone into the house for a chat with her."

"That's against the rules, isn't it?" I looked sharply at him. He laughed and said, "Will you have a bit of sense? All pleasure cannot be called luxury. As for the other matter, a man is a savage without a woman friend, and he needs refinement from a woman's company. Dick has no other notions when he visits her. Oh, not at all! He'd never think of such a thing!" He smirked quietly as he uttered these words.

The rules were strict on alcoholic drinks in my time. They stated, "The use of ardent spirits such as whiskey, brandy, rum or gin is strictly limited to those who have a written permission for their use". Beer and stout were not mentioned. In Greystones the three others had a drink of 'ardent spirits' in Dick's bedroom before dinner on feast days. I never saw them drinking 'ardent spirits' but guessed that they imbibed whiskey or brandy upstairs. They drank wine with the meal. I was told how lucky we young lads were. In the nineteenth century young Brothers were given a daily bottle of stout at dinner, when there was little money for food especially in the cities.

My First Steps as a Teacher

Maybe I was naïve but I loved teaching, where I enjoyed the children and the bustle in the classroom. My classroom looked out on a field sloping up from the school where a stream came hurrying down. Cows came here to drink and some put their flat noses and mouths against the window glass to gaze into the room. During the first week I never slapped anyone, but I never discovered who was whispering and I did little teaching. One day Declan walked in. He questioned the children about what I was teaching. To those who did not know, he doled out slaps with a black leather. This was a different Declan, who turned and whispered, "Turn your back to the class!" I did so.

"You're too soft," he said. "They'll walk up your back because you can't do your job as a teacher until you keep a class quiet."

From that day onwards when I used the leather occasionally, I felt that I was a cruel tyrant. Fergus asked me how I felt about teaching.

"I hate hitting the lads but what else can I do?"

"I know," he said, "but what happens when they disobey their parents?"

"They get a few wallops for it."

"There you are then. Do as the parents do! That's a good guide, isn't it?"

However, I made one rule for myself. I must not slap during Religious Instruction, and I extended this later to the teaching of Irish.

That autumn it rained continually so that wheat-crops were in danger of being lost, which were grown as they were during the war. Soldiers were sent to help with the harvesting and children stayed out of school. Grain harvesting needed many hands. When it was late autumn, we had fires in the classrooms and mine had a barrel stove with its flue stretching up the wall, which it also heated. That stove heated both the room and the old wall of stone and yellow clay, which it climbed.

We went silently to and from Mass and Dick bought the newspapers. I can recall one day that he beckoned to Declan and Fergus, when he left the shop. A south-west wind was driving the rain and sweeping leaves from the trees.

"The German leaders were hanged in Nüremburg!" Fergus said to me at the door.

I heard that the hangman was an American, fulfilling the wish of his life. I shuddered.

"They should have hanged Stalin in Nüremburg and Churchill also!" Fergus said.

Declan muttered.

"You'll say next," Dick said, laughing, "that Roosevelt should have been on the gallows."

Both Declan and Fergus denied this.

"He was completely different from the other two," Fergus remarked.

I never read about the executions in the newspapers because I obeyed a silly rule, and I felt in the wisdom of eighteen years that religious authority was just.

One night I heard 'Lily Marlene' for the first time on the radio, which Fergus called, "That mawkish German tune!" I knew practically nothing about the misery of the war after 1942, which this song symbolised for me because I was kept in ignorance of it.

There were some wealthy English people living in Greystones since the war, who left the devastation of their cities to seek peace and good food, when peace came. The man had been an air raid warden and his wife an anti-aircraft gunner. She was light and slim and became friendly with Dick, who called her the Duchess but her husband was a powerfully built man. The couple recalled Francis Ledwidge's lines, "*The moon and its following star, / Like the cuckoo and its little mother.*"

When Fergus and I went for a walk through the village, he told me never to give way to young Protestants, whom he knew well after five years.

"When we came here first," he said, "some of them tried to force us off the paths." He asked me then, "Do you know Sister Anthony in the convent?"

"No!"

"She's eighty-four. One 12th July Eve when she was a young nun years ago, Prods came yelling to the convent at night, 'Get out of here, you lousy papishes!' The other nuns were scared but Anthony came out ringing a large hand bell. They fled thinking she was sounding an alarm and they'd have their throats cut before the night was out."

One morning I received a letter from Whisperer. He was in O'Connell's Schools, where he was transferred from St Patrick's, Marino, one month after leaving the college. The letter was given to me unopened, as was all my mail.

"Dear Revd Brother," Whisperer began, "I am buried here among many brethren of our blessed Congregation but can have discreet fun." He spoke of his school. "Of course, I am teaching brats who don't know B Flat from a bull's foot. I miss all the professors in Marino, especially Dermot, who liked me to pray on my knees during breakfast. We must meet sometime for a few whiskeys!"

Declan loved news and gossip.

"You had a letter today," he began. "Did a monk write it?"

I told him what it was and I read the letter for him.

"Oh, it's from a young fellow, and he hasn't any news. Oh, I'm told he's crazy but he's harmless."

Christmas

Before Christmas we had the yearly retreat, which we made in the college at Bray where I spent the best year of my life so far. I felt content there, where Pop was still the Superior and Brendan was a staff member. During the retreat I tried to understand how my colleagues in Greystones could break rules openly and yet be good Brothers. As the director of the retreat put it, "After all, the Scripture says, 'The letter kills and the spirit quickens!'"

I was confused and decided never to think of a problem, unless I had a solution. I had applied to renew my annual vows but not even the smallest doubt occurred to me about remaining with the Brothers. I was staying and that was that.

Before Christmas Day we returned to Greystones and received our Christmas mail. Declan had few cards but he had plenty monastic gossip. He was a taciturn man but he spewed out news about which applicants for annual vows were rejected or left.

"Do you remember a lad called Bruno, who was in St Patrick's, Marino?"

"Yes. My group."

"Well he's gone. Failed the scrutiny...There's no hope for the likes of him!"

"Charley writes: 'Do you remember that young monk, the most powerful swimmer in Kilkee last year? Dismissed for visiting a pupil's mother. He can have all he wants of mothers or women at home in Wexford now. No harm in the lad but who knows?'"

Declan added, "My friend Charley's never wrong!"

I stole a look at Dick who was studying the tablecloth. Fergus gave me a sidelong glance, coughing discreetly. Declan rambled on with the monkish gossip.

Our Christmas vacation was sedately happy. We were invited to a concert at the O'Connell's Schools and I went there with Fergus. It became a young monks' reunion. Whisperer brought me upstairs with the other young men to his room. When we went in, cigarette smoke greeted us. I shook my head, when Whisperer offered me a cigarette.

"Good God," he exclaimed, "so you don't indulge in the weed?"

I muttered something about my lungs.

"Oh, suit yourself," said he.

They started talking about hurling and Gaelic football then, which provided their staple conversation, as I knew. They spoke of Bruno whom Stick had banished from the Brothers.

"He should have asked for a transfer as I did," said Whisperer. "I was a minion of Stick, but went from the frying pan into the fire. Our boss, Stan, is a tyrant. However, I'm here."

There was a brief titter but at least he could live safely in Stan's house.

Before they went to the concert, each of the five smokers took out toothpaste and shot a little into his mouth. They entered the hall exuding the fragrance of dental hygiene, and not the smell of unholy tobacco. After the show finished, we had plenty to eat. I do not care what I ate because I came to meet Whisperer and have a break from routine. He gave me the news.

"The boss, Stan, lives in another world. He comes out sometimes to accuse us of talking in the corridor to show who's boss. He watches trivialities but does not know we offer incense to the goddess, Nicotine. Stan goes off – to our delight – for days but he treats us like kids. How's your boss?"

"Dick is not too bad, he's…"

"The day I climbed up the drainpipe to my room, all that Stan saw were the young monks urging me on. I went aloft like a monkey."

"You climbed the drainpipe?"

"And wouldn't you if you had Stan, as I have here? He's a pain in the behind!"

That day I met Timothy, a mild fellow who was in Marino with us. He pretended to lock a child in a classroom and when the child looked out the window, his friends chanted, "Dan Dare! Jump out! Jump out!" He did so and injured himself. A headline in a Dublin evening paper informed readers that the child was falsely imprisoned and the brutish teacher forced him to jump from a first-storey window. It was the first time that I saw untruth used to inflict hurt. Timothy was labelled in public for years as a kind of ogre, which he was not, but he had shown a lack of judgment, so the press made a 'Roman holiday' of him. I wondered was all that happens in life, good and bad, based on luck and accident?

The Great Snow

January 1947 was at first mild and wildflowers such as Lesser Celandine bloomed prematurely. In the third week of January on a Sunday night snow came in blizzards across the Irish Sea. More snow followed and hardly a quarter of our pupils came to school on Monday. The countryside was white and the streets of Greystones were covered with stretches of ice, when some snow melted during the daytime. The school was closed for a fortnight. This snow proved an unexpected blessing. I had chilblains, which tormented me every winter since childhood. After a snowball battle with the pupils on the day that we closed the school, my hands were senseless. Following painful re-heating, the chilblains on my fingers disappeared and never appeared since. I hurt my foot slightly on the street and spent some days in bed. When the local doctor visited me, I was reading Cicero's work *De Senectute*. He looked at the book.

"Well, well! So you're reading Cicero's treatise on old age, by heavens!" He looked at me. "What are you doing here, with men who live in a different world?"

I shrugged my shoulders.

That month the scarcity of wheat caused bread to be rationed. In Marino, as I heard from Whisperer, porridge and not bread was served at teatime, but Dick used the status of his clerical collar to provide us with enough of that. During this time, a ship of commercial timber was wrecked on the Kish Bank north of Greystones. For weeks large beams of timber floated on to the beach. During the day men went into the water to bring in the timber that was reeking of diesel oil. I thought that Dick was wrong to pay young men to fetch timber to use as firing.

"Why doesn't he leave it all to the poor, who need it?" I asked Fergus.

"I think you'd better ask Dick about that and not me!" he answered briefly.

I never did.

All Brothers not finally professed were obliged to study. A course of reading was drawn up, divided into five grades. A Junior chose two subjects and studied them over six months, and the boss received the examination papers and then returned the answer papers for correction. I took Latin and Social Science for my test in spring 1947 during the snowstorms. When the examination papers arrived, Dick gave them to me and left. It struck me that I could cheat easily, but some odd pride forced me to do the test honestly.

"I did the study," I thought, "so let's see how I can manage!"

After a while Fergus came in and looked over the Social Science questions.

"Japers!" he exclaimed. "Who's Malthus?"

Both of us knew nothing about him, so he sat down and checked the textbook that I had.

"Malthus isn't even mentioned here," he remarked. "He must be some Italian or Jew or someone who made stinking cheese."

He threw away the book saying, "Let everyone stick to his own poison!"

Latin was no trouble. I had studied *De Senectute* well and enjoyed it.

I heard Fergus say to Declan outside the room door, "That young man is a genius or a fool, or maybe, good God above, he likes studying."

I passed both papers.

Declan smiled as he said, "You're one of the few to do the exams honestly, because no one takes these things seriously."

I was quietly pleased. It has struck me since that someone inserted the question on Malthus to see what could be illicitly dredged from the rest of each community.

On the night of Patrick's Day rain moved over the country from the south west. The streets were wet with rainwater, which flowed where ice had been in the morning. When we reached the school the yard was flooded, because the swollen stream had invaded the ground under the floorboards of the old building. It rained incessantly for months afterwards and spring work on the farms became difficult. My memory is that it never stopped raining until the end of July. I do not recall when there were dry days and sunshine – there had to be some in that time, but I forget.

The Easter Vacation and Afterwards

Easter arrived and Fergus went to see his parents for his five-yearly visit home, and I was due to go the following Easter. When he was leaving, he took me aside.

"You'll have a replacement for me this evening and do you know who 'tis?" I could not even guess. "It is the old Novicemaster, Berchmans Reid," he grinned. "Enjoy his company if you can! The Provincial Council is meeting at St Patrick's, where he lives, and the whole community is being sent here and there for Easter Week."

The old man came in limping that afternoon clutching a little suitcase and filling the house with the aura of conformity. I never realised how tall he was.

"Oh, God!" I muttered to myself, "We're back to the narrow road to Calvary!"

Dick and Declan avoided the old man, and Dick advised me to bring him walking every day. Both absented themselves during Easter Week as much as possible, and where they smoked on the other days, I do not know. I suppose they visited other monasteries or spent time in the hotel next door. The radio was retired for the time, so I had to obey every little rule. Oh, these walks! The old man limped along slowly. One day he spoke about the merits and demerits of shoe polishes: I heard that his shoe polish penetrated the leather but you had to brush it diligently. I barely muttered "Yessir!" when he said, "I once bought a polish that was only pigment with no substance at all!"

How he continued talking for an hour and a half on this subject, I shall never know.

Another afternoon we went to the railway station, where we saw livestock in rail-cars that were being sent to Dublin. He went from car to car bumbling about the animals. He was an expert on trivialities, who lived on the limits of verbal expression. The old Novicemaster left us on Saturday and Fergus returned that evening. He threw his suitcase under the table and silently smoked cigarette after cigarette.

In May we had the Provincial visitation, when a Provincial Consultor interviewed each one of us and enquired into our spiritual well-being. When my turn came, I faced a kindly man, who asked me whether I had any complaints. No! I did not have any!

"I suppose all the rules are strictly observed here?"

"Yes sir!"

"I can take it, then, that there is no wireless set in the monastery?"

"No sir!"

"And nobody smokes cigarettes or tobacco of any kind?"

"Yes sir! Oh, sorry! No sir!"

"And I can take it that nobody visits the houses of seculars under any condition?"

"Yes sir!"

"Oh, you're blessed to be living in an edifying religious house, reverend Brother!"

He smiled broadly, even roguishly, as I left him. I wonder did he know the truth? I followed Martin Luther's advice on this occasion: *Pecca fortiter!* Sin bravely!

Year End

During the end of the month of June I was depressed. Depression grew over me like a fungus, and I thought the skies were about to crush me. It seemed to rain every day and everything seemed drab. I felt trapped under the sky. I thought that if I killed myself, I could escape from this darkness and wondered how I could do it. One night as I was in bed a mighty thunderstorm awakened me. If I stood at a window, I thought lightning might kill me, so I jumped out of the bed to inspect the windows in the oratory, the dining and sitting rooms and stood a while by each. It appeared that the blue-and-red fulminations had no designs on me.

One school day in June, when the rain ceased for a while, Fergus went to supervise Dick's pupils, while Dick was providing fuel instead of buying it from scarce stocks. He spent a few days on the bogs of Wicklow, where he, with the Duchess and her husband, rented bog land. He enjoyed this. I do not know who did the turf-cutting but it was not Dick or the other two.

As Fergus said, "Dick does not work, but he loves work when someone else does it!"

Dick rambled on about his friends when he returned.

"The Duchess is the boss in that house, and that great heap of a husband has as much say as the cat. She is one of the gentry, but he was a civil servant, who passed exams to get his job…"

Declan added to this casually "…just like our pupils!"

Fergus was looking sidelong at Dick between cigarette puffs but remained silent.

"Her type of women," Dick said, "dominate everyone to show them that they are the rulers. Ordinary folk rise when her people allow it in the goodness of their hearts."

At the end of month on a Saturday we three went to the bog and footed the turf, standing each two sods together. Dick was not there while we three worked. I found the work back-breaking. Declan saved turf at home in Clare and Fergus knew how to achieve results with the least energy, which I did not. Declan knew how to use the sparse shelter in the bog, when a shower reminded us that this was Ireland. I noticed the remains of decayed vegetation in the turf, a source of heat in its death.

"This is Ireland, isn't it Fergus?" said I.

He grunted as he put two sods together.

"I think that turf is like our people, who arose from the ashes of the eighteenth century…"

"Begor, you're right!" Fergus answered. He hardly heard me.

The Provincial Chapter, which finally professed Brothers in Ireland elected every few years, reviewed the rules. They sent suggestions to the General Chapter, which took place in July and members came from all over the world. The Chapters were parliaments, which met for a week or longer every six years. When I first heard of active and passive voice, I thought they were grammatical terms, but here 'passive voice' was the right to be elected and 'active voice' the right to elect. Fergus told me the story of the changes in the early 1940s.

"You see," he said, "the Superior-General years ago appointed ten of the twenty delegates to the General Chapter and another ten were elected, but he could block change with his casting vote in a division. In the 1930s some men in Ireland decided to draw up a programme of reforms secretly, which are now being put into action. They were all Republicans opposed to the older men's British Imperial sympathies."

Some Brothers met Cardinal McRory, Archbishop of Armagh and gave him reform proposals to be forwarded secretly to Rome. The Sacred Congregation for Religious appointed a Jesuit, Revd John J. Hannon, to visit Christian Brothers' houses in Rome, England, Gibraltar, South Africa, India, Australia, New Zealand, USA and Canada. Hannon completed this in the first years of the war. He suggested change and Rome replaced members of the General and Provincial Councils in the spring of 1943. The Superior-General was furious when he had to accept the new men, but he alone remained of the old regime because he was elected for life. Brothers were forbidden to canvas for votes in the election for Chapter delegates. One Brother, who was proved to have done this in 1947, lost active and passive voice. He felt so wronged that he left and taught in a little school dressed in black as a Christian Brother, but did not wear the clerical collar. The most successful candidates were skilful conspirators.

"Democracy in the Church?" as Declan put it. "Just wait and see how this democracy will turn out!"

Achill Island

During the General Chapter in July we went on holiday to Achill Island. The journey across Ireland by train was slow, and I saw the Shannon for the first time when the train crossed it through Athlone. The midlands were another Ireland to me because I never lived far from mountains. When we reached Westport, we went by bus to Achill. The beauty of the island overwhelmed me. I loved the blue distances of sea and mountain across Clew Bay when sea and hill hovered in dramatic colours. That first evening I dipped my hands in the seawater on the rocks, my depression melted away and I felt freedom of mind, which I had not felt while depression smothered me.

I loved the food. There were fish meals, especially of pollock, which sometimes was fished off the rocks before mealtime. All the vegetables and food were produced in the area, and it all had the strangeness of what was outside a town or city. We stayed in Dooagh, the most westerly village with the recruiter, Markey and his men from Brunswick Street nearby. Markey was a roly-poly figure with a smarmy manner and scant respect for most people. His men from Dublin did not like the food.

"Look at that meal now!" one said. "The fish are pulled off the rocks and the vegetables are from the area."

This attitude seemed fatuous to me then and it still does.

Most houses in Achill were thatched then, and the lime-washed walls shone in the sun. Each house seemed to have a reek of turf near it, a donkey grazing nearby and a sheep dog about the place to keep a wary eye on people and guard the property. I often served morning Mass in the church near Keel village, when the Mass-servers were absent. One day after Mass the old priest gazed through the window at the sixteen Brothers walking back to Dooagh. I heard him mutter: "Look at them, all dressed like priests and not one Mass between the whole lot of them!"

Declan disliked both Achill, which he called "Achill of the hundred showers", and Markey. One evening when I and an older monk arrived late for tea, Markey said, "Young man, you're late. Is that what the new Novicemaster taught you?"

Dick was silent.

"And you've nothing to say," Declan retorted, "to the senior man of your house who kept him late, Br Markey? Well?"

Markey pretended not to hear him.

Declan's friend in Dublin sent him news of the General Chapter, which was in progress in Marino. As he read it, bright and pleasant smiles transformed him.

"Men, the chief conspirators are now on the General Council!" he announced.

"And everyone is given his thirty pieces of silver!" Markey commented.

"This place tests your faith, which must be strong enough to accept some of what goes on at the Chapter'," Declan quoted a delegate as saying.

"Hush, Br Declan! Don't be scandalising the three young Brothers!" Markey piously observed in his unctuous tone.

Declan gazed at him over the rims of his spectacles.

"If there's scandal in what others do," he said, "so be it, but I've no intention of lying to the young men. Unlike you, Br Markey."

This silenced Markey for a time. Declan always addressed him as 'Brother Markey' instead of using his religious name. We enjoyed his reference to Markey's lies.

"What I predict is this:" said Declan looking at a letter, "The new council and the General can never agree and there will be conflict until the old man dies. Then," he continued, "the ice-cream sellers will rule the Order."

Markey asked him sharply who they were.

"Oh, yes, it's well you know! They're the Italian Cardinals and we know what their devotion to truth is!"

I enjoyed Declan's disrespect for Markey. My three companions respected each other, but Markey deserved Declan's barbs. We certainly had respite here from the comfort of the middle-aged lifestyle, which we led on the eastern coast. We heard the news that radios were now permitted and that smoking was permitted to all finally professed Brothers.

When Markey exclaimed, "The ship is sinking!" Declan added, "If it is, it's going down in a smoke screen!"

The Goat Hunt

Wild goats lived in the most westerly part of Achill Island on Croaghaun Mountain. Someone said that these herds were descended from domestic animals. Dick suggested to cull their numbers.

"I know they harm no one but why not shoot a few?" he asked.

Dick agreed that I should accompany them, so I was given a sheathed knife.

"This knife," Dick told me, "is to be used to paunch any goats we kill!"

As I thought of what I might have to do with the murderous-looking knife, I felt sick for a moment. When we climbed up Croaghaun Mountain, Dick was armed with an old Lee-Enfield service rifle and some .303 ammunition, which the Gardaí gave him. He took it all so seriously that he promised fresh meat to the owner of our holiday home.

Someone made a comment about Declan's .22 rifle.

"With that thing he'll bounce lead on a goat's horns to make him go faster, if he's lucky."

About seven in all were coming. When we reached the 1035m-high summit of Croaghaun, I saw the Atlantic Ocean stretching to the west towards Canada and the USA. As I imagined the infinity of the ocean, I heard, "Wake up! We're off to hunt wild goats, the Lord save us!"

From the summit, the ground inclined slowly at first and then became precipitous. Northwards there was high ground leading to the northern cliff, where we glimpsed a herd of goats, led by a puck. He rushed off, followed by his women and kids. Dick was so excited that he sat down to fire a few bullets, but they hit the heather and sent echoes through the area. Declan also loosed off shots but his rifle was too light. The goats were gone and their retreat outdid our laborious trudging. After some time Dick looked at his watch.

"They're gone and we'll be late for the meal. I've had enough."

We went to Keem Bay and returned by the pathway to Dooagh. I saw rough amethysts in a rock face there, where I broke off small crystals to bring away. I have them still.

The stories of this day's adventure were recalled by Fergus as farce.

"Our adventurous Dick is a great hunter before the Lord, whose ineptitude protected the goats where they were not harming a soul!"

He almost sounded like Whisperer, who said in a letter, "How privileged you were, to be led by Dick the Great White Hunter, who sits down to fire a gun!"

Our holiday in Achill ceased at the end of July and Declan breathed contentment. In the final days he was like someone escaping from a reservation.

"We'll soon be far from the rain, rocks and bogs," said he happily, "as we return to civilisation."

From the train to Dublin from Westport, I had a last glimpse of the West. We left Croagh Patrick and Nephin behind us, bearing veils of cloud that day, which caressed their summits. This other Ireland was quite a contrast to where I lived in the east. The rainy summer ended violently a day after we returned to Greystones, when a three-hour thunderstorm broke out. After the storm August and September were months of warmth and of sunshine. On the first day after the holidays I read a newspaper from beginning to end, for the first time since August 1942. I read it avidly. I was slowly returning to a kind of normality.

The New Chief

In the first week of August Dick finished his two three-year terms of office, the maximum that a Superior could serve before he was replaced. Dick was transferred to Dublin and Declan regaled us with lists of transfers and newly appointed Superiors. At the beginning of the school year, all appointments were made. The day before Dick left we heard that Br Colman was the new Superior.

"Oh, he's a tough schoolman," Declan commented. This meant that he was severe on his pupils.

"Declan," I asked, "what kind of person is he?"

Declan removed his pipe.

"Oh, you'll see for yourself when he comes."

Colman was a brother of Cal, the teacher in Baldoyle, who emphasised his teaching by beating us with his fists. When Colman came, I noticed that he was a little man, whose face was wreathed in smiles and bubbled with bonhomie. He shook hands with Declan and Fergus but he nodded to me.

"So you're the young fellow here!"

When I turned on the radio after tea, he barked.

"Who told you to turn on the wireless, young lad? Put it off!"

When I did so, he turned it on again.

"Where you're concerned, young fellow," he declared, "I decide what happens here!"

During August and September the little man began pestering me. Why, you will ask, did I not report his conduct to the Provincial? The answer is that I liked Greystones, and was certain to be moved out if I complained. I had absorbed enough in the Novitiate to consider all this as persecution to be borne 'for my sins', which were many as my sense of guilt suggested. I never did discover what these sins were, at that time or afterwards.

It was quite clear that Declan disliked the new boss. They never went walking together, as he and Dick had. Fergus accompanied the little man and I was alone. In my first year in Greystones Fergus had gone out with me every day, but Colman now went with him. In this way he learned about the area and was introduced widely.

At meals Colman talked 'shop' and we heard his views on teaching. He made such statements as, "That young whelp of a Parsons takes an odd day off. I'll tan his little arse for him if he does that again, the pup!"

"The more you beat them," he said, "the better they learn. There's no mammy softness in me. No pups walk up my back!"

As Declan stated later about the little man, "That fellow practises Solomon's saying, 'Whom the Lord loves, he chastises and he scourges every son that he receives'."

If I expressed an opinion, Colman treated me as a 'young pup'.

"So you want us to listen to your schoolboy wisdom, do you, young fellow?" he said. "Fancy all that talk from a lad who can't kick a football or swing a hurley!"

At this time I became very exacting on my pupils. If I slapped anyone, I did not regret it but I never realised until later what happened. I remained calm, but I crumbled sometimes under what this man imposed on me. Some have fun on a football- or hurling pitch in the afternoon; others find comfort in a woman; but every day I was alone with that miserable person – myself.

I had a respite. Colman required surgery for an inguinal hernia, which had been his closest friend for a time, so he spent five weeks having surgery and convalescing during October. Peace descended on Declan and myself in his absence. While Colman was away I taught two groups of pupils, my own and Fergus's and he taught Colman's. I had about seventy lads, and felt exhausted every evening but was happy because I had peace in the house.

About one quarter of our pupils came to us by bus from Bray. One morning the lads from Bray complained that the Protestant school boys had harassed them at the bus stop the previous afternoon.

"The people here suffered persecution from Protestants in the past," I preached to them, "and bowed before it like slaves. Did that happen in Bray?"

There was a chorus of "No, never, sir!"

"Go on now," I trumpeted, "all you lads from Bray and teach these bigots a lesson!"

"The Garda Sergeant called an hour ago," said Declan that evening at tea, "and told me about a riot at the bus stop, when the Bray lads showered stones on the Protestants. The Gardaí were told that you incited the Bray lads to do this."

I was surprised.

"But Declan," I explained, "I had to tell them to fight for their rights!"

"You should have told me first," he remarked, "and we could have gone to the bus stop and settled it all peacefully. You acted wrongly, I'm afraid!"

I had caused a sectarian riot.

Next afternoon Declan simply told me, "March the Bray boys in ranks to the bus stop and wait there until the bus has taken them away."

There were no more hostilities. Two Gardaí and Catholic and Protestant parents were at the bus stop when we reached it. I shepherded the boys on board the bus, and was obliged to be on duty there every afternoon until peace was confirmed. When Colman returned, I expected to be flayed alive.

"This," he growled, "is the one worthwhile thing that the young fellow ever did!"

Now I was certain that I had been in the wrong.

Christmas Once More

We had the pre-Christmas retreat in Bray and I revelled in the silence and absence of bickering from Colman. I spent time in the Beech Walk, considering the gospel teaching which urged us to love one another. If turning the other cheek to an attacker was Christian, I wished it were otherwise. If I had forty cheeks, I should have to turn them to that man in Greystones to be slapped. On Christmas Day we had full and plenty of everything. Colman was maudlin after his many whiskeys. I wondered did the Holy Spirit's tongues of fire land on him.

"You're a hard worker in school!" said he. "There are few young fellows like you. Do you know, it's a pity you can't play a decent game like anyone your age!"

Two of us visited Carriglea Park Industrial School near Dún Laoghaire after that Christmas. We arrived at one o'clock and a young monk brought me to his room and offered me a cigarette.

When I refused, he said, "No one bothers about this anymore. Nowadays you're in the right 'til you're found out!"

All visits to a monastery after Christmas followed a predictable course. A junior visitor spent time with the local junior, while senior men went to the boss's room for drinks. The later merriment of the older men was conceived in the bellies of bottles.

When it was time for lunch, where I saw a Brother – his soutane hidden by an overcoat and hands in pockets – in charge of about one hundred and eighty silent boys, who walked in from the yard. I turned to my companion.

"God protect me from the likes of this place!"

"If you're sent here," he smiled as he answered, "you'll have to go."

"I'd rather leave altogether!" I blurted out.

He looked sharply at me.

"Forget it!" said I, "I'm only joking!"

By this time Declan was ignoring Colman as far as he could. One day we heard him expound his theory of school discipline, which filled Declan's face with distaste.

"The best way to ensure that they remain quiet when you're away," said Colman, "is to beat a few before you go. They'll be like mice when you're away!"

He laughed heartily. Declan's mouth curled in an expression of contempt.

As he said later, "Hitler, Stalin and Mussolini were also of small stature – just as our Brother Superior is."

The Local Priests

The parish priest, who lived in a large house near the church, was Monsignor Curran. His voice was so weak that I wondered how anyone heard him when he preached. He seemed to be a kind man, whom the President of Ireland, Seán T. O'Kelly visited, a little man whose wife, Phyllis, towered above him.

They attended the Monsignor's Mass in the church and then had breakfast with him. The Mass servers liked his visits because Seán T. gave them shillings, which were excellent pocket money. The present in 1948 was the three-penny coin – not a bad present for a young fellow.

A few doors down from us lived the two curates, a middle-aged man and a young priest, a student at the Irish College in Rome, when our parish priest was President. The priests mingled socially with us except when one came to say Mass once a week, and we did not visit their houses.

I remember a Catholic girl marrying a member of the Church of Ireland in its local church after Christmas. When she tried to reach an agreement with the Monsignor, it failed and she went on with the wedding in the other church. He was furious.

"My dear brethren," he spluttered in rage on Sunday, "what a scandal we had in our parish last week!"

Everyone listened to him because few had heard about it.

"A child of Holy Mother Church abandoned the true faith to marry a heretic in a heretics' church. May she and those who supported her be spared Hell-fire, but I doubt it. Wilful disobedience to church law leads to infernal punishment." The philippic went on and on.

Colman spat out praise of the Monsignor for his attitude to the Protestant church.

"Where I grew up," he opined, "there were black Protestant farmers near us. We had nothing to do with them. They hated us but couldn't persecute us, as their lot did to our people long ago!"

Declan said nothing but afterwards remarked, "I wonder what's biting the Monsignor? This is not how he acts usually because, he's a mild old fellow."

That Spring

In February 1948 Eamon de Valera, the Taoiseach, called a general election. After the election his party – which had been in power for sixteen years – lost its majority, and a coalition government was formed on 18th February. A new political party, Clann na Poblachta, founded by former IRA internees, helped to unseat the government. Even some sons and daughters of Fianna Fáil supporters voted for Clann na Poblachta. When the voters' register was formed, the Brothers' names were entered, because we were presumed to be twenty-one or more, the legal age then to use the parliamentary vote. I voted although I was under twenty-one.

I heard one Saturday morning during the election campaign that Seán McBride, leader of Clann na Poblachta, was holding a meeting in Bray. I set off on foot for Bray at 1pm but when I reached it I heard that he was speaking on the following Saturday. I trudged back in disappointment by the cliff path to Greystones. On the day of the election I voted for the two Clann na Poblachta candidates in Co. Wicklow. They failed to be elected and lost their deposits. After the count was completed, Colman said that in Greystones no one voted for these two.

"I did!" I blurted out.

Colman stared at me and declared, "No wonder voting is limited to over twenty-ones." Fergus teased me for disgracing the Brothers.

One Sunday at the end of March Colman announced that we were invited to a school concert in Dublin. He, Fergus and I went by train and I spent the day with Whisperer and the young monks. Whisperer and I had a few words alone and he called Colman a cruel and tyrannical Tartar.

"He's in Greystones to try your spirit of faith."

I laughed weakly at this mockery, and denied that Colman was a nasty little man. Whisperer smiled.

"Your words say one thing but your face speaks differently!"

Colman spent the evening socialising with some older men. We left late and the smell on his breath suggested that he had taken plenty of whiskey. We missed the last bus from Dublin to Greystones and took a bus to Bray instead. There was no bus to Greystones at that hour, and we walked the rest of the way over the hill, because our boss did not hire a taxi. It was more than 9km, and trees stood on both sides of the road on part of the way. It was moonlit and windy that night. Colman was frightened that a tree might fall on him and did not hide his fear. I found his cowardice amusing. It was midnight when we arrived at the house, and I had to hold up my pants for the last kilometre because my braces had broken. I asked him for a new pair.

"Go to hell, you pup!" he shouted. "Cord can hold up your pants, and is good enough for you!"

Later on Declan came to my bedroom.

"Here is a pair of old braces for you that'll do you until I get a new pair. I heard what he said. Take no notice of him."

My Visit Home

Easter Monday 1948 was the day I visited my family in Dungarvan. It was five years eight months since I last met my father and mother, my three sisters and two of my three brothers. I looked forward to it very keenly. Declan asked me to come into his room the night before I left. He was house Bursar and he gave me a £10 note for my expenses.

"Here is a little more," said he handing me another £10. "Sit down and we'll talk." He lighted his pipe. "I've to tell you something about one of our men in Dungarvan, which you didn't hear. It's like this," he began. "A young Brother took a fancy to a teacher's daughter a while ago, who often came to visit him at the school. He left Dungarvan last week with her and went to England. You should know it so you'll be prepared."

It did not faze me because I could not comprehend it. I shrugged my shoulders and muttered a simple "Thanks!" as I went out the door.

The journey by train to Waterford was a delight. Unlike the wartime journey to Dublin, I forget who was in the carriage with me because my mind was on my people and the town where I was born and reared. When we reached Waterford City, I alighted and went to take a bus to go home. I boarded the bus going to Dungarvan, which was painted a heavy green as all the public buses were. As we passed the Comeragh Mountains in the lands of my Power ancestors, I recalled how much I was one of the people of this countryside. When the bus reached the centre of the town square, I looked around at the sights of my childhood. The buildings seemed to be dilapidated, shopfronts looked as if they had not been painted for ages and many shopkeepers' names were in Irish, a change since I left nearly six years before. The town of my homesick dreams looked very shabby.

When I met my father and mother, they seemed like strangers. I did not know what to say to them. Worse still, when we reached home, I only recognised one of my brothers and sisters, two of whom were young adults. The others were so changed that I did not recognise them, and I was ill at ease with them. I felt a stranger.

The five years and eight months' separation from them all and my training and experiences had alienated me from my own. I wanted to touch them and hold each one in my arms but could not. I felt that Whisperer might comment, "The monks made another person of you; now you belong only to them." As I see it now, I was part of another family with no issue of its own, which renewed itself from other wombs, but rejected its fleshly origins as sinful. I was entombed in a spiritual cell with a slit to admit light and air and food and drink.

When I went to Mass the following morning, I intended to accompany my mother.

"Now," said she to me, "you must go ahead of me and I'll go at my own pace."

I thought this was because of the monk who had eloped. It was not. Years afterwards I discovered that my mother was trained never to accompany a cleric or any male except a child, her husband or a near male relative on the streets. I thought it bizarre that she accepted that the clerical clothes had cut me off from her. I did not know then why she acted as she did, with attitudes which belonged to another age and generation. I find it odd that the only morning I felt at ease in Dungarvan was when the Brothers invited me to breakfast after Mass. I remember what the boss said as I left.

"That Colman is a savage but don't let him get to you. He should be serving in a gaol and appointed hangman!" He laughed at his own wit and I shivered inside.

As I spent the next few days at home, I began to know my family but on Saturday I had to return to Greystones. A feeling of misery filled me. I heard my father say to my mother, "Isn't he very thin? I hope he's not delicate." This was a typical reference to tuberculosis, which killed so many of my age then. Was I frightened of it? No! I admit that I felt that anything which could prevent me from living in a house with Colman was good, even if it were tuberculosis.

On Saturday night I returned to Greystones, where I met Declan as soon as I arrived.

"You're welcome," said he. "The other two were away for the last three days, and I was here in happy solitude."

I was glad to be with him. Later I handed him an account of the money he gave me.

"There's no need for this," he said. "I know the rules say you must provide details of expenses for the Bursar, but we needn't be so petty as to scrutinise every item. Anyway, you hardly spent any money."

He took the written details as well as the cash or notes I had left over after the few days. I spent little because I had forgotten how to spend money since 1942.

On the next afternoon Fergus and the boss returned. As they went upstairs, Declan was smoking his pipe.

"You'd be better away out of this house, wouldn't you, young man?" Declan said.

I never replied and he said no more on the subject. I found that the sanctuary lamp was not lighting and I remedied the matter. Colman looked into the oratory and saw me. "Oh, so you're back, young fellow! We spared a week's oil on that when you were away."

Last Days in Greystones

On the following Wednesday, when I returned from school, Colman's face was a-beam in a grin like grease over cold chipped potatoes.

"Well, young fellow," he addressed me. "You're leaving us."

I looked at him. He had to be allowed to have the first and last words, when he spoke to a young person.

"You're off tomorrow morning to Westland Row and we'll be rid of you."

My head was in a whirl. What had I done to deserve being transferred? Did the boss say that he wished to be rid of me? I had not complained about his conduct to anybody, not to a single person of any kind, even to Whisperer.

That night Declan came into my room.

"I suppose," he began, "you're pleased to be going away?"

I did not know how to respond to this. He told me that the Sunday we went to Dublin, a Provincial Consultor called, the tree-feller in Marino.

"Well," he asked Declan, "how is Colman getting on?"

"Vile temper in school and house," replied Declan.

Mulholland inquired how I was.

"He's very nasty to him. He treats that young lad worse than a cur dog!"

I was astounded to hear that Declan had reported Colman's treatment of me and felt resentful of it. I was prepared to bear the endless bullying although as I discovered later, it was sapping my spirit and forming within me a deep suspicion of authority. I was being trained to become a rebel and distrustful of all with authority over me.

Now that I was being transferred from Greystones, I hated being dumped into the centre of Dublin City. What on earth, I asked myself, did I do to draw down on myself the nastiness of that man, that I was expelled from Greystones, its countryside and its seaside, and condemned to live in the smoky air of the streets of Dublin City? My sin in Colman's eyes may have been that I never showed any resentment of him, compounded by the fact that I never played games. I turned the other cheek to a bully and earned the wages of tolerating him – or so I thought.

In Dublin City Centre

When I arrived at Westland Row about 10.30am, the discordances of city traffic and the smell of dust in the air surrounded me. A lean middle-aged Brother with gaunt jaws framing a pale face met me, and as he looked at me through steel-rimmed spectacles he introduced himself as Br Columba, the Superior. I heard later that he was nicknamed 'George' but never enquired why that was. George nodded to me and asked was I the man he was expecting to fill the vacancy in his community, but did not bother to welcome me. He hurried me out of the railway station to the monastery nearby, and I followed him lugging my big suitcase along.

The monastery was a house of three storeys. The kitchen and the refectory were in the basement, and at mealtime you could see the school playground and behind it the tall grey school of two storeys. The house in Greystones was a dwelling house with wallpaper on the walls, but now I was in a real monastery with cold blank walls. St Andrew's parish church and the curates' house were between this and the railway station. George told me to leave my suitcase in my room at the end of the corridor on the top storey, report to the School Principal and begin teaching at once. I dragged the pack upstairs, threw on my soutane, clipped on the cincture and hurried out to the school.

At 11.30am I was standing in front of fifty boys in 3B Standard in a very large room with poor ventilation and barely adequate lighting. The unshaded electric bulbs were alight most days, even when it was bright outside. The 3A Standard class shared the room, and all day it seemed there was competition between the two teachers and the hundred-odd pupils in two groups to outtalk and outshout one another. The other teacher was Jim Hynes from Co. Galway, who seemed an easygoing but very effective teacher: I learned a lot from him.

"Welcome, Brother," said he. "I hope you like it here. The health of the man you replaced was not good, so he applied for a transfer to a rural school."

No one had told me this. Like much in our life there was no explanation for most things, questions were seldom asked and if posed, less seldom answered in full. When it was 1pm and dinner-break, I went into the monastery and met the others.

I was the junior of three young men, who sat at the end of the table. I knew one of them, O'Neill, in the colleges and in Booterstown, and I also knew his companion, Sexton, who had been with me in Baldoyle. O'Neill congratulated me on being sent to the Row, but I did not feel pleased.

"You can go to Croke Park every Sunday if you wish," he told me. "None of us is ever charged at the turnstiles because we do more for the GAA than any others in Ireland."

Yes indeed, I thought, that was always my opinion.

"After school every day we go to Ringsend Park and referee games or train teams or we kick a football around," continued O'Neill. "What did you do with your time in that awful dive in Greystones?" he asked.

Without waiting for an answer O'Neill said, "You'll like it here. They say that the boss in Greystones is a lousy hound and you're well shut of him."

I noticed that the other young man, a Clareman named Sexton, did not join in the conversation at all because O'Neill, the six-footer from Co. Meath, dominated it. He was well built, looked as strong as a horse and seemed pleasant. O'Neill had become a nice fellow since we had left Marino, where I remembered him as a rough type.

After the lunchtime break my pupils lined up in the dark corridor, which was faintly lit by a little lamp at a picture of Our Lady of Perpetual Succour, before going into the classroom. As the pupils passed, each one blessed himself.

"That's in honour of Patrick Pearse," Hynes explained, "who went to school here with his brother Willy. They were in the room where we're teaching for the only year that they spent here."

Only one year in the school, I thought, but why? There was not time to question anyone about it as we ushered the pupils into the room. That school was the hub of many noises. Throughout the day the whistling of the trains could be heard and the grinding of cartwheels in Westmoreland Street on the cobblestones, where large shire horses pulled carts loaded with goods from the railway station to stores in the city.

After school we had a cup of tea and O'Neill and Sexton prepared to go to Ringsend. I demurred a bit.

"If you don't come, you must stay in the house. The boss insists that we never go out alone, so you'd better come with us." Sexton advised in a semi-whisper, "Go to George and ask for a shilling for the bus fare this week."

I did. George complained like Scrooge, while Sexton supported me, so George grudgingly gave me six pennies. I noticed that the Clare man haggled like the countryman he was, and was training me to do so. It struck me that a hard skin could have helped to deal with the bully in Greystones but I was too soft, or to put it another way, too sensitive. In Greystones I always had to take a walk alone, while here I was being dragooned into a type of cameraderie that I disliked. I was too tired after the day in school and felt more fatigued than when first I began to teach.

We returned from Ringsend at half past five to face the usual quarter of an hour prayers in the oratory after reading saints' hagiographies in nineteenth-century books full of signs and wonders. This was an arid quarter of an hour, which I did in Greystones in my own time, but here everything was regimented. When night prayers concluded in a monastery, the Superior read the page for the next day from the *Liber Mortuorum*, 'The Book of the Dead'. The names of Brothers who died on each day were all recorded here and when these were read, we were asked to pray for them. This was done each night in all monasteries. We heard place names that varied from Cork and Belfast to Johannesburg in South Africa, Kalgoorlie, Woomera and Ballarat in Australia, St John's in Newfoundland, Gibraltar, and the Calcutta Male Orphanage in India, which must have been a horrible place. The children in the orphanage were mostly of mixed blood, I heard later, some of them the results of white soldiers' fun. The Irish Christian Brothers provided education for the Irish Catholics in India who served in the British Army and other occupations there.

When night prayers were over, I was glad to tumble into bed.

Hemmed inside a City School

In May that year we had a few days of very dry weather. Early each morning a vehicle awakened me, which dampened the street to keep down the dust, a token activity because it returned in the later hours. We lived with dust in all its forms. It was a nuisance, when it hung in the air during a drought and on the streets and everywhere but when the rains came, it reverted to various forms of mud.

"Oh, this dust!" I remarked to O'Neill a day after I had arrived at the Row.

"Forget it, boy, but get on with your life."

I looked at his burly and well-built frame.

"It's alright for you, O'Neill, because you have all that you want here. All I'm looking for is the countryside," I said.

"You can keep your countryside with the cows and muck and all the hard work on the farm. I had enough of all that at home," said O'Neill. "This is a great life, so it is."

My 3B class of boys was composed of those who were not bright enough for 3A, because the fast-learning ones were in the A Standards. My successor in Greystones taught 4A, but the teacher of 3B took it over when he went, leaving the others to me because I was a junior. Of the fifty boys in 5B about fifteen of them were in a local Boxing Club. They were described as "hard chaws" and believed that a teacher was either strict or not worth respect. They gave me a hard time at first and then I gave them a harder one. They tried everything and I retaliated until we respected one another. I noticed that the tough lads, especially the boxers, never bullied the quieter fellows and I admired them for that, when I discovered that a bully is usually a coward.

The teacher Hynes decided to give me some advice.

"Do you mind me saying that you work too hard, and rush around using up unnecessary energy?"

"Really?" I queried. No one had said this to me before and I was surprised to hear it.

"Indeed you do," he continued, "and there's no need for it."

"But I like it that way!" I retorted.

"Oh, indeed you do, young man! Did it ever occur to you that in thirty years' time when your pupils expect you to teach them well, you'll be burned out?"

I never thought of that, but I thought that he was exaggerating. As I saw it then, to teach under our conditions, I had to have good lungs, be almost impervious to noise, and rush about like a scalded cat. I had experience of these forms of activity while I was teaching at Westland Row.

There was a Secondary School attached to the monastery, where three Brothers taught with as many laymen. One Brother was a tall blond-headed man, who seldom raised his voice and was always gentle and soft-spoken. One morning he was not present at prayers or breakfast and in the afternoon O'Neill asked me whether I noticed his absence. I did but what about it?

"Oh," O'Neill informed me, "he was moved off to Cork. And do you wish to know why?" As I muttered something he said, "He broke a boy's jaw with a blow of his fist yesterday!"

I did not believe him but it was true. O'Neill probably heard of it from members of the GAA club, which had contact with the school where they recruited boys for minor hurling and football teams. None of the older Brothers breathed a word of it to any one of us juniors.

Life was different here in Westland Row than it was in Greystones. George, the boss, probably intended to be kind but he was mean. He conducted endless haggling with us juniors over pennies for bus fares, which enabled us to leave the city centre in the afternoons and weekends. He often moaned about the change in monastery life since his young days, when a monk walked everywhere and never received a penny. To me he was 'Skinflint George', while O'Neill muttered that he begrudged us the fresh air.

"Fresh air, is it?" I exclaimed. "What fresh air do we have in the city dust?"

There were continual complaints from my companions. The weather was too warm or too wet. The food was never good or well cooked, because the boss was too mean to buy enough of what was good. I never heard so much whinging and complaining. Once I interrupted O'Neill with "Pity you didn't have to put up with the boss in Greystones and you'd have plenty to moan about!"

After a month, however, I had become as great a complainer as anyone else.

One Sunday when I went to Croke Park to leave the monastery, I met Whisperer there.

"What has entered your soul?" he murmured, after a few moments' conversation. "You're groaning under the weight of complaints, but when there was reason for it, you never complained: so why do you darken your whole life with groaning?!"

I began to feel unsettled. Nothing was right and instead of being bullied, I was annoying myself and allowing others to upset me. I could face a bully stoically but had no defence against this new menace, which ate into me like a poisonous parasite.

In June the Secondary School teachers' vacation began but we had to teach until July. The Secondary School Brothers had university degrees but some of us were not even qualified teachers. Nearly all Superiors were graduates and if you were a Secondary Teacher, you became a Superior. Here I experienced discrimination between teaching Brothers for the first time, because in Greystones we had only a Primary School. Secondary teachers in the 1870s were the first to ease the poverty of the Brothers, when the others had to depend on a yearly public collection. The Secondary School teachers were the privileged and curled darlings of the Order.

Our Principal, Tony, was a Cork man who laughed at one moment and swore angrily the next, whom I liked and so did the others. There were a hundred places yearly for new pupils in Second Standard, who were chosen from two hundred applications. Tony arranged interviews on a Saturday to choose fifty pupils from two hundred boys.

"First of all, if the boy has a brother in the school or his father was a pupil, note the names. Examine the boy in his tables and ask questions in Irish and give him a spelling test. Decide whether he'll be well conducted. We don't need barefaced pups."

He handed us the names of three boys, whose brothers in the school were troublesome.

"One bad apple from a barrel is enough; we don't need a second."

The last boy of the twenty that I met was John, who was with his mother and I saw his name on my black list. I found him intelligent and sharp and wondered what on earth I should do. It was clear that he was quite a star, which put me in a quandary.

When I finished, I agreed with his mother.

"He's good, isn't he?" she said casually. "I'm a teacher, who taught him last year. He's not like his big brother, who caused trouble here."

I agreed that he should be admitted instead of saying that the Principal made that decision. How could I tell Tony that I did not fail this boy because he did very well? If I rejected him, how could I face myself? His mother suspected prejudice against him.

Next morning we met in the community room. As each boy's name was mentioned, Tony took notes and the two other boys on the black list were rejected. I announced, "I examined John Byrne."

"Oh, that hoor's milt, is it?" barked Tony.

"He's a well-mannered boy!" I blurted out.

Tony laughed and decided. "Too bad for him; he'll never come to our school."

I gulped and said, "His mother's a teacher and heard everything. We must take him!"

I saw Tony grow pale with fury and angry words cascaded out of his mouth.

"You pup!" he shouted. "You're hardly out of the nest and you're dictating policy. Didn't I tell you to reject him?"

"But Tony, listen to me!"

"Silent waters run deeply and you are the shittiest silent…"

The other senior Primary School monk stood up and said, "Our business is ended. Come on men; let's move out. Tony, come out in the yard and we'll have a smoke."

It was the first time that I defied an order since I joined in 1942.

"Tony's bark is worse than his bite," O'Neill whispered to me. "Keep away from him 'til to-morrow!"

John Byrne was admitted to the school, where he began a distinguished career.

None of our five National Teachers interviewed applicants. The school was a centre of Roman Catholic promotional work and they were seen as being on the fringes.

The Shadow of the Skirt

Our cook was a young pretty girl. As O'Neill put it, "An old stick like George, who knows nothing about women, put this temptation in our way." I thought it funny that I considered that if she was not a temptation to George, neither was she to anyone else. One June evening I went to the kitchen to stoke the AGA cooker and as I entered I saw the cook talking to Tony. Her hand was on his shoulder but he drew back and she said, "I'm off!" She tussled my hair with her graceful fingers, before she hurried out the door and up the steps to the street. She was humming a tune as she made her way out. I began to stoke the cooker. I wondered why she had not gone since six o'clock.

"Some women would pull the pants off you!" Tony whispered to me before night prayers.

Our chaplain, who said Mass for us, was Father Benedict, a Carmelite and a native of Connemara. He also heard our confessions. I discovered that he a very fatherly figure, who liked to have a chat after the confession. I remember one occasion:

"The Irish Christian Brothers Congregation was founded at the end of Penal Days. The Brothers' duty in a school was religious although they taught reading, writing and arithmetic – but they kept children out of proselytes' clutches." He slowly went on. "There was resentment against the Protestants especially in the west."

He went on to talk about a song that his father sang in Gaelic, which ended:

"Avoid the Protestant minister and his mindless empty prate!
Whose church has no more foundation than the bollocks of Henry the Eighth."

I was shocked at the sectarian bawdiness.

"Everything has changed since then," he continued, "and the work of the Brothers in Ireland is done. You people are now needed abroad and not here."

I reminded him that we needed to defend the faith in Ireland.

"Really?" he queried. "Your pupils and ex-pupils have made this the most Catholic country in Europe. Your higher superiors should turn their attention to the world outside Ireland."

O'Neill guffawed at this, when I told him.

"How would we do, if we left our country and the GAA? We were trained to obey the boss and the rules, to teach school and let others do our thinking! Thinking is bad for you."

When I came to Westland Row first, I found a chess set in my bedroom. "Oh, that was Frank Meagher's," O'Neill remarked, "who had a serious type of heart disease."

I heard Declan in Greystones talking about Meagher, who was leaving under a cloud.

"That 'cloud'," explained O'Neill, "was caused by his heart. I believe you haven't a notion what I mean. Frank Meagher left us with heart trouble – a nurse with a pretty face. It could happen to anyone."

"But he had taken final vows, hadn't he?"

"That won't stop a fellow. He was refused a dispensation from his vows but when he walked with her in public, it was reported. So he had his dispensation fast enough!"

Summer Holidays

I was glad when summer holidays came. I wished to go to Achill but we went to two adjoining houses in Wicklow town which George rented. He called us Juniors aside and warned us not to go out walking unaccompanied.

"It's unfair! This condemns me to the football field as a spectator," I said.

"Don't you know," O'Neill replied, "that the boss is afraid that a woman will snare you!!"

I felt that Wicklow town was dull compared to Achill with all its dramatic scenery. I went swimming each day between showers of rain, although it was not as rainy here as in Achill. We swam in the Murrow near the football pitch. The Murrow is a sea inlet with a narrow peninsula cutting it off from the ocean. I remember watching O'Neill swim for an hour at a time like a walrus in the water. When I watched the football games, he was the best of them all, which included men from the town. In local games, whenever a team needed a player, he joined the team and played like a star.

Sometimes I slipped off alone saying that I was visiting some Brothers in the town. One afternoon I called at a house and found only Derry there. When I arrived, he took six boxes from the boss's room, when there was no need for a senior man to do this. Derry – who was over fifty – acted like a naughty schoolboy. He had been on the Chinese mission, and some of them were sent to Gibraltar afterwards. During World War II they went to Tangier with their pupils, where Derry and another former China hand put up an Irish flag on Patrick's Day. When they were sent back to Ireland after this, they were nicknamed the "returned empties".

During holidays I noticed that I never heard O'Neill or anyone complaining as they had in Westland Row. O'Neill swam and kicked football, and seemed very happy away from that monastery in the city centre. I cannot remember the sun shining, although it sometimes did. The Irish weather at times gives tantalising tastes of how life might be in a slightly different climate, I thought. The holidays were not great but returning to the city was the worst of all. On the way to Westland Row on the train, O'Neill was complaining, and I was depressed as it puffed its way to Dublin. As we passed through Greystones, I longed to return there, if only the little man were gone.

When we returned from Wicklow, we went to Rathfarnham, which was a Jesuit house where we had the yearly eight-day retreat. This yearly retreat was held in summer for the first time, when vows were to be renewed and final vows taken. During that retreat I thought about the change in my life. I had been inwardly content in the misery of Greystones, but that inner peace had now gone. I felt I was in a barracks, where complaining is a part of life, because such conditions were not natural living.

Was this the religious life, I asked myself, which I had been taught? Was I sure about anything anymore? I saw in Greystones that a person could be treated unfairly without redress, and that moving one from where he is wronged does not right that wrong. As I walked in the gardens in Rathfarnham thinking of what I heard in lectures, I found a tiny stream surrounded by bushes, where the moorhens rushed around. I came here many times a day, where it was peaceful. Westland Row began to look to me like an outpost of a religious French Foreign Legion.

The City Exacts its Price

On the Saturday before we returned to school Tony brought us together to the community room, to enter details of the pupils' progress in the school registers for the year. We all brought the roll books of our own and the secular teachers' classes. When the work was finished, I asked Tony how old the original registers were.

"Oh, the oldest are about eighty years or more," he answered.

"Tell me, Tony," I asked, "did you see where the Pearse brothers' names are registered?"

He laughed as he answered.

"Yes, I certainly have. You must see this or maybe you will not!"

When he found the register, the pages were removed where Patrick and Willy Pearse's names should have been, although it was forbidden to remove a page from a register. The names of the de Valera boys in the 1920s were scored with lines, which did not appear in cases when children left the school before they ended their course.

"You see," said Tony, "the Pearses were executed as criminals and the Brothers in 1916 felt they were a disgrace. In the case of the de Valera boys, they drew lines through their names because the monks regarded their father as a public enemy during the Civil War."

"And what do we make of the shrine to honour the Pearses in the hallway at your classroom? I think we're a lot of hypocrites aren't we?" he nodded. "I was told that Willy Pearse was given a beating for some error in lessons and Patrick came across the schoolroom to support him and so both were beaten. Their parents moved them to another school the following day."

Life in the monastery resumed and discontent was filtered back into our life like a slow poison during September. O'Neill complained constantly. A constant depression seemed to envelop him now, so that he looked very unwell. One Saturday I decided to go out for the day and asked permission from George to visit my aunt in Clontarf, where I stayed until seven o'clock. From her house I could see the Wicklow Mountains, the two Sugarloaves near Greystones and Bray, where I wished to be, although that Wicklow paradise had been ruined for me before I left it. Fly like a free bird, I thought, but who might shoot me or what hawk may tear me asunder? There is an enemy over all, as I was beginning to see. I arrived back after 7pm refreshed and I went to put on my soutane.

As I passed O'Neill's bedroom door, I saw a notice, '*No admission except to authorised persons*'. Good God, what is this? I thought. I asked Tony,

"What happened to O'Neill?

"Are your eyes sealed or something? He's in the sanatorium with a dose of TB."

"TB?"

"Yes, you eejit! I didn't say BC! He was taken away after you left today, and the Corporation men came and fumigated his room."

It was a great shock. The strong man, the swimmer and footballer, was laid low and I never guessed that anything was amiss. I speculated that tuberculosis must have been linked to his frequent depressions. At teatime we and Tony were silent. Poor O'Neill! How I missed his noisiness! He now had something to complain about at St Patrick's, Baldoyle near the monks' cemetery. A retired National Teacher was appointed temporarily and George moaned about the loss to monastery funds. He expressed no sympathy with O'Neill.

"Why did O'Neill contact TB?" I asked Tony.

"How do I know?!" He snarled. "Ask the doctor, will you?"

I waited a day or two before I asked again.

"Did the dust and smoke cause it?"

"If that's it, we all face TB," Tony chuckled.

I speculated that discontent triggered the disease, which was consuming the youth of Ireland then. Whoever, I thought, knows anything that is of importance anyway?

I felt unwell after O'Neill left and went to see our general practitioner. He had rooms in Stephen's Green and I had seen him a few times in the monastery. He had a type of X-ray machine and asked what I ate before I came.

"Oh, a normal meal," I replied.

"Oh, well, now," he said, "What I know is that you ate little. I don't see a trace of much in your stomach. You must eat!"

I went away with a prescription. When I told George about the prescription, he was querulous.

"Oh, I suppose you must. In my day we soldiered on and kept our pains to ourselves."

Oh, yes! I heard that they did and that many died of untreated illnesses. I wondered what his attitude to O'Neill was. O'Neill was very talkative but was really a more reticent fellow about serious matters than I suspected.

Whisperer told me he visited O'Neill.

"Oh, he'll be fine but it'll take time. He's as much shaken by the idea of having TB as by TB itself. Why didn't you visit him?"

I explained why I did not.

"Ask one of the older men for bus money," he said. "They always have a few pence to spare. That's what I did."

"I'm not begging for what I should have by right!" I answered sententiously.

"Oh, wonderful are the joys of holy poverty!" replied Whisperer with a grin. For once Whisperer was serious, when he added that he doubted that George was a Christian. "You certainly have lousy ill-luck with that little dragon of a boss in Greystones," he concluded, "and now George is exhaling the halitosis of parsimony over you."

I could not bring myself to beg a few pence from anyone and never visited O'Neill.

Whisperer was living hardly three kilometres from where I was but our movements were so restricted that often I had to write to him. The phone in the house at Westland Row was in George's office because he distrusted any young man using it.

The Memory of the Dead

That autumn all schools participated in a commemoration of the rebellion of 1798. We prepared for the ceremonies by teaching the children ballads about the fighting in Wexford in 1798, because the rebellion was almost completely confined to Wexford. On the day of the commemoration each one marched his pupils from Westland Row down Pearse Street to Aston Quay. As they walked, they sang ballads under the grey sky, from which the sun had taken a day's leave. Rain was also absent.

I remember 'Kelly the Boy from Killanne', 'The Croppy Boy' and 'The Memory of the Dead', all nineteenth-century ballads. We knew nothing about the fighting in Wexford and if the politicians knew anything, they did not speak about much about it. When we came near the lawn of Croppies' Acre, where the men were hanged after courts-martial in the Dublin Barracks now known as Collins' Barracks, there was not space for all who wished to be there and we halted far back. Anyway, I had no wish to hear the uninformed patriotic rubbish of the politicians.

After the ceremonies the children went home and we walked back for want of bus fares. We young Brothers had nothing to eat from breakfast until 5pm, when we reached Westland Row. Our cook was absent and we had bread and butter because none of us could cook. The older men went to hotels and some went cabin-hunting. We were used by now to this and also proud of it, which was part of our junior status in our type of society, although I cannot remember why. We were young and could live with what came with youth in that religious Order.

As Tony said to us afterwards, when he returned, "Most people know that the Catholic Church and the Protestant Church disapproved of the rebels." When I retorted that some priests led the rebels, he laughed saying, "They had no support from the bishop but got it from bottles of whiskey every night!"

The celebration or commemoration was an expression of beliefs that patriots should support, but was contrary to what our church taught. Little did we know or care about the bloodshed, hangings, floggings and appalling misery of the 1798 rebellion.

I recall not only that November but many others that I spent elsewhere. The feast of All Saints is on 1st November but after it comes the Feast of the Holy Souls. Many good Catholics may have to forego the delights of Heaven after death until venial sins are purged, in what the Church called Purgatory. We prayed for their release. To help the Souls in Purgatory we could gain indulgences for them, a 'spiritual ransom' earned by prayer. A plenary indulgence was gained when a person visited a church on All Souls' Day and said certain prayers. We made twenty visits in the Novitiate that day but as the years went by, we made less and less. I never forgot the gloom of the visit to Dean's Grange Cemetery in the Novitiate year, when the army of tombstones depressed us. The Socius gibbered on about being made of dust and returning to dust after death. As we returned Whisperer spoke gloomily about thinking of death. Later on in better spirits he muttered, "*Ashes to ashes and dust to dust, / If God won't have you, the Devil must!*"

Rome Speaks

After the end of breakfast one morning George chose a letter. He seemed a little surprised as he looked through it silently and then he read it aloud.

"This is important!" he croaked. "Revd Ferdinand Clancy, our Procurator in Rome, is Pro-Superior-General. Very well, that's enough now!"

The Roman authorities had appointed a Pro-Superior-General and relieved Revd Pius Noonan, Superior-General, of the powers of his office. Noonan retained the title and dignity of Superior-General, but Rome sacked his assistants as well as all the Provincials and their Councils throughout the world.

There was a look of disbelief on some older men's faces and sly smiles on others', as George read what was in the correspondence. The good man took no part in the discussion, but his face was disapproving. Grace after meals had not yet been said.

"Let's remember," he remarked, "that we're either in the service of God or we're not!"

The truth was that the Church in Rome regarded democracy as a political error, and had never accepted the liberty, equality and fraternity of the French Revolution. The Pope is Europe's last autocratic monarch.

We Juniors went into Tony's bedroom later and he said our job was to teach, and it did not matter what the ice-cream sellers did. I inquired about the new chief.

"Oh, you mean Clancy, the lad from Clonmel?" Tony snapped. "He was our Procurator at the Vatican. Revd Noonan is now upstairs until he joins the angels, if they'll have him!"

The story of what happened became known. Noonan resented the democratically elected councillors and did not co-operate with them, so complaints were made to the Vatican.

"Neither side would lead or drive," Tony said, "so the ice-cream sellers appointed Clancy chief boss, and he's taken Noonan's job and fired all the other elected men."

I overheard the older men discuss the situation.

"This has breached our constitution," one man said, "and we took our vows under it and not under Roman rag-bag orders!"

Someone suggested that we should take vows anew under a new constitution.

"If there's any such thing!" commented one. "We struggled for democracy and we got it, but Rome has thrown out the new constitution!"

Clancy began visiting the monasteries in Ireland and abroad to meet the Brothers. When he called to us after school hours, he shook hands with each one. He spoke with George in his room and spent time with two other senior men. I heard that he visited the sanatorium and the old Brothers in Baldoyle. He went to see a few men who had been forced out of the Order for canvassing for the General Chapter election, and suggested that they could return but they declined. Clancy was popular, a polished diplomat with a cosmopolitan air that was foreign to us. A person such as he was never elected to this high office, because the Roman authorities never interfered before this time so openly in the Brothers' affairs.

Clancy loved to have the altars in the oratories covered in flowers, and gave the impression that he cared nothing for petty rules, which most Brothers could not understand.

"The ice-cream sellers in Rome trained our Br Clancy as one of their own," said one man as he joked about a future Cardinal.

Clancy established his residence as Pro-Superior-General in Rome.

"The ice-cream sellers want to keep an eye on him," Tony said, but the reason for this was to have Catholic religious Orders' higher Superiors living in Rome. Revd Clancy appointed Valerian Ryan as his Vicar General in Marino. Val, as we called him, valued learning and culture and he wished to move the Christian Brothers from their narrow attitudes.

Val did not like the educational stinginess on which the Irish Province was built, and did not wish partly trained Brothers to teach or Brothers to attend university night classes. Nowadays, he said, there was no need to abbreviate the Brothers' education as there was when the Brothers lived in frugality. Val had been kept out of higher office by intriguers because his breadth of view was alien to some. Val's attitude was Clancy's, but had Clancy come too late to reform the Irish Christian Brothers? Were they already irrelevant in the twentieth century?

Christmas and Afterwards

In 1948-49 I spent my only winter in Dublin City centre, where the calm and misty days palled on me. I could smell the coal fires and I thought of the consumptive O'Neill who spent three winters here. I thought that I was facing TB and after it I faced ill-health, a lingering recovery or maybe an early death. I realised years later that I wished to be ill, to escape from the wilderness of the spirit that I felt in this house at Westland Row week after week. Christmas was vacation time and in every monastery the celebrations lasted for days or more than a week afterwards. In Westland Row, George saw to it that it lasted one day. George was so parsimonious that there were few leftovers.

I heard that two of the older men received presents of a few bottles of whiskey and they drank these in their bedrooms. They were invited to monasteries for lunch, where they drank what was called, "alcoholic beverages of a reasonable nature". We two Juniors went to a concert at O'Connell's Schools monastery where we met people of our own age. Whisperer was there. He thought it funny that I considered the Vatican intervention important.

"Our monkish lives will not be changed one whit by the sweet-tongued Clancy, my friend," he began. "We must teach school," he added mockingly, "obey with blind obedience and bow down before the Blessed George, Holy Stick and Venerable Stan."

Whisperer's Superior, Stan, was an even meaner skinflint than George, as all young Brothers knew. He even limited the amount of sugar in the bowls on the table, and he doled out the butter even more sparingly.

"When Clancy came here to dinner," Whisperer went on, "we received soup. Afterwards I noticed that the four cats outside the house were no longer there. Ah, I thought, I know where Stan found soup! How delicious was the feline soup on which Ferdinand supped."

I did not even laugh at Whisperer's sally but began defending George.

"At least we have soup every day, although I don't eat much. Look here, my friend, at least you have diversions here, but I'm in a smoky tomb at the Row. Can't you see that I'm gradually falling asunder!"

"You're right!" replied Whisperer. "Fitter for you to be looking after yourself than thinking of Clancy the politician! You're not eating and cannot live in George's niggardly regime. Before very long George will have some of you looking like survivors of Belsen."

We fell silent. When I think of that conversation, I realise how everything had gone awry. Was this the spiritual life? Was this how a monk should act; by complaining, circumventing rules, and acting in mind contrary to the ideals which he was to cherish? Was it for this that I left home and family? I tried in vain to evict these notions from my mind.

After Christmas I enjoyed teaching 3A up to a point, while Hynes taught 3B across the room. My pupils came from fairly comfortable families in the suburbs and some from York Street and Fenian Street, the last of the Dublin tenements. There was a little boy there who wore a light overcoat. One day I suggested to him that he should take it off because the room was warm.

"Sir," he whispered, "I'm ashamed to take it off."

I was surprised.

"Why's that?"

"My shirt's torn," he whispered with a blush, "so I must cover it and I'm wearing nothing under that."

This group also included John Byrne, whose entrance to the school I had secured in spite of Tony. Whisperer laughed as I boasted about him and intoned solemnly, "Holy Saints, pray for us and guide us well on the paths of education! Amen!"

We spent more time teaching Irish than we did Mathematics and English. The attempt in the Primary Schools to revive the old language after 1923 had failed after two decades and a half. We had to teach it, but some parents disapproved of it or were neutral. It was not a happy situation for anyone who loved the older language to see this, and I found myself swimming disheartened against a torrent. The churchmen were against the Irish language, and with the merchants were a major influence in its decline. George once said something about the English language, which was central.

"The truth is that knowledge of English has enabled the Christian Brothers to work for the Church in English-speaking lands in the British Empire and in the United States."

The Irish language had not been fashionable for more than a century after the Brothers' foundation, because it was the language of the rural poor. It was the badge of poverty and inability to speak English was seen as total ignorance. In our time teachers were compelled to teach Irish in school against the parents' wishes in so many cases. I felt trapped; what I loved was being sent to destruction.

Illness

In the beginning of February I made frequent trips to the doctor. One day he told me after an examination to inform George that I was to go to bed.

"Tell him that I'll come to see you later, and meet him."

When George discovered that I was absent from prayers before 6pm, he sent Tony to me, who laughed when he saw me in bed.

"Cripes, man," he exclaimed, "this isn't bedtime. George is having kittens in the oratory. What's wrong?"

When I told him, he went off without a word but soon returned.

"George says that you must get up, and that the doctor is not your Superior!"

When I went to the oratory, I realised after a while that I was lying on the floor and Tony was lifting me up. I think I heard George mutter, "Bring him back to his room!"

The doctor came later at 8pm and mentioned about sending me to a nursing home. Later Tony called.

"George is furious at the waste of money," he said, "but you're going there tomorrow and I'll come with you. We couldn't allow you go alone, you young snipe! In that place they might think that we're all as mean and hungry as George is."

We took a taxi to the nursing home. I gave my aunt's address in Clontarf to Tony, to tell her where I was. When I went to bed, I lay back and felt blissfully lazy, as I had not for seven years, and I slept without a break until 3pm next day, except for brief meals. My rest cure started with three days of almost uninterrupted sleep.

When my aunt came to visit me at the end of the third day, I was drowsy. I began to tell her about Westland Row and Greystones. She was the first person to hear it all.

"Well," she said curtly, "may I take it that you're leaving these people? I'll look after you for a while, if they don't agree at home with what you do!"

When I realised the conclusion she drew from what I said, I protested.

"I don't wish to leave them at all! I shouldn't have spoken of what happened in Westland Row or in Greystones. I never complained of it to anyone before!"

It was now her turn to be surprised.

"I've misjudged your intentions," she slowly said. "If your mother and father thought I said that, they'd blame me for enticing you to leave. Will you keep it secret that I spoke about it? Your parents regard me as a lax Catholic anyway, and will think that I undermined your religious vocation."

I never mentioned her name because, anyway, she had no part in it at all.

This period in the nursing home was the first time since 1942 that women – the nurses – cared for me and I thought that they cosseted me. It is difficult to believe that, although I was almost twenty-one years old, I was not attracted to any of them or any woman. I suppose I could say that I was retarded emotionally. George never came to visit me but Tony came often, and each of the others turned up at least once. One evening Whisperer came in and stood at the end of the bed. With the voice of a priest at a High Mass, he began.

"And whom see ye in yonder bed? A wretched monk whom Colman despised and George belittled." I could now laugh at this word-juggler's remarks about the pair. "Forsooth," he droned, "thy tribulations will soon be ended and thou wilt be sent where birdsong as well as downpours of rain are in the ascendant."

He sat down and for some reason I started laughing so much that muscles at the back of my head began to ache. I began to feel that I had not laughed for a long time, at least for a few years. The back of my head ached with this unaccustomed feeling. Whisperer stayed for an hour and I wished he had stayed for the day, and a few other days as well.

"That nurse," he said, as he was leaving, "who came in a few minutes ago, is a bonny lassie. Oh, behold how we suffer from the wretched miseries of the blessed vow of holy chastity!"

I laughed and saw it as something funny, which it was not. Such sayings then were idiotically comical to me, when I was still unaware of Nature's urgings.

During my time there I was sent to a hospital to have a chest X-ray and some medical checks. I travelled by taxi and imagined the anger of George when he received all the bills for these trips. Since he never visited me, I did not have the opportunity to hear what he thought of me and my waste of good money. One day the doctor had definite news, when he visited.

"You'll be pleased to hear that your chest is sound and your health is not basically affected. Although you're well physically, you're very run-down and underweight. You've escaped a breakdown, so do not push yourself too hard in the future."

"When am I going back to Westland Row?"

"Not now and never again, if I can arrange it. I'm recommending that you should be free from teaching duties and live in the countryside to convalesce for six weeks. I recommend then that you should be sent to a country town away from Dublin. What do you think of that?"

"I hardly believe it! Will George…oh sorry…will my Superior agree to all this?"

"Oh, yes! Someone informed your Provincial about you, and he phoned me asking for a copy of all medical reports to be sent to him as well as to…what did you call him? Ah, yes! I remember it now…George!"

He smirked and began laughing quietly.

Tony called for me and I left the nursing home by taxi for the short journey to Westland Row to spend the night. As I sat at table for the after-school cup of tea, all the Brothers welcomed me back, and George nodded to me from the head of the table. Tony saw to it that I was in bed early. He told me that I was going for a time to Celbridge, where an orphanage was being built.

"Was it you that told the Provincial about me?" I asked, before he left the room.

He seemed surprised.

"Who told you that?" After a pause he said, "Yes! I did. I couldn't leave you at George's mercy, could I?"

In the Plains of Kildare

The following morning I set out for Celbridge by bus. I had never been there before and wondered what lay before me. Whisperer sent me a letter, delivered by hand the night before I went.

"It was a kindly one in Heaven," he informed me, "first cousin to your Guardian Angel, who inspired the Provincial to give you such an opportunity to live in Celbridge on the banks of the River Liffey. I wish showers of blessings upon you! Amen! Alleluia!"

The Superior in Celbridge, a tall and lanky man, met me at the bus stop. He told me that he was Canice McGoldrick, and that he and another Brother lived in an old mansion while a monastery and an orphanage were being built there, which was to be called St Raphael's. He was about sixty years of age, a good businessman with limited interests, but I found that he was a very kind person. The other man in the household was a "lay-Brother", who managed the large farm. This was Davy, a Kerryman, a small and hardy man who was accustomed at home to working unstintingly on the family farm. I seldom saw him dressed in a soutane.

"So you're the young fellow who nearly died of hunger in the Row!" he began when I was introduced to him and McGoldrick had gone.

"I wasn't that sick, was I?" I retorted.

He smiled as he said, "You need to be fed, so you do! In this place you'll have such an appetite after a while that you'll be fit to eat a horse. That is, of course," he added as an afterthought, "if you'll get him!"

We ate simply and adequately. I felt a little lonely. In the nursing home I had many visitors and the nurses were always in and out of my room, and in Westland Row there was plenty company, ranging from the boring George to the lively Tony. On the second day in Celbridge I decided to go to the kitchen downstairs to meet the cook. I told her that I had come for a glass of water. She was a strong and well-built country girl, who flushed a deep red when I met her. She seemed reluctant to talk, although she answered me when I tried to make conversation. After drinking the water, I retreated upstairs.

"The cook who's downstairs, is it?" queried Davy when I said how taciturn she was. "She's here to test her vocation."

He explained that she intended to be a Carmelite nun, but was told to live a solitary life for a while as a monks' cook, where she preserved strict silence to test herself for the life of a Carmelite. I had read of the Carmelites and admired them; but now began to think of them with repugnance.

However, as Davy put it, "Every donkey to its own load!"

I was alone for most of the day. There was a room full of large bookcases in the house where every book had been published before 1920. Nowadays these could be worth a fortune, but then they were the rejects from monasteries where some senior men never appreciated books. I read widely in that room during the spring of 1949. I was aware that Celbridge was where Dean Swift's friend, Vanessa, lived but I had little interest in Swift then. Seán Hogan, a former IRA leader from Tipperary lived here, and Davy told me that he went mad at the full moon.

"The ghosts of the dead are haunting him, the ghosts of all his dead comrades, and all the fellows that he shot down in return."

The wonderful Castletown House was also here but, as Davy said, that was another "bloody landlord's house and should be burned down or sold to us," so I never visited it. Davy thought that my taste for reading was an idiosyncrasy at best and at the worst a waste of time.

Davy tried to tempt me into the fields with him.

"You could help me check the animals," he explained, "and keep an eye on the workmen for me."

I made all kinds of excuses for not doing so. One day after selling cattle, he asked me, "Where's the boss? Is he gone off somewhere?" He had indeed. Davy took out a roll of £5- and many £10- and £20 bank notes, and counted them. He put one tenner in his pocket.

"That's for an odd drink. If you come out on the farm, you could have a few pounds on the quiet. I must give the rest to Canice and arrange the cattle prices for him, when he returns."

I just smiled. I knew enough by this time not to witter on about our vow of poverty because I was becoming tired of the whole matter.

I became fit enough to go for walks and went further every day. One day I kept going until I saw a round tower by the roadside with its usual elevated doorway. The sight of the little Romanesque arch charmed me and I stopped to admire it but, of course, I barely knew the word 'Romanesque' then. I heard from a passer-by that it was 8km from Celbridge, so I walked

16km that day at least.

I spent most of Lent that year in Celbridge until Easter Tuesday, which was forty days in all. After three weeks I travelled to Dublin to see my doctor.

"How do you like your rural retreat?" he said, smiling. I was surprised at that query.

"It's quiet there," I answered. "The two men with me are over sixty years of age, and I have no one else to talk to."

He shot a glance at me, but made no comment. We had a long chat about how I fared in Celbridge.

"In spite of where they've sent you, you've improved immensely, but I never intended that they should send you to that kind of place."

However as he condemned both George and my place of convalescence, I listened with half an ear. He did not know that I had peace there in the countryside. How could he know that I was as happy there as I ever could expect to be as an Irish Christian Brother? I just held my peace and listened. Before I left his surgery, I was pleased to hear that he was recommending to the Provincial that I should be sent to a country town in the south. He told me that he was sending a report after each visit to the Provincial as well as to George. I returned without visiting Westland Row, which was not far from the surgery.

I seldom saw Canice McGoldrick, the Superior, except at meals and prayers. A few times he came to the library and sat down to chat with me. One time he spoke of the orphanage building, which was to be completed in a year.

"Then I'm out of here," he said. "I've no taste for places such as Artane, Letterfrack or Carriglee Park and the likes of these, which are prisons for the children who are there, and prisons for the monks who serve there. Everyone suffers in those places."

I just listened as he spoke.

"There is another side to that story, isn't there?" he nodded reflectively. "If these places weren't there, where could the poor children be put? Someone must look after them and their needs!"

He advised me that whenever I was correcting children's written work, I should keep them at a distance.

"You never know what germs of fever they may have," said he.

Here was wisdom, which came from the crowded nineteenth-century schools, as I realised later. At the time I thought that McGoldrick was referring to something else. In Baldoyle and elsewhere we were constantly warned against any bodily contact with a man or boy, and above all with a woman or girl. Our mentors quoted the Latin saying, *Noli me tangere*, which means, 'Do not touch me'. This expressed not only a distrust of all expressions of love and affection but also fear of homosexuality.

McGoldrick began to speak of what the monks did in Australia, when they first went to Sydney in the second half of the nineteenth century, after a failure in 1843-47.

"The men who were successful went out in 1869," said Canice, "and the captain had to anchor at night off the coast, waiting for a wind to bring the ship into Sydney at first light. When our men went on board before dawn, the sails were flapping and they caught the scent of the eucalyptus trees in the air. The men, who left Cobh for Sydney, were tough old timers," he continued. "I heard about one who was leaving the North Monastery in Cork one morning for Cobh, when he saw a boy who escaped a beating. He stopped the sidecar, administered there and then the chastisement and went off to Australia. You see, he thought that it was his duty to punish the boy before he went to the other side of the world. Ah!" said he thoughtfully, "they went there for life and few came home for a holiday. The truth is that most of the first Brothers who went out to Australia at that time suffered religious transportation for life!"

On Easter Wednesday I returned from Celbridge to Westland Row. On the previous night I telephoned George asking when I was expected at the monastery.

"Any time, you madman!" he answered.

I arrived for tea at 4.30pm. Tony greeted me with gales of laughter.

"George is having a fit," he almost yelled, "because of the money you and O'Neill are spending on him. You'd imagine it was all his own money."

When I told him about being called a 'madman', Tony stopped laughing.

"By the living Jaysus!" said he, "You must report that at once to the Provincial, I'm telling you. He can't be allowed get away with that kind of talk!"

I never reported it. Why should I? After all, I was leaving this Foreign Legion post and going, I hoped, to my own Ireland. I was always a foreigner in Dublin.

In the four days that I spent at Westland Row I came and went from the house, without having a companion as George had ordered. I intended no longer to do what he ordered because I had more than enough of him by this time. Of course, he never had an escort himself when he went out and, if you think of it, who might ever wish to accompany him? As Tony said, "That old bastard bores the pants off me!" The companion rule was not enforced on or observed by senior Brothers, so George's enforcement was bullying, because we could not retaliate against him. As men under annual vows we were carefully re-assessed each year.

One day I went to Clontarf to see my cousin, and Tony gave me sufficient money to pay my tram fare. The rule was that I had to have my Superior's permission to visit "a secular's house" but no one obeyed this rule, except those freshly out of Marino and Juniors like me. George saw me leaving but kept his peace as I went off. My cousin had an English visitor staying with her and introduced me as a teacher.

"We hear that you teachers are obliged to teach children Irish, whose parents disapprove of it," he began.

"Some do, but that doesn't trouble me!"

"Why don't you come over to us in England, and I'd get you a job at once. I'm on the local school board." I saw my aunt smiling. "You're paid much better there than they are here," he added.

"You see, I cannot. I'm under vows."

"Under what?"

"Vows of poverty, chastity and obedience, which a monk must take," I answered.

"You look too young to be a monk. You're not a monk, are you?"

"I am."

"Leave them, young man. Life is too short for that kind of thing. You should be having fun like all young lads of your age."

My cousin kept her silence. I was well aware of what she thought, and during her twenty-five years in England I felt that she moved away from the piety in which she had been reared. After a while she explained to him the obligations of vows but he looked puzzled. I remember the tale of a

Dublin lad who went to London in 1940 and fought in the war, but was amazed when he first returned to visit to Dublin in 1946.

"The place was religious," said he, "Ireland was the only place I knew apart from Muslim countries, where religion mattered so much." Roman Catholicism dominated our people in a so-called independent republic.

George told me on Thursday night that I was going to Tipperary town. I was so pleased to hear this that I felt faint. That same evening, I found Tony talking to the cook in the kitchen, who had a hand on his arm as I walked in.

"Oh, I hear you're leaving us!" she exclaimed.

She and Tony looked very friendly together, and he did not move away from her when I arrived. She was a little flushed and he looked so relaxed that the explosive man that I knew so well lurked happily behind his smiles. As I went out, I heard her saying to him, "I'm glad you're not going!"

I should not have wondered in my innocence what on earth was going on between them, because later events proved what it was. They were in love.

A year later I heard that Tony went to England with her, where they married in a registry office. Celibacy never suited him. I wonder how many does it suit? Is there a positive side to chastity as the Catholic Church teaches? I doubt it.

"We have appetites for food, drink and women," Whisperer had said. "Why starve the appetite that urges you to love a woman?" He sniggered as he continued, "As the Novicemaster said, 'We're ignorant of many things but Holy Church guides us infallibly through.' Isn't it great to have a guide who can't be wrong?"

It must have taken Tony quite a time to clear his mind of the indoctrination against love. How long did the permafrost of religious chastity take to thaw fully within him, when he left the Brothers? I never met or even heard of this loveable and volcanic man again.

My days at Westland Row had come to an end and I was very pleased that my stay in the 'big smoke' was about to become only a part of my memory.

The Golden Vale

I was travelling to my seventh residence of the Christian Brothers since 1942, almost a transfer a year. Whisperer explained the reasons for frequent transfers in this way, "If your health fails, you're decently transferred. If someone can't tolerate the company of his Brothers, the Provincial will send him elsewhere if asked. If a wretch tells the Provincial that he can't agree with the boss, he could be sent to give holy edification elsewhere but, a Brother in love with a woman is hurried away from her charms."

The happiest transfer was when a man was appointed as Superior, unless there was some troublemaker where he was going who could make life a bed of thorns for him. It was pleasant to be recalled to study in the training college or the university. It was hardly pleasing when someone too severe on pupils was 'shunted out', under the threat of legal proceedings after injuring a pupil.

Just before I went to Tipperary the Irish Republic was declared on Easter Sunday. All of us that day were conferred with Irish citizenship but if I wish, I can still claim British citizenship and a British passport – which I certainly do not. As the train approached Tipperary, when I saw the Galtee Mountains, I felt that I was coming nearer to my native roots. Behind me were the ghastliness of Westland Row and the dullness of Kildare. I was now in the Golden Vale of Munster. At the inaccurately named Limerick Junction I alighted and went on the Waterford train to Tipperary town. I was met by a taxi driver there who was to bring me to the monastery in his boss's large pre-war Bentley car, which that I grew to know very well during the next few years.

Boss of All Bosses

When I reached the monastery, a low-sized fat man with spectacles and a pudgy smile on his face waddled out to meet me. He took me by the two hands.

"Ohsha young man, you're welcome! Come in and we'll start putting flesh on you. You're as thin as a rake! Zhee?" Thus did Albert O'Mahoney, the Superior, introduce himself. Is he real, I asked myself, or is he playing a part until his real nature breaks out? He took me by the arm to the refectory and opened a little door at a hatch in the corner.

"Biddy," he bellowed, "bring our new young man tea and a few sandwiches and plenty of butter."

Butter? We had little of that in Westland Row and Colman in Greystones snarled when he thought that I was indulging myself a little. Albert heaved himself into a chair at the head of the table and I sat near him.

"So there you are!" he began. "I'm going to call you Benjamin! The Provincial says to feed you well. Oh-be-the-hokey, man, you won't die of starvation here! Full and plenty, that's what you'll get here. Zhee?" He meandered on through thickets of words, half-articulated phrases and grunts.

I never met anybody who equalled his verbiage at that time or since. It was approaching two o'clock and I felt that I ate more than during the year I was in Bray. Albert led me upstairs to my bedroom above the hall door, which overlooked the town and faced the distant Galtee Mountains. In their agelessness the mountains seemed to slumber on the horizon in the sun as they had over many millennia.

This monastery had been built just before World War II and there was hot and cold water in each bedroom. Even my room, the junior's quarters, was equipped with it. Good Lord! What luxury is this, I thought, splashing warm water on my face. When I looked out the window I saw the Primary School, which was built before World War II, a one-storey building with a large playground. I forget how I occupied my time until the others came back from school later. The Primary School men came in first.

Austin Connell, who was a thin and average-sized man, was the temporary Principal.

"The Principal has been ill and is convalescing in Dublin," he told me, but he was not sent to Celbridge but to better quarters.

Al Guilfoyle, a dark-haired person whose features looked Spanish, had an air of nobility and gravity about him and had come from Marino a year after Austin, but he was with him in the Second Year Training group and both returned to Tipperary. There were four lay teachers in the school and I was to be the teacher of Fourth Standard until the summer holidays.

A little later in the afternoon the men from the Secondary School, the Abbey, arrived at the other end of the town near the railway station. The four of them were seniors and sat at the upper end of the table. During the meal it became clear to me that the community seemed to be a happy group of people. We had dinner at 4pm every day except on Saturdays and Sundays, when it was at 1pm. Albert rambled on uninterrupted at first.

"You zhee now, we have young Benjamin here from the Big Smoke. He needs feeding and we'll feed him up…"

I heard someone comment in a whisper, "*Like some kind of bullock!*"

"…and he'll be right as rain in no time, won't he now? Zhee?"

All of them began to eat while listening to the great man, who shovelled quantities of food into his mouth and spluttered out words punctuated with "Zhee". No wonder he was known, as Guilfoyle whispered to me, as 'Zhee Mahoney'. After his initial meandering he confined himself to eating, and the others began quiet chats. They spoke of hurling and Gaelic football. It was Friday and the Primary teachers were looking forward to the weekend but the Secondary Teachers, poor souls, had to spend a half-day teaching on Saturdays in these times. After the meal, we all went to the oratory, which was a small room built for the purpose and cool in warm weather. In winter its northern aspect made it cold, but we wrapped ourselves then in our monastic cloaks against the damp cold.

The four of us Primary School men sat in the community room. Austin and Guilfoyle lit cigarettes and after a few puffs of smoke, they asked about the men in Westland Row. I remarked, "Isn't the boss here very pleasant?" The two smiled quietly.

"Oh, you'll find him that way for a while," remarked Guilfoyle after a short silence.

"One day you'll do something to annoy him, whether you know it or not, and he'll be a different man," added Austin. "I'm afraid we found that over the years."

"I don't understand," I said.

"Our abbot, Albert the Great, is a man who sees intended slights where there are none. You'll learn that for yourself, but don't complain that we didn't warn you," Guilfoyle concluded. "The two of us know that after eight years here."

I enjoyed teaching Fourth Standard but the boys were wary of me.

They responded slowly and never volunteered an answer unless pressed.

"Oh, you can blame Paddy for that!" Austin explained. "He's one of the best humoured men you could meet, is good company here but a different person in school. He was teaching your pupils."

"I don't understand you, Austin!" I retorted and he made no reply for a moment, but crossed his legs and threw a part of his soutane to join the other on his knees.

"To tell the truth, Paddy terrified the boys." Guilfoyle continued. "Some refused to come to school, and their parents sent them to the town National School. No wonder they're wary of you, and hardly trust any of us after dealing with Paddy."

I was not teaching them for long. The school was closed for "fever holidays" when a fever epidemic broke out in the town. Fevers were endemic in Irish towns then, until housing with sewerage and running water in modern dwellings ended them.

Among the lay teachers in the school was Bill, a National Teacher who taught there for over forty years. When he retired later at sixty-five, the Principal Teacher was a Christian Brother aged twenty-seven. There was no promotion for lay teachers, who were treated as junior in rank to Brothers and never allowed to become Principal in a Brothers' school then. Bill was a skilful teacher but once a month before he married, he drank well after his salary arrived on the 10th.

"Poor Bill loves the bottle and everyone knows it. Ah!" said Albert often, "Bill's heart was in the right place but he gave bad example before he married, staggering to his digs from the pub legless for three nights after pay-day and absent craw-sick with whiskey for two days."

Enjoying the Countryside

The others were happy to have 'the fever holidays' but not I, because I had taught little since February. Guilfoyle was amused at my enthusiasm for school.

"Our new Brother," as he put it, "loves to be punished and prefers time with his pupils to enjoying the leisure which the fever gives us. Isn't enthusiasm wonderful?"

That summer of 1949 was one of the sunniest that I remember. I was twenty-one on 14th May and the cards that I received from home and from my aunts with pictures of keys on them puzzled me. 'Twenty-one' meant nothing to me. During May I was at a loss what to do with my time, so I decided to explore the countryside. I often walked to Bansha and back, 16km in all, and sometimes went into the Glen of Aherlow, whose valley and the bare hillsides above it delighted me. It was so different from the dust of Dublin city and the ceaseless din of the city centre.

In the Main Street of Tipperary town there were two statues. One was John Hughes' statue of the writer, Charles Kickham. At the west end of the street was the 'Maid of Erin' who should not be leaning on a harp, I thought, but carrying a bucket of milk! An ungracious writer described her as "that hefty piece of dumpling-breasted statuary, expressing the weariness of bodily effort and the belly laughs of sin". A lorry toppled her in the 1980s but did not smash her, so she is now further on by the street-side where she is safe from the traffic.

The farm at the monastery kept us supplied with milk and vegetables. Albert was a farmer's son, who knew how to farm and he employed Paddy Fitzgerald. You could gauge Albert's mood from his remarks about Paddy.

"Ohsha now," he might say, "that Paddy out there gives value for money. He knows where his bread is buttered on. Zhee?" Sometimes he growled, "That fellow is lazy. When I was his age, I could dig out a drill of spuds in clock time. I don't know what I'm paying him for, so I don't."

Paddy earned his pay to the full by working hard and weathering Albert's moods.

When I was in Tipperary at first, another man was paid to help Paddy and Albert thought him the best workman that he ever hired. As Guilfoyle remarked, "What's new is bright! Wait 'til the shine wears off this paragon."

Eventually one day at dinner Albert's face was clouded with anger.

"Ohsha, the best of hens lay out!" he announced. "The fellow working with Paddy should be gaoled."

"Ask the abbot what the paragon has done!" Austin whispered to me.

"Ohsha, Benjamin, you'd be shocked if I told you." He devoured a mouthful of food and we had a brief silence. "I'll tell you. That brat was rough on the carthorse and what do you think he did today? He kicked the poor horse in the belly and she between the shafts. Zhee? Paddy told me. I told the pup never to show his nose here again, when I hunted him without a halfpenny of what he earned this week."

Since I came to Baldoyle in 1942 I relaxed for the first time in a monastery. I read books, which someone collected in the early 1900s, and often I sat with Guilfoyle in the community room and listened to music on the radio. I was listening to music again as I did at home each night, when as a boy when my father played O'Neill's Irish music and pieces such as Gounod's *Ave Maria* on the violin, which I had not heard since. The only music that touched me since I left home before this time was Plain Chant, which Brendan Donovan taught us.

Albert the Abbot

The rules of the Order were kept in the house but there was no tension here, as there was in Westland Row and in Greystones with Colman. One late afternoon Albert announced, "Would anyone of you like to go to our place in Cashel?" Two of us did and after half an hour Mick Murphy arrived with the Bentley, the sturdy pre-war vehicle. It was able to take the bulky Albert, who filled the place of two, and ourselves. I sat in the front.

Before we went, Austin declared. "Why should I go to Cashel? We'll have peace here without Albert!"

We journeyed to Kilfeakle through beautiful country, and in Cashel the Superior welcomed Albert and took out a bottle of whiskey and glasses. The young monk took me to see the town because we did not drink alcohol.

"How are you getting on with old 'Zhee'?" asked he as we left the house.

"Fine but why shouldn't I? He's better than the last two bosses I met."

"He's an old gramophone, isn't he? Uses acres of words to say nothing."

We walked through the streets of Cashel until it was time to return. I was awe-struck by the Rock, which is crowned with buildings that were constructed during more than one thousand five hundred years earlier. When we returned and entered the sitting room, a smell of whiskey and cigarette smoke hit us. Albert was lolling where he had parked himself for the previous three hours at least.

If our abbot was garrulous after umpteen whiskeys, on the way back drunkenness fuelled his loquacity. He spoke of Belfast in the 1920s, when Loyalists terrorised Catholics with sectarian pogroms. One evening he was in a street when a Protestant mob came towards him.

"What did you do, sir?" I enquired.

"Ohsha, Benjamin, boy, I jumped in a shop window and escaped out the back of the place."

Someone whispered, "*Why didn't they cut his tongue out?*"

Then I asked, "Did the glass hurt you, sir?"

The driver laughed quietly as Albert bumbled, "The Blessed Virgin saved me, so she did!"

When we reached Kilfeakle, the abbot was asleep and muttering incoherently. Normal conversation then began about a hurling match on the following Sunday in Thurles. The car trundled onwards in the dark, as scared rabbits fled ahead and into the roadside, frightened and blinded by the headlights. When the car halted outside the door of the monastery in Tipperary, I was asked to awaken the abbot, and he decanted himself from the car. When I offered to help him, he grunted, "Ohsha now, don't I always climb up them steps be meeself, zhee?"

There were no night prayers and I found the lamp in the oratory quenched, but I was too tired to light it. The Canon Lawyers can keep their mortal sins, I thought, and I was so tired that I left the Lord in the dark until morning.

Before night prayers Albert generally slouched in a chair with a cigarette in his mouth. As he said, "I like to sit and think of nothing," which was complete relaxation. With his eyes half closed at last like a cat resting, his cigarette burned down and its ash fell on his black soutane, where it added to a permanent grey slick. Someone who disliked him once asked me, "How's your boss, that dirty heap of cigarette ashes?" Whether he ever fully smoked a cigarette is unknown to the nations. Some of us read books or newspapers, others chatted and a few played cards, while the cigarettes filled the space between Albert's lips, which were thin hard lines formed for judging and ordering. His head had only wisps of grey hair in its suburbs.

The original "abbey" was an Augustinian friary, which was built on the banks of the little River Arra and dissolved at the Reformation. One arch of its buildings remained. Erasmus Smith was the founder of the Abbey School, which was a Protestant school in the seventeenth century but now it was Albert's pride and joy. It was "Me Abbey", as he called it. When he took it over after a case in the High Court, most of the old buildings were burned down one night and classes were held in the outbuildings. As Guilfoyle put it, he could have called it "me stables and me coach house and me outhouses" after that. Albert hated school games, because pupils were injured on the field, and as for sports meetings or athletics, Albert abhorred them for the same reason. Austin held a secret sports meeting yearly but not in 1949 when the school was closed in May and June. Albert did not allow himself to hide "me Abbey's" light. Each year the better results of the Secondary School examinations in the Abbey appeared in *The Nationalist*, the Clonmel newspaper. These were printed on long sheets of paper and Albert sent to the parents of pupils in National Schools. As Guilfoyle put it, "Well now, it is that time when the abbot sends out circus posters to trumpet the greatness of Me Abbey!"

Oh, yes! I can see Albert as he waddled to and from the abbey, his hands clutched behind his back with his huge frame moving forwards as he gazed at the ground. Spiritual values? I supposed he had them, but they were hidden and not apparent to anyone. Dedication to his religious Order? Yes!

"We're the best teachers in Ireland, so we are," he trumpeted with satisfaction. "We put our lads into the best jobs if they do what we say and learn what we teach them. We're the best, so we are. Zhee?"

Yes! That indeed was Albert the Great, the Abbot of Tipperary.

The Good Monastic Life

In June the sunny weather continued. Each morning I was out of bed at 6.30am and walked the dormitory corridor ringing the bell to arouse the brethren to assemble in the oratory at 6.45am for prayer and meditation. From the beginning of June Albert was no longer present, but sometimes toddled to the convent for Mass at 7.30am. The Secondary School teachers' vacations began in June and the Brothers, who taught there, went on summer courses. When I went to prayers in the mornings Austin was sometimes there but often I was alone as fewer listened to the bell or ignored it.

Some days Albert hired the Bentley for the day when he felt the urge to travel, and once we went to Mount Melleray Abbey. I heard speculation about the austere life of the monks.

"No one can persevere in this kind of life," someone said, "unless he believes it's worth it."

It never struck me that this was also the basis of perseverance as a Christian Brother, which was called "the spirit of faith". Any trained teacher could teach, but we bound ourselves by vows to teach for a religious objective. It was an unnatural and strict life.

One day a Brother from Australia visited us and stayed a few days. A native of the area, he had not been in Ireland for thirty years. Every morning he and I were the only ones at prayers and only three of us went to Mass on weekdays. Often I had to serve the Mass, when none of the Mass-servers attended. We drew up the rosters for the Mass servers in school, which was closed since May so no lists were compiled. The convent chaplain was Revd John Ronayne, who retired from parish duties during the Civil War and lived with his sisters. I noticed that he acted oddly.

"Ronayne? The priest who says Mass in the convent?" asked Guilfoyle. "He went to attend a man condemned to death during the Civil War. The poor fellow clung to him and could not be pulled off, when somebody shot him there with a revolver. That's why poor Ronayne was disturbed afterwards, and could never carry out parish duties."

At this time most of our prayer routine had been thrown to the wind. Prayer was as regimented among the Brothers as school was, and there was no room for private prayer. If the boss or deputy did not bother with prayers, they were not said privately. That summer I experienced this for two months at least. We all thought that the Irish monks in Australia who returned to visit their Irish homes, were strict. I wondered what the Brother from Australia, who looked as if he saw nothing but sin in the world, thought of our non-observance of rules. He depressed me.

We set off for holidays to Kilkee, where we went with others in July. Albert hired the Bentley from Paddy Spring and we enjoyed the driver's stories as well as Albert's.

When we reached Moyasta, where there was a junction of the West Clare Railway, I remember the little train approaching the level crossing at a relaxed pace. It seemed to glide and to sail gently over the boggy terrain as if there were cushions under it, which sunk slightly as it passed onwards. All rail services ceased when winds reached 80 mph. What a pity that this railway was ever closed!

We lodged in a house on the sea-front facing the inlet, which was separated from the sea by George's Head and the Pollock Holes, a range of rocks across much of the mouth of the little bay. I felt at home in Kilkee. Large numbers of people from Limerick came there, who seemed to see it as their own holiday home. We went to Mass every day and nobody seemed to be absent, but for all other prayers and pious practices we were left to ourselves and we seldom thought of them. It was unlike what George did in Wicklow. The abbot's relaxed regime appealed to me.

The warm dry weather made wearing black clothes a burden and in their sombre folds I felt uncomfortable. Of course, there was only one Christian Brother in Kilkee who wore a hat, and our abbot wore a black cap, which covered his bald head. We generally went swimming at a cove near George's Head. Many priests came but I noticed that there were no young priests present, at what was strictly a male bathing place. Our men wore bathing suits but the middle-aged priests swam naked. One day some girls arrived on the high ground above the cove and giggled loudly as they viewed the priestly nudity. A few priests starting firing showers of pebbles at them and they scurried off.

I remember a priest saying, "The filthy hussies! Couldn't they have a bit of respect?"

"Aren't the priests drawing this on themselves," one of our men whispered, *"or am I wrong about it all?"*

When I asked Guilfoyle why only middle-aged priests swam naked, he thought for a moment.

"You know I think that they are flaunting what is of only one use to them!"

Someone laughed and then added, "You see, we have all been brainwashed by the likes of that Duggan priest. Our attitudes to ourselves are hardly sane, are they?"

"As far as I'm concerned," said Guilfoyle, "our Mother Church seems to know of one sin, the general sinfulness of anything concerned sex. What's wrong with our naked body anyway?"

Austin had a final word on it.

"We wear clothes because of the weather and we all need to have those sensitive parts of us protected. Am I right?"

For this disclosure of wisdom, he received a slow handclap. Nobody made any further comment on the matter.

As well as swimming in the sea nearly all the young Brothers went at least once a day to the football pitch, where were not sufficient fellows to form two teams, so they played seven-a-side matches. Albert growled at it.

"Zhee now, if one of you fellows gets hurt, you'll be on the flat of your back in hospital, Zhee? You might be injured for life and what good are you to any of us?"

No one took any notice of him but continued with the football.

This was the first time that I spoke to a priest serving in a parish, who spent some time at the Irish College in Rome, a far superior place to the Diocesan colleges and the gloomy establishment in Maynooth, as he called it. He told me that Revd Michael Curran, the President, spied on them because he did not think that they studied in their rooms at evening. He suspected that they were playing cards.

"Were they?"

"A few were, maybe, but not many. I never played cards during study hours."

He told me that he was late coming to his room one evening, and saw the Monsignor looking through the keyhole.

"I gave him an injection of shoe leather up behind," he boasted, "and he bumped his noble forehead against the door."

I laughed, "Were you fired?"

"Of course I was!" he laughed. "I was guilty of blasphemy by assaulting a priest. It was lucky that I had an uncle, a parish priest who knew and disliked the Monsignor. He arranged to have me admitted to the Diocesan college."

This was Monsignor Curran who was recalled to Ireland because of his public support for Benito Mussolini during holidays in Ireland, and in his letters to the newspapers, I heard. As parish priest of Greystones I knew how genial he was until the sectarian matter about a mixed marriage arose, as I have already mentioned. I always had the feeling that the diocesan priests despised us as semi-clerics and as scullions in the Lord's service and considered us inferior because we were neither priests nor common laymen.

I enjoyed the first ten days of the holidays like a child building sandcastles. Our meals were on time and well cooked, served at table by a young woman, who also tidied the bedrooms. I noticed that while she did chores after breakfast, Albert sat in each of the two reception rooms from which the bedrooms branched off. While I was reading a book one morning, she passed and gave me a darting glance, with her eyes seeming to look into me. I took a sudden breath and for the first time in my life I saw this young woman in another light, but did not understand it. I had not felt this way before and its newness confused me. I put away the book that I was reading, took my bathing togs and a towel and went to the cove. As I went, I felt that I needed her or some woman. At that moment of twenty-one years of age my boy's innocence or, even more so, my ignorance, left me. What did I do about it? Nothing. What was her name? I do not remember. How often did I speak to her? Never. It was the first time that I fancied a woman, but it was unsubstantial and I paid the price of that empty exercise. It changed my life. She never spoke to me but sometimes when she passed by, she sneaked a look. I did not know what it meant but I sighed within myself. I understood why Albert spent time there in the morning, where he guarded our virtue against female enticements.

For the rest of the holidays I said no more prayers and when I went to Mass, I was daydreaming. If I must have a woman, I told myself, I must leave. An affair never occurred to me because I felt that I must have all or nothing. Of course, to leave the Brothers was a disgrace to our family, but to leave for her was heinous. I remember a Brother saying of one who left, "Oh he was one of the finest fellows, but look at what he did, the poor devil. Don't you feel sorry for him?"

Albert held court every evening in the sitting room and sat on an easy chair chain-smoking. Some young Brothers from other communities came to join the card school, which was in progress after our first evening. Albert usually threw a cigarette over to anyone who seemed to need it among the young men. Those of his community kept clear of the card players to avoid Albert, and I dreaded meeting that girl because what could I do? I suppose that she did make a move towards me, but I never gave her a chance. I was alone in my emotional wilderness. There were some retired Brothers on holidays in Kilkee also. Old Carey, who wore a hat, went to all the Masses he could in the morning, which could amount to twenty because most priests celebrated Mass at high speed during holidays. Carey was a retired and sharp-tongued man, whom Albert held in contempt.

"That old fool," as Albert informed us, "was always a fool and still is. Zhee?"

Albert's black cap in Kilkee attracted Carey's attention.

"With his black cap," he growled, "that smoky Zhee Mahoney is secularising the Congregation."

I heard that Carey was a well-read intelligent man, but he pretended to know so little that many Brothers treated him as a fool. Others saw him as outrageous but very few knew his brilliant mind.

One night after a dance in a hall, a couple stood in the doorway of a house entangled in one another. Casey, who stayed here, was angry at being awakened by what he considered to be heinous sin, and he emptied a basin of water on top of them. As a result of his zeal for Christian virtue Carey was asked next day to leave. Albert was adamant that he was not staying with us.

"Who'd bother with that ass? He won't come in here to pester us, I tell ya! Zhee?"

We all laughed at the grotesque incident, and Albert had material for his sarcasm, as he dished out lots of verbal liquid manure on every occasion that he could.

Back to the Monastery

When we returned to Tipperary we had petty monastic order once more. We made up for our months of laxity and first of all had an annual eight-day silent retreat. A vocation to the religious life, we had been told, was God's gift, but to reject it was to face eternal damnation. As Whisperer summed it, "How sad, dear sir, that we're bound for Hell if we leave the monks. We're conscripts for life in the eternal army."

If this were true, I thought, is it not an odd punishment for not accepting a gift imposed on a wretch who ceased to want it?

"God is good," Whisperer stated, "but he permits the cruelties of living and he punishes those who refuse his gifts."

After the eight days' silence I decided to remain a Brother and, was renewing my vows for the fourth time on 15th August. I never knew what the vow of chastity entailed for me until now. My experience in Kilkee never commended that particular vow to me again as an inviting prospect, so I was at last facing a harsh reality.

We had an unusual man as new Sub-Superior, Columba Meares. If the Provincial trawled through Ireland for Albert's extreme opposite, Meares suited what was required. He was well-spoken and well-read, loved music and painting and was a man of vision and polish. He was also a photographer, who printed his own pictures. Meares seldom described Albert as "the abbot" as we did but as "our agricultural Superior". When he did say "abbot", it was with withering sarcasm. One day Meares smiled wryly as he almost muttered to himself.

"Oh, that high dome of Abbot Albert's forehead hides no great intellect nor any love of form in the universe. It is the bony guardian of a mind which has more kinship with muck and cows than it has with thought and with life."

Our abbot seemed to be concerned only with agriculture all the year, and the results of the Secondary School examinations in the autumn. On the other hand, Meares' conversation at the dining table reached a new height when he spoke of books and above all, of ideas. Whenever Albert was absent, discussion of games was now quite restricted. Young Con Flannery often yawned as Meares spoke, for example, about the work of Compton Mackenzie, whom he once met at the Wexford festival. Meares often spoke of the need to reform the Order along strict religious lines.

"All the trouble that we had in the Order in the last few years," he said, "was driven by Irish Republicanism. That scarcely befits religious ideals, does it?"

As Meares spoke, Guilfoyle had a look in his eyes of a vision of truth. He gazed at his long slender fingers, as he smiled at our life's contradictions, while Meares was speaking. Guilfoyle admired Meares but he was so reserved that at first we hardly guessed it. One afternoon Guilfoyle pointed out to us in the community room that we were Irish Catholics of the National Church.

"Don't be pulling our legs!" said Flannery. "I bet you can't tell us what the National Church is?"

"The National Church, dear Brothers," Guilfoyle answered promptly, "consists of the unholy trinity of the Irish Catholic Church, the GAA and Fianna Fáil!"

We had another new arrival, Bill O'Donnell, a Kerryman who survived tuberculosis after lengthy treatment. He was a dedicated teacher, who had the Junior scholarship class in the Abbey, boys who studied for a County Council scholarship. Bill was a hard man, who substituted personal humiliation for physical punishment of pupils. One day a boy so annoyed him that he ordered him to remove his boots and threw them out of the window.

"Go down," he said, "find them and put them on before you come back up the stairs!"

Bill cared for the welfare of his pupils but the difficulties of his illness and recovery did not breed much understanding of their sensitivities.

Flannery was sent from the Training College and was a native of Co. Westmeath just as Guilfoyle was. He was good-humoured and more likely to smile than to frown. A relative of his worked in Kilbeggan at Locke's distillery. His stories about it, I suspect, owed much to his imagination.

"Everyone in Locke's gets a few free drinks every day," he informed us, "and some are great boozers. On Saturday evening many's the man that's wheeled home on a handcart, who hardly knows his own name."

Guilfoyle, whose people were neighbours of Flannery's, smiled.

"Your stories, Con, are like chickens' legs, because they travel fast and exist much in fantasy."

Christmas

Christmas and the school vacations were near. Austin asked Con Flannery and me to set up decorations in the community room, while Bill spent much time trudging the roads. I heard at that time about his tuberculosis and his unexpected restoration to health.

"Isn't he as mad as a hatter pounding the roads alone?" remarked Flannery.

We went to midnight Mass at the convent for Christmas Day. I served Mass for Revd Ronayne, who was in a tormented mood.

"It must be the phase of the moon!" said Bill later.

As he gave the nuns Holy Communion, Ronayne grunted his liking or dislike for each nun, as I noticed when I served Mass and Communion for him. He never said "Happy Christmas" to me, or "Thanks" for serving Mass. Christmas Day was as miserable as other days in his life for this Civil War victim.

The Christmas meal was typical of what we could expect from Albert; a plentiful, huge feast which had the freshest of foods and the finest of drinks. Austin, Flannery and I did not have alcoholic drinks but Guilfoyle liked wine as Meares did. Bill drank copiously and became as garrulous as Albert, who guzzled food and emptied glasses while staggering verbally through sentences. Each sentence was less complete as the meal proceeded and he meandered finally into linguistic obscurity. After the meal Meares suggested that Flannery and I should help the housekeeper to wash up. I could see the disapproving look in Albert's eyes.

"What are we paying that one for, zhee?" he growled. "Making our young fellows pot-wallopers, is it, zhee?"

After the wash-up, Meares gave Biddy a bottle of port wine.

"Happy Christmas, Biddy," he said, "and enjoy the wine. God bless you!"

Our abbot regarded her as a skivvy, who was paid as little as possible. To him she was only a woman, who was widowed before her son's birth. He described her as "Judy Suds" and she was going off to take her boy home from a neighbour's care.

We had no community prayers on Christmas Day and Austin, Guilfoyle, Con and I played games of bridge. Albert went for a few hours of sleep, Bill for a three-hour walk and at 8pm we came together in the sitting room. I had already gone for a walk through the town with Flannery. There was not a soul on the streets but the lights on Christmas trees brightened windows. I was assailed by a longing to be in my house with my wife and children, the first time that I felt this. When we returned at 8pm, there were bottles of stout and ale lined up on the sitting room table as well as port wine, sherry and two bottles of Irish whiskey. There were also two dozen bottles of mineral or "windy" water as Albert called it with contempt. I enjoyed all Con Flannery's stories about those at home who got regularly drunk on 'first shot' whiskey. By 10pm the abbot had staggered to bed, and the others were tipsy except Meares who drank a few glasses of sherry, which had no obvious effect on him. Flannery enjoyed teasing Bill, who was becoming rather drunk.

The two of us lifted one senior man "drunk as an ass", as Flannery said, upstairs to his bed. We laid him on his side in bed, as Flannery advised me, removed his shoes and took off his collar. He had learned at home how to deal with drunks, he said. I wondered was his father one of these? The others went off to bed one by one but both of us stayed with Bill.

Bill was talking in his cups about men who left us.

"After teaching for nothing for years, they're treated like dirt, dressed badly after teaching without getting a penny, and sent off with little in their pockets. It's not Christian, I say; it's not Christian!"

Flannery blurted out all kinds of opinions to keep Bill talking. He summed it up with this, "I'm often thinking how can anyone be a boss and remain a Christian?" Bill's speech was becoming incoherent.

"Come on!" said Flannery. "Get him out!" We reached the end of the corridor, when Flannery said suddenly, "Quick! Bring him out the hall door!"

It was too late and he covered the boards with evidence of drunkenness and the food that he had eaten. We dumped him in bed, and returned to the community room. Flannery took two boxes of cigarettes and I put a cigar in my pocket, which I smoked before I went to bed. I felt queasy after it and saw in the mirror a green face and felt like a wet rag. Next morning Flannery and I arose before Biddy arrived.

"There's a job for you in the hallway!" Flannery said brightly to her.

She went out and I heard her shouting.

"What dirty divil left that mess on the floor. The boss, I bet! Holy God, what a dose that old fellow left me after Christmas! I had too much of him all the years!"

We never told her the truth.

That day I went with Flannery for a walk to clear the cobwebs from our heads, as he put it. He considered Bill's over-indulgence in alcohol comical but suddenly he asked me, "I wonder is Bill an alcoholic?"

I was startled.

"What's an alcoholic?"

Flannery became serious as he said, "That's someone who cannot control his drinking. I knew a few."

"Well," I countered, "I never saw Bill drinking until tonight, but isn't it more likely that the abbot is an alcoholic? I hear him moving around in his room talking to himself at night, whenever I wake up."

"You know," said Flannery, "There was a fellow at home who finished a bottle of whiskey when he got it, but felt guilty. He made hot whiskeys until the bottle was empty, and had a glass of booze in one hand and the Rosary beads in the other. I suppose that he thought that God would forgive him if he said the Rosary while he was taking the hard stuff. He must have said dozens of Rosaries in his time!"

After Christmas during very wet weather Austin, Guilfoyle, Flannery and I played so much bridge that we became like addicts. We, as the Scripture says, "sat down to eat and drink and rose up to play." We went to the "spiritual exercises", which were not as numerous as the rules had prescribed. And so when we had vacation from many prayers, we used it to play cards. What the others thought of it, I did not know but I became absorbed in bridge.

New Year with Its Troubles

When we returned to school after Christmas, Guilfoyle did not appear in the morning for breakfast. We heard at midday that he was admitted very ill to a nursing home in the town. Albert never spoke of him but Meares did to Austin, Flannery and me.

"Our dear agricultural Superior is trying to ignore Guilfoyle's illness," he began.

"What then is the matter with Guilfoyle?" Austin asked almost idly.

"He has pleurisy and pericarditis," Meares continued. "You should have been told that he is in a very critical condition."

I was shocked and I blurted out in some confusion. "And why doesn't the boss tell us?"

"He hasn't visited the nursing home and will not accept how serious it is. You must not visit Guilfoyle for a few days; he's too ill to have any visitors at present."

As I have said, Bill loved walking. Rather late one Saturday evening after Christmas I went out with him and we returned in the dark. I mentioned Guilfoyle's sickness, when Bill snorted with disdain.

"Some doctors," said he, "say that kind of thing to take the credit when the patient recovers."

"How do you know that?" I asked.

Bill stopped walking for a moment and resumed his pace as he said, "One time I was so sick that they said I was dying, but here am I now full of beans!"

When I remarked that I heard he had nearly died from TB, he stopped and barked at me in anger.

"And who told you that anyway?" I told him that it was Flannery.

Bill stopped suddenly, and I heard him announce out of the darkness:

"May my curse fall on that villain who told you! May he die in agony with no doctor to ease his pain, or priest to give him the sacraments! Amen!"

I was shocked at this outburst. I had heard about cursing, but now I witnessed it on a roadside in the dark. It was the ultimate negative, the spawn of hate and hurt and the weapon of the helpless. I shivered within myself. Years later I heard that no evil befell Flannery, so Bill's cursing was dissipated in the night. It was a grotesque exercise in the dark and belonged to the dark, when I think of the innocent and pleasant young man, who was the object of the curse.

One afternoon Bill sidled towards me obsequiously.

"Will you help me two nights a week checking History in the Scholarship class? You're a genius at History, but all I know about History is what I find in the school book."

Why not help him, I thought.

"Where will I meet these boys?" I queried.

"In your own classroom twice a week, where you'll feel at home with them," he answered. It was quite an experience for me.

Bill gave his pupils the text of an examination question before going home from school at 4pm. I showed them how to answer it on paper. Bill's theories on a journey through Examland were revealing. He believed that "If a lad doesn't know anything by heart, he doesn't know it at all!" Rote memory was his principal teaching method – although he was partially correct about this, there was another facet to it. As Bill put it, "Don't waste your time telling them too much. Take the straight and narrow way at all times!"

On Holy Thursday five days before the examination, the boys arrived very listless. I allowed them out of the school quietly after half an hour. When I went out, I heard Bill questioning them in the bicycle shed. He had waylaid them as they silently left the school building. They all sickened between Friday and Monday, but on Tuesday morning they all had recovered for the examination. Bill was almost insane with worry during that Easter, until he saw them all on Tuesday. I am sure that there is no need to say what I thought the origin of their sickness was.

Guilfoyle recovered slowly but remained in the nursing home until May. Albert never referred to him, and seemed to regard him as an outcast. What it had to do with Christian care for the sick I did not know. As Austin put it, "Apparently, old Albert believes in a different Christianity!" I recalled how kind Albert had been to me, when I was unwell. The more I thought of this, the less I understood his attitude to Guilfoyle's illness. I wondered if he felt guilty about Guilfoyle's health, who had been in his care for a dozen years and more?

One day Flannery remarked, "Did you hear that some people thought Guilfoyle might marry a nurse, when he left the nursing home?"

"A nurse?" I asked in surprise.

"I'm talking about the nurse who saved his life," Flannery replied. "She even spent her free time beside his bed as well as her nursing hours."

Guilfoyle, however, remained a monk until death.

Late Spring to Summer

Austin loved his own privacy. He spent time in the garden tending his strawberry plants and some blue lupins on the outside of the school wall, but did not like anyone talking to him while he worked. He made it clear to me that I was a nuisance, whenever I came out to chat with him or tried to help him. As April slipped into May, a feeling of unease grew among many of us. The glories of spring were on the trees and in birdsong. I was becoming tired of this male society. Some men in their forties were snappish at this time and some spent their free time in their bedrooms. We young lads stayed in the community room at evening. Meares was otherwise, imperturbable except when he spoke of Albert.

"He has been too long a Superior, twice in this house and twice in Drogheda; he's over seventy and should not serve another three-year term. Why doesn't he stock the library with modern books? Has he bought any book in the past year? Show me a book published after the 1920s in the bookcases."

As far as I knew then, this was true.

There was a locked room in the monastery, that we called "the pig's parlour". Whenever we needed anything – from stockings to toothpaste – Albert had it here. In May he allowed me into this room, a privilege that he granted to nobody else. I saw flitches of bacon strung along parallel bars that belonged only in a gymnasium. Boxes of cigarettes, clothes, shoes and other items were here. Spiders here had secure domiciles, their webs slung from ceiling to floor, from boxes to flitches of bacon. One day I saw a stack of volumes and noticed modern authors' works. Good Lord! I thought, so he bought books – but why did he keep them here – unless he decided that they were not suitable reading for us? None of us read Compton Mackenzie's books but I saw five of them here. I took them out, read them and found them interesting, but Albert must have thought them hardly fit for our virginal eyes. I often described the pig's parlour to the others. As a result Meares never again ate bacon in the monastery.

"We have a house larder," he once said, "the abode of spiders, flies and creatures that may be carrying, and are indeed prepared to spread the ten plagues of Egypt."

The year 1950 was declared a Holy Year by the Vatican. Crosses were erected on hills and many shrines built. I heard that my aunt, Sister Otteran, a Dominican nun in South Africa since 1916, was now managing a hostel in Rome, but was now visiting Ireland for a few days, for the first time since 1934. When I asked Albert for a day off to see her, he agreed. She was very proud that I was teaching.

"In South Africa all these years," said she, "I taught in Boksburg convent."

I asked if she taught non-white children, and she surprised me.

"I never taught a black or coloured pupil; we never admit them."

So she was not a missionary but was like many priests, nuns and Christian Brothers who went to countries of the former British Empire. They all cared for the European settlers and the white people including the Boers' descendants in South Africa.

After my short visit home Albert decided that I needed to be taught a lesson. For ages he had ceased calling me Benjamin, but now he acted as if I was not there. At mealtime he made a point of addressing everyone except me.

Austin simply said, "Sorry, but I knew that you could have months of ostracism imposed on you."

Meares addressed me and spoke to me but Albert? Never. I felt isolated. What had I done? The community was my social life and I had none outside it. Guilfoyle and Austin pointed out how inevitable it was.

"This is what Albert does to all young people," said Austin.

After a week I could not tolerate this anymore. One night after prayers I went into Albert's bedroom, where nobody ever went. Either you knocked on the door or else met him elsewhere in the house. Albert looked almost stunned as I walked in.

"Sir," I began, "why are you making a leper out of me?"

His voice stumbled as he muttered verbalisms.

"Sir," I announced as I looked into his eyes, "I am supposed to renew vows soon. If this goes on, I'll write to the Provincial, telling him I'm leaving because of you. Don't you recognise me as a member of this community? You'd take more notice of a dog!"

He was speechless. Then he began muttering, "Ohsha, zhee now, me good fellow, it's alright, me good fellow. Your imagination is throwing you down, so it is, young fellow! 'Twill be all right now. Zhee! Be off with you and go to bed!"

I whispered to Austin next morning after Albert addressed me, "Who said that you can't halt the wild bullock's run?"

It struck me that Austin and Guilfoyle were too tolerant of this abuse of authority in the past, as I had been of Colman's behaviour.

Seaside Holidays

The summer vacation came and we prepared to go to Kilkee. The weather was not as fine as the previous year but as long as the skies did not spill down water on us incessantly, I was satisfied. I had comparative freedom for a month and was out of the monastery confines. Late on Sunday nights or early on Monday mornings in Kilkee I could hear couples near our holiday home entangled in loving embraces. Bill thought it hilarious but I envied the men.

"Ohsha," Albert often muttered, "zee now they're in heat, so they are! I'd like them to go somewhere else, but they're waking me up and they deserve a basin of water to cool them down, like the fool Carey did last year!"

He remarked with a horselaugh that water could quench their heat. Carey, the cooler of amorous ardours, was on holidays in Kilkee that year again, and he walked along the seafront a few times a day leaning on his stick.

I saw an old man called Reilly, who lived in Kilkee, rambling down the seafront. A former member of the Royal Irish Constabulary, he escorted Roger Casement into custody in 1916. He was old, had his own part of Irish history and walked rapidly with a soldierly stride, but he wore no stockings. During World War II Reilly's son was parachuted into the area from Germany but spent the rest of the war interned in the Curragh, when the Gardaí were informed.

As someone said, "He came home for a holiday in the middle of the war in a Luftwaffe bomber, but was glad to be parachuted into his own backyard."

There was a circus in Kilkee that year, which provided an eating competition for small boys. On our first Sunday the two finalists competed on the roof of a wagon at the seafront. I went to see this display of schoolboy gluttony. Each of the two boys was given a huge loaf of bread, two large onions, a pot of jam and half a pound of butter. I can still see the loser suddenly rush over to the side of the wagon and be sick on some of the crowd underneath.

"The winner must have a stomach like a concrete mixer," Bill laughed heartily. "Isn't it all great gas?"

Meares considered it otherwise.

"It is all reminiscent of a sickening Roman custom," said he. "The only thing that these circus men lacked during this disgusting display was a vomatorium!"

Bill whooped before he asked, "And what is that? A 'vomiting tome'?"

Meares shook his head as he stated, "Dear Br William, 'vomatorium' is a place to vomit, which was in a well-off Roman's home just as our bathrooms are nowadays."

One morning someone informed us, "Andy Quirke is appointed as your new Superior, and the abbot is sacked! After all his years in Tipperary the Provincial pushed him!"

Quirke, I heard, was an easygoing man, who was also on holidays in Kilkee. Albert did not hear the news until lunchtime because the Provincial had not informed him. He sunk into a morose silence. Meares was appointed a Superior in a Dublin monastery. Young Brothers ceased coming to play cards to our house and cadging cigarettes every night. Albert was seen as powerless since he had been replaced. Let me state that Andy avoided our sacked abbot until he arrived as the Superior in Tipperary a few days after we returned from holidays.

The evening of the new appointment I remained inside as Albert rambled on about the good he did for pupils over the years, as he smoked cigarette after cigarette. I listened to him because of his kindness to me when first I came to Tipperary, and he was alone now because the card players had deserted him. We heard a hesitant step coming outside and Albert ambled into his bedroom but left the door open.

I saw Carey at the window, who trumpeted in, "Where is the great man…" There was silence until the mischievous words were shouted, "…*that was?*"

During the last few days in Kilkee Albert remained silent. Guilfoyle and Austin never made any remark, but were glad that their tormentor was going. Most men on holidays said that Meares reported unfavourably on Albert to his Provincial Council friends.

"Ah!" said one man. "Meares is Judas who earned his thirty pieces of silver."

I did not regard the matter in that way at all, and neither did Guilfoyle and Austin, because Meares was a gentleman. Now that I think of it, our agricultural abbot was also a gentleman, but in quite a different manner and of a different calibre.

The New Era

Albert left Tipperary in the beginning of September after spending sixteen years there, nine as Superior and seven as Sub-Superior. He was sent to St Patrick's in Marino to be 'let out on grass', as they said, where his companion was the retired Novicemaster. If ever two opposites lived cheek by jowl, it was this pair. We had lost not only our inimitable abbot but also Meares, another a contrasting pair. Andy Quirke was a man without any pretensions.

"Andy is a decent man," Bill said. "As long as we don't hunt skirts, rob the bank, come down the street mad drunk every night or shoot some eejit, we can do as we wish where that man is concerned."

Andy was never absent from prayers and was present always at morning meditation, prayers and at Mass. He acted quietly and he ruled by his example. Andy talked incessantly at table about hurling and Gaelic football. No longer did anyone mention books, but rather the merits of every GAA team in Ireland. Austin, Guilfoyle and I carried on our own chats at the end of the table, although Flannery preferred the endless talk on games and predictions of the results of future contests. In our National Church, as Guilfoyle explained one day, the GAA was a safe haven for priests and young religious men.

"In the GAA," he pointed out, "chastity is safe because women are absent, and let's admit that interest in anything artistic is rather dangerous for our virtue. And we must remember," he continued, "that it's safer for us to read only the sports pages in the newspapers. All in all, as I think over it, I become convinced that it is better that a monk should be a thick ignoramus! His vocation is safer that way."

"But how will we teach," Flannery interjected, "if we have nothing stored between our ears?"

Guilfoyle looked solemnly at him.

"Dear reverend innocent, learn only what you must teach, never think for yourself, and you'll always be a good monk. As for you," Guilfoyle said, looking at me, "I fear for your future. You think too much and that's bad."

We all laughed at his sally but what sounded humorous was very serious.

Change from Rome

In early winter rumours were going around about the reforms that were planned for our Order or Congregation. It was said that Rome was imposing a constitution on us, to allow some of us to be ordained priests. I could see Meares becoming a bishop, if not an archbishop and a red-hatted cardinal. If Albert had not been old, he could have been a Monsignor but it struck me that he could not fit into any mould except the one he had filled all his life.

One afternoon Guilfoyle took the lead in a discussion among us Juniors.

"I think," said young Flannery, "that these changes they're talking about are only yarns spread for fun!"

Someone pointed out that we had taken our vows under a constitution but if a different one was imposed, we could leave. Three agreed that this was true.

"Oh, isn't that a wonderful turn of events now?" commented Guilfoyle with some asperity. "It seems that if this is your attitude, you already wish to leave the monks, but all you need is a respectable pretext. Am I right?"

There was no straight answer to that but some bantering.

"We're not strictly speaking a religious Order," Guilfoyle continued, "but an association of laymen in clerical garb and some cardinals in Rome may wish to change this by ordaining some of us. After all, we're Irish National Teachers attired as clerics. Let's remember that we made our vows to God and not to any constitution or anything like that."

What need was there for us anymore, I thought? There were thousands of Catholic men teaching needlessly in clerical garb. It struck me that I should leave now and teach as a National Teacher like my two brothers. I was a bogus cleric, so why should I continue to appear to be what I was not? Of course, it could give me a 'respectable' motive for leaving the Brothers, if a new constitution were imposed and I refused to accept it.

Guilfoyle asked someone later that day did he remember what was in *The Directory*.

"I suppose you remember the opening words," he reminded those who were listening, "which go this way: 'The spirit of this Congregation is a spirit of faith.' Remember?"

I recalled the Novicemaster saying that this was the most important sentence in the book but I had not realised the importance of what he said then. If you did not believe that your teaching was a sacred religious duty, you did not have the spirit of faith and you ceased being a Christian Brother. I believed fully in this 'spirit of the Congregation' once, but believed it less now.

"Catholic religious orders like ours," added Guilfoyle, "originated when a priest, Jean-Baptiste de la Salle, founded one in France. From 1804 our men began to provide religious and secular education for the poor. Did you hear of the Franciscan Brothers in Connacht?"

I never did.

"Franciscan Brothers?" I asked.

"Oh yes!" said Guilfoyle. "There are a few living on the west coast, and the Order is almost extinct at this stage because they had no recruits, postulants or novices!"

I was in charge of Fifth Standard that year from August 1950 to June 1951. I liked teaching History and Geography, which were not taught to younger children, but I was obliged to teach them through Irish. A few years earlier all subjects were taught through the Irish language but since English was the language of most homes there, this was not a good idea and Mathematics was taught henceforth through English.

As Bill put it acidly, "Most monks can hardly speak good English, can they? How the hell can they teach Irish or anything else properly through Irish in that case?"

Practically all knew only a sanitised version of the Irish language, because they knew neither swear words nor terms for natural functions such as love-making, urinating or defaecating. Most parents do not favour Irish. It was very obvious that the movement to revive Irish had failed, but no one admitted it. I loved Geography and History, but had to explain everything in English before translating it into Irish. It was frustrating.

As Austin said to us one afternoon, "In 1916 and afterwards they fought for an Irish Republic and the revival of Irish. We have a so-called republic here in one part of Ireland but few people want Irish and those that pretend that they do, speak English."

As to parental opposition to Irish, Guilfoyle stated, "We know nothing at all about family life and we've renounced it, haven't we? A person must know Irish to pass public examinations. If he doesn't, he must work with the pick and shovel here, or take the boat to England to work as a navvy there, unless his family has money and a business."

Someone mentioned the 'democracy' movement in the Christian Brothers, which provided for proper elections, but we now had a temporary or a Pro-Superior-General appointed by Rome.

"These democrats brought politics into our religious Order with republicanism," Guilfoyle retorted. "Look at our prayer book where all prayers are in Irish! What about men over fifty, who want to pray in English? The Christian Brothers is a branch of bogus republicanism."

One day Guilfoyle handed me a paperback.

"Read it and maintain your sanity about Irish!"

It was *An Béal Bocht*, 'the Poor Mouth', written by Myles na gCopaleen. I read it avidly. It was rough and hilarious and I laughed at the crazy world of the Gaeltacht and the Irish revival movement that Myles created in Irish. It was a relief, and laughter tempered my bitterness at the pseudo-Gaelicism that governments created, and that we tried to promote in school. Catholic priests were generally against the Irish language revival, but gave allegiance to the new Irish State which they saw as a powerhouse of English-speaking Catholicism, to support the church in English-speaking countries. As I thought over what I heard, I wondered whether I had renounced normal living not for the love of God, but for the 'National Church' of Catholicism, Fianna Fáil and the GAA. What if Guilfoyle was right?

When Albert left us and went to Dublin, I noticed a change. It struck me that the new Superior liked the priests of the parish: Albert was somewhat anti-clerical.

"Ohsha, Archdeacon Cooke," said he, "is a fine priest but he has no say here. Zhee? We're responsible to the Sacred Congregation of Religious and not to the Archbishop!"

It may seem odd that Albert was the first anti-clerical Catholic that I knew. Cooke was a fine but straight-laced person. Someone unfairly complained about one of us and he defended the monk.

"Ohsha man," said Albert, "you shouldn't have drawn him on you. We look after our own and we don't need the likes of him. Zhee?"

As Austin remarked, "Albert is capable of letting one of us down in spite of his talk, but Archdeacon Cooke is different. He has strict principals, unlike our good abbot."

There was a priest called Dick Quinn in the parish, whom Albert kept at a distance. Once during a parish mission, he came to say Mass.

"Well, the Sixth Commandment is getting a rest," he said, "and they're talking about the Seventh."

The Sixth dealt with sex and the other with general honesty. We taught the children that "we must pay our lawful debts and give everyone his own," but Dick Quinn held that dishonesty was not considered serious, and everything was exaggerated about the other. As a Catholic priest Richard Quinn was before his time in his attitudes.

We come to April 1951, when the bishops dictated government policy over a social welfare bill, 'The Mother and Child Bill'. Children were to receive free medical services from birth until teenage years, which they badly needed. During the debates in the Dáil, which led to the fall of the government, Revd Dick Quinn visited my classroom.

"What do you think of the Mother and Child Bill?" he asked.

I said that I knew the church opposed it but it was not mentioned among us. If Meares were there, 'The Mother and Child Bill' was certain to be the major topic but games interested the Brothers while Andy was the boss and little else. Revd Quinn explained that the Minister for Health, Dr Noel Browne, was introducing the Bill to undermine the Catholic faith.

"Browne was trained in Trinity College, and means no good to Catholics just like the others in that college!"

I agreed completely with him. I never gave the matter thought at that time, but accepted unconditionally all that the Church decreed.

Confirmation

Dr Noel Browne led the campaign to eradicate tuberculosis in Ireland, but it was too late for my pupil, Danny. That autumn I thought that he had tuberculosis symptoms, which I had seen in others. I decided to advise his mother to have him examined but feared I might insult her, especially if he did not have it. Tuberculosis in those days was often a blot on a family's honour, social standing and respectability.

The Wednesday before Easter I heard that Danny had been sent to the local hospital. When I visited him, he was silent and inert. Two days later he was listless as he lay slumped in bed. A few nights after this Andy told me that he was dying.

"If you want to go to the hospital, go over there now and comfort his mother!"

I can never forget the last hours of Danny's life as I listened to his laboured breathing, because I had not seen anyone die before this. His mother and aunt were by the bed, inconsolable, and I began saying Rosaries to overlay their misery.

His father stumbled in drunk after midnight, nodded towards the bed.

"He's making no battle, is he?" he said to me. "He's finished, so he is!"

He began to discuss the following Sunday's games and ignored his wife, his sister and his dying son. Seeing the boy die horrified me and I felt that I was to blame for his death. What kind of a coward was I that I did not speak out? He had gone barefoot selling milk each winter morning in rain and frost, to earn the price of a Confirmation outfit, when he was riddled with TB but was the first of his classmates to receive Confirmation.

There was no one to talk to in the grief that I felt. I longed for a real friend, and for the first time I felt that I needed to talk to a woman – but there was no one.

It seemed to be raining always and the wind seemed to blow from the north west. It struck me gradually that prayer and spirituality were of no help whatever, when I needed them. I wondered had I lost the spirituality, which I cultivated in the Novitiate.

I threw myself incessantly into teaching the candidates for Confirmation. They learned all the Catechism by rote and selections from the Bible. I used a handbook, a form of junior theology text, as I discovered when I read some Latin works later. Archbishop Kinane examined the candidates publicly in the church, and he turned a few times to the priests near him as he quoted with a smile the Latin version of the answers he received from my pupils. He was the bishop at home when I was a boy and had confirmed me in Dungarvan.

I have wondered since then whether all my efforts at teaching religion were worth anything at all. I spent all day in school for the last two weeks before the ceremony teaching this religious material. How much of it did the boys understand at all? I do not know. Did all the theology that I gave them better their lives? I do not know. I thought I was doing wonderful work and tried not to think about the dead boy whose memory haunted me constantly. His death was a memorial to my guilty grief.

Final Days

Vacation time came and we were in Kilkee once more. Before we left, I knew that I was going back to Marino to finish my teacher training and began to wonder how it might go. I was glad to return to a year of study but did not relish being "*cabin'd, cribb'd, confin'd*" in Marino again but there was a month of freedom in Kilkee. This year Andy did not hire the Bentley to transport us across the Shannon to Kilkee. We were given the times of buses to reach the village, with a little money for expenses and each of us planned his own journey. I received five shillings for meals but bought a little German dictionary in Limerick instead of some food. With that money in those days I could have bought myself a decent lunch. I have no special memory otherwise of this holiday at Kilkee, except for the rich baritone voice of Guilfoyle singing duets at the Cove whenever we had a singsong.

My two years and four months in Tipperary were almost over and it was the longest period of time that I spent in any one place since I left home. Although very few Christian Brothers spent a lifetime in one place, this was unlike the nuns, who spent their lives in the same convent. I loved the town of Tipperary and regretted leaving it.

St Joseph's College

The morning that I left Tipperary was as sunny as the day I arrived. When I reached Dublin in the early afternoon, I was surprised to meet Whisperer at the station.

"My dear sir," he remarked, "we have at least five hours to kill, haven't we? Why go back to gaol earlier than we should?"

What a silly fellow I was not to think of delaying my return to Marino but to arrive at half past seven, as I was instructed in the orders that Andy received. Whisperer led me to a hotel and we went into the bar.

"What on earth are we doing in this place?" I asked.

"You're here," he sighed, "to have a little drop or a glass of something, and no rubbish about rules."

At this stage he was a permanent Christian Brother, since he took final vows on 15th August but yet he could not avoid confinement as a Junior for a year in the Marino hothouse. I had never been in a bar before and it felt strange. Whisperer called for a glass of ale and I took a cigarette with a mineral. He blew the smoke skywards "to the Holy Ghost", as he said, while I coughed as I smoked for the first time since I had tried it first, when I was a youngster. I did not know how to deal with a menu but Whisperer was adept. He laughed at me.

"Well this is the way to enjoy brief freedom before we return to prison. Let's see what we'll do after this...Yes! We'll go to the pictures! And I suppose you were never at them as a monk, just as you never smoked either! Did you live at all?"

Certainly I felt that we belonged to two different kinds of monks. When I left Tipperary, I was given money for my fare and a modest lunch but Whisperer seemed to have plenty money. He muttered about "that boss of yours who sent you off with pennies". He looked quizzically at me.

"You've the wrong bosses, haven't you? I often wonder what made you such a humble doormat."

I felt socially inept. However I did not choose a boss because the Provincial appointed all of them, and I did not have a choice where I was sent and who was boss there.

We went out to Marino from O'Connell Bridge by bus some hours later. It was after seven o'clock when we dragged our cases up to St Joseph's, the former missionary college. We went into what was once a gym where our fellow students were assembled. A man whom I later knew as Morrison sat at the piano where he played music non-stop, which filled the chinks in our conversations. There were fifty Brothers there from three consecutive Novitiate groups. I knew about forty, some of whom I had not seen for five years. Their faces were no longer boyish with varied adolescent skins, but they looked like the adults they were. They stood around in twos and threes with their hands in their soutane pockets.

After some time the Superior came and called for silence. It was Malone. His hair was scarcer than I remembered it some years before, and some stray tufts the remains of the mop that he had. He stood in the middle of the gym and spoke in Irish.

"Brothers," he began, "you're all welcome back to Marino!"

I winced as I heard this.

"The fox welcoming the hens!" said Whisperer grimly. I could see a zealot's glint in Malone's eyes behind his spectacles.

"Brothers", said Malone, "you're not youngsters any longer but experienced teachers, and some of you are finally professed. We rely on each of you to make our time here happy with no friction. Oh, yes! The six of you with final vows are not allowed to smoke or to take the drinks normally allowed to you on festive occasions."

He read out a list of our names and seniority numbers. My number was twenty-five and Whisperer twenty-four, so we sat together at table. We then went to the refectory for tea. I was surprised to find O'Neill on the other side of me. He looked strong but thinner than before he went to the sanatorium. After tea he went to bed as he did every evening until Mass on the following morning.

We speculated about those fellows, just seventy at most, who should have been with us but who left during the years. Of the one hundred and twenty who came to Baldoyle in 1942 about twenty were still Brothers in Ireland or abroad. Many of those who left went voluntarily, but more were weeded out before the yearly renewal of vows.

"They never nabbed me for breaking rules!" Whisperer chuckled. "I'm here in spite of the Pharisees that watched me over the years."

We heard an odd story about the young man Joe Walsh, to whom I was 'guardian angel' in Booterstown before we went to Marino. I was surprised to hear from my friend Paul that he left, because he was normally so gentle that nobody noticed him. Farrell, our supercilious History teacher in Marino, became Superior in Mullingar after Joe Walsh went there. Farrell treated him with disdain and humiliated him in front of others. One afternoon after teatime, Farrell raised his eyebrows.

"Will someone tell that young lad, Walsh," he said with a sniff, "that he must brush all the bowls in the toilet later?"

Walsh raised his head and shouted, "Do it yourself, will you?"

The word 'shock' hardly describes what everyone felt.

Farrell looked at him and said, "Well then, reverend young sir, you will come to my office in five minutes and we'll discuss your conduct and frame a letter to the Provincial."

The others began to think of what the young man faced with Farrell, but instead they heard Joe Walsh shouting abuse at Farrell in his office. As Paul said, "He became a raging lunatic". Until the end of the school year Farrell lived in dread of Walsh, and locked himself in his bedroom and office because the reverend man was a coward. When Walsh left the Christian Brothers in the summer, he became a rational person once more. Farrell aroused within him a fighting resentment, which was unique in the Christian Brothers.

As Whisperer said, "After years making dirt of lads in Marino, Revd Toffee-Nose Farrell, met his match. Beware of the anger of a patient man!"

College Living

At first I felt it odd each morning that I was not going to school but was being taught. I felt it odd not to be with lively children but instead of that I was accepting daily rations of knowledge. I thought to myself, "Now I should know what it is like to be a pupil in front of an all-knowing teacher."

We settled down but I felt the lack of freedom. We were forbidden to go to the city centre when we went for a walk in the afternoons, but that did not deter Whisperer from going because he had his own supply of petty cash, which paid for bus fares. We were out one evening, which was damp and dark with the decay of November on the trees and in the gardens.

"I'm nearly sorry I ever took final vows," Whisperer suddenly said to me. "Why didn't I dump my vocation and choose Hell? I wish now that I was caught flirting with that girl on holidays from Galway like Frank was!"

He told me about young Frank, who took a shine to the seventeen-year-old daughter of the house where they were staying on holidays.

"He brought her to the pictures a few times, and gave her a few squeezes and chaste kisses when nobody was looking. Instead of forgetting her when he returned to his monastery, he wrote to her and she came to see him once a month."

I wondered how it was discovered.

"Oh, that was simple," said Whisperer. "A woman in the Legion of Mary, whose son he was teaching, saw Frank and his girl together twice, and she reported his sins by anonymous letter to his Superior. The boss and another man raided his room when he was in school and found letters from her. He was shipped out that evening."

"Fired?" I asked needlessly.

"Yes! Fired eventually! The sinner was sent to another monastery far from where he was, and before renewal of vows was sent home to his parents."

Later on I thought of asking whether he married her.

"Married? You're an innocent ass! His boss wrote to the girl's parents and sent the letters. She had to lead a quiet life after that, until she disappeared later to England, the refuge of Irish sinners!"

On weekday afternoons when classes were over at four, we had a cup of tea and most fellows went out to the playing pitches. As they ran out to the field, I could hear the whoops of high spirits at being released from confinement. I generally went to my room to read. Morrison spent the time playing the piano, and always played a piece by Tchaikovsky at the conclusion of his daily practice. In a bedroom near mine was Smith, who had a concert flute. For the first time I heard the ocarina solo from the Overture to 'William Tell', which was so beautiful that it brought the songs of birds into my life. As I listened to the mellow flute notes – dewdrops on blades of grass – they were countered by the cascade of piano notes arising from the gymnasium. That gymnasium had neither equipment nor gymnasts, since the Brothers training for foreign service were no longer trained in this college. We in Ireland were expected to live the same life as the Brothers in Victorian times, when gymnastics and the like were understood to be practised only in foreign schools and colleges.

I had a daily chore in St Joseph's, which was to care for the altar and the sanctuary. This meant among other things that I should see to the flowers on the altar every morning, and replace them when necessary. I had to go to the farm where there was a flower garden, and I struggled to wrest flowers from a sour-faced monk gardener. One time he complained, "You're taking too many gladioli!" or "The colour is going from the garden!" Another comment was "The garden looks as if cattle were trampling on it!" I was not very zealous in my duties and noticed that the Christian Brothers' senior men did not fancy too many flowers in the house, just like the priests. As I come to think of it, I was not so keen on them either in these times.

"We need more flowers on the altar," Malone said one day. "Our Pro-Superior-General likes them!"

Clancy loved flowers but he was mostly in Rome or somewhere else on the face of the earth, where flowers were prized and loved.

There was the sanctuary lamp, which demanded my attention in Greystones and in Tipperary with varying results, but I was very careful to keep it lighting at all times in this college. I had to be careful here, as I discovered. One day Malone called to the classroom, where I was at a lecture and he called me out, so I wondered what catastrophe had hit my people. Outside the door he bent towards me.

"Brother," he said with drawn lips in a tight voice, "did you realise that the sanctuary lamp is quenched?"

Did I? Oh, damn it! I thought to myself.

"Oh, is it?" I muttered innocently, "I'll light it later."

"Oh, no!" answered Malone with trembling voice. "You'll do it now! Remember that you must obey Canon Law."

The poor man was afraid of being involved in a mortal sin, so I hastened away to light the lamp and save his immortal soul.

Being Taught

We had two outstanding professors. One was Br Paddy Muldowney, a tall athletic man who taught Mathematics. His method of teaching was to give a short lesson, then set problems arising from it. He went about from one to the other discussing it with each one individually. He taught quietly and effortlessly. Paddy Muldowney loved music and taught us Music and Singing also – we enjoyed his classes in a special way. He was a skilled pianist just as Morrison was, and for the first time we tasted the delights of true musical expression in our life in the Order. Muldowney acted generally like a person with only average intelligence and little cultural background. That year I discovered what a superior mind he hid behind this, how well-read he was and how far his intelligence reached. I thought highly of him, but the strange thing is that I cannot recall a single expression of his.

The other man taught History and was Br John Campion, who was always smiling or about to smile. We all knew him as Johnny.

"Ah, dear Brothers," he often said, "you read History here to regurgitate at the examination day, but you must learn to do research. Ah, yes! Brothers, private and deep research must be your object later as scholars!"

He announced that we should study European, English and American history on our own, but he was concentrating on Ireland. Whisperer howled with laughter at this advice.

"What'll we research?" he said one day. "Isn't that some stuff found in old newspapers, but maybe also in the secret places of a pretty woman?"

Johnny strayed from one subject to the other as a bee flitting from flower to flower. One day he said, "You know, young men, that we all need women." This was greeted with amusement by some and loud derision by others.

"And how can we have women with our vow of chastity?" Whisperer said to him. "Maybe Clancy will ask his ice-cream sellers for a dispensation for a fling from holy celibacy now and again?"

Johnny laughed quietly as he listened to this.

"You don't have to break your vow of chastity," he commented, "to be friends with women. We're in a male society, which can be crude, so we need women's friendship to civilise us."

There was more laughter and Whisperer quoted from Thomas à Kempis:

"Be not an intimate of any woman but commend all good women in general to God!"

To this Johnny retorted quietly, "You don't need to be intimate, but friendship is never forbidden. I imagine that no one ever took trouble telling you that in the Novitiate."

I felt amused as I imagined the Socius talking about that or anything like it. Later on some of us had a chat on the subject. I defended Johnny against those who regarded his notions just as fun. I felt that he never knew that he was advocating the abolition of chastity, but nobody agreed with me on that.

Besides these two men mentioned there was the boss, Malone, who taught us Rural Science, a mixture of basic physics, chemistry and botany as well as gardening. He taught us as if we were in a Primary School by methods that were boring examples of lessons for ten- or twelve-year-old pupils. I could scream at times. A subject called Hygiene, which included physiology and biology was part of Rural Science. We received a new textbook published in England, but Malone either inked over or removed the section on human propagation. I went with Whisperer to Eason's bookshop in O'Connell Street, where we inspected a copy of the book and read about men and women's genitalia and viewed the diagrams with great attention. Here we found interesting details.

"Will you look at that?" said Whisperer, "I never thought that women had so many interesting parts but anyway I never saw a naked woman."

I remained silent.

"I'm wondering," commented Whisperer, "did Malone enjoy the diagrams before he destroyed them? Fifty-one times he covered this part of womanly territory with ink, and he tore out one hundred and two pages to safeguard our virtue!"

For a few minutes Whisperer's levity disappeared as we considered such a petty waste of effort.

"This destruction of the diagrams," Whisperer muttered to me at last, "and all the interesting information makes Malone appear as a desiccated man, doesn't it? This good man is a wind-blown bone thrown by the roadside, but what on earth does he stand for?"

Jan, our former lecturer in Education, still held that position. He asked us to inform him what we thought about the educational methods which he taught us in First Year. He had earned an MA in Educational Studies when others had not gone beyond the baccalaureate, including the talented and refined Paddy Muldowney, who did History. As he told us with a grin on his pudgy face, we now knew more than he about practical education. Jan stood with his left hand and arm behind his back as he lectured us and he wrote on the blackboard with a chalk, which lost itself in his fleshy hand. He was the only one to speak on the inadequacy of our education but it never struck us to query why he, Professor of Education, did not raise this matter with the rulers of the Irish Christian Brothers. He accepted it in practice while he complained about the *status quo* to his students.

Our Marino

Whisperer and I went to visit an old cowhouse in the farmyard, where we smoked in the afternoons. I could now inhale cigarette smoke. I acquired this smoking habit to defy what I considered a silly rule, but it was a struggle to wean myself from it years later. It seems odd nowadays that the Brothers, who were permitted to smoke cigarettes, described them as relaxing and necessary for a person to unwind after school hours, but we all discovered later that they were dangerous.

"Great place, this Marino!" remarked Whisperer as smoke rings dispersed among the cobwebs in the outhouse. "Imagine, my dear sir, how it is with us! I'm a fully fledged monk and you're about to be one, and here we're skulking among dried cow dungs to smoke illegally like two naughty boys. Oh," added he with a sigh, "how much my dignity suffers from it all!"

"It does like Hell!' I replied. "But you're certainly right that we're treated like naughty boys."

As we spoke, we could hear the thump of a football on the playing pitch not far away, and the shouts of our fellow students as they rushed about the field. He began to laugh in quiet self-mockery as he absorbed his own statement with the smoke.

"My dear sir, if we were proper monks, we'd be out chasing a ball full of wind along the mucky ground, and we'd have no time for whinging and whining like this."

The shouting began to fade and Whisperer carefully quenched his cigarette and hid the butt between stones in the wall.

"Come," said he, "let's go back to the holy monastery!"

He was silent a while on our way back.

"Oh holy God," he said between his teeth, "why did I take final vows? Why didn't I pack my bags and go across the Irish Sea to the pagan land of Britain? Too late to shut the stable door when the horse has bolted!"

I remained silent, but I had time to decide because I did not have final vows as yet.

"Oh, what a mess I have made for myself!" he said, more to himself than to me.

"A mess?" I asked. "What mess?"

"I wasn't going to take vows because of Elaine," he announced.

I stopped walking, I was so surprised.

"Elaine? Who's she?" I asked.

"A teacher that I knew, who's great fun; that's Elaine."

We went the rest of the way in silence and I did not query him any further.

We celebrated the Feast of All Saints on 1st November with the suspension of all classes, and I paid a brief visit with Whisperer to my relative in Clontarf. That night we had a concert in the gym, where Morrison and Smyth with others played music. The high point of a wonderful two hours was when one Brother sang three operatic arias. Then Malone stood up and played Irish tunes on the violin with passion. We never heard him play before and we gave him enthusiastic acclaim. We listened to him playing the Cúilionn, as I had never heard it played – it sounded better than my father's version. He concluded with Irish dance music, the usual lively airs with the simple pattern of repetitive musical phrases on dance rhythms, but the Cúilionn was the most beautiful of them all. This was to be the finale but I saw Whisperer rise and go to the piano with Paul, who loved music. There were giggles as Paul tortured arpeggios from the instrument and Whistler took out a tinwhistle. Then we heard Handel's 'Largo' rattled out on the piano to the plaintive squeak of the whistle and as the music was coming to an end, laughter drowned the final notes. It was the last item of the night, ending in buffoonery typical of Whisperer, which had its own serious intent, also typical of the Whisperer that I alone knew.

The variety of talent among us marked us out as an unusual Second Year student group. Paul discovered that he could compose a humorous monologue interspersed with piano pieces and songs to entertain us on feast days. Our teaching staff was the butt of much of the caricature, and they enjoyed it or pretended they did. Whistler sounded a tinwhistle comment on each subject like jibes scattered as chaff in the wind. One night we were invited to St Mary's across the road, where we had spent the year after the Novitiate.

Before he was due to appear Paul came to me, "I left the script over the road in our place. Get it quickly for Christ's sake!"

I found the house locked. Then, clothed to the heels in my soutane, I climbed a drainpipe to a window, which had a steel railing in front of it. I jumped towards it and prised open the window. As I rushed out of Paul's room with the script, I found O'Neill in the corridor holding a hurley, because he thought that a robber had broken in. He was amazed that I, who was not an athlete, could climb so well and come in. For a few days I became the talk of the college, but O'Neill proved that I did this.

"You are the silliest of a donkey's progeny!" Whisperer observed. "Why did you risk this? They'll say now that you're mad as most of us really are."

O'Neill, as I said, was not at the revue because he went early to bed. He had been a tough physical type but was kinder than when I first knew him. He had recovered from TB but no longer played football and took many hours of bed rest. He also visited and cared for anyone unwell, because illness made him the kindest of men.

The Jesuit

In 'spiritual books' that we read in the Novitiate we learned that each should have a spiritual director, a guide for our spiritual life. I never had a spiritual director but this changed a little in St Joseph's College, when we had a spiritual director who came weekly to hear our Confessions and speak to each of us privately, if we wished. This was a Jesuit priest, Revd Tom Counihan, whose past endeared him to us. Revd Counihan as a Jesuit Scholastic visited Kevin Barry to support the young man as he awaited execution in Mountjoy Gaol in 1920. Barry was arrested ambushing a military unit and though he did not kill anyone, he was sentenced to die on the gallows.

Counihan was a blunt man, who wasted no words in coming to the point.

"Our native government," he began, "has based much of its attitudes on three hypocritical policies. The first is that the Irish language must be revived; the second is that emigration from this country to England should be stopped; the third is that Ireland must be re-united. Don't be fooled! You have under your care the next generation of Irish schoolboys, so don't let this rubbish misdirect your work."

All this was anathema to Malone but Counihan was invited to come to Marino because Malone's superiors decided that he was needed. Malone received orders to engage Counihan speak to us every week.

"The Dublin government doesn't care a hoot about the Irish language. How many TDs speak Irish? Very few! Let's look at the second aim. Our government is delighted to have an outlet for idle workmen, who would cause revolution if they stayed here. England absorbs them and potential rebels go where they won't harm our Republic. As for the unity of Ireland, the government doesn't want to rule the Six Counties of North-Eastern Ireland, that fractious and divided society in the north of the country."

As I listened, I thought of Guilfoyle's forthright views but they were nothing like this. These three opinions were typical of what, according to Guilfoyle, the National Church believed and supported. We never heard this point of view on the three 'great aims' before, and I am sure Malone fumed when he heard from the back of the chapel this anti-republican heresy. Malone supported a Fianna Fáil government dedicated, as we were told, to reviving the Irish language and halting the evil of emigration; he believed that Fianna Fáil fully and seriously intended to unify Ireland.

"My dear young men," pursued Counihan, "you've all dedicated your lives to the service of God and not to Ireland. God is our creator and the Lord of all things but the nation is a political structure. I am convinced that if you as Christian Brothers hold strong nationalistic beliefs, you're serving at the altar of a false god."

He went on in this strain for twenty minutes. Since I was in Marino in 1945-46 I had heard very favourable comment on the opinions that

Counihan condemned. For the under-forties they were the highest ideals that an Irish Christian Brothers could hold. One day, as I turned over these matters in my mind, I remembered that the Novicemaster never expressed opinions like these. He had spent most of his life as a Brother in that other Ireland of the north-east in Newry.

Whisperer was excited after this forthright talk and expressed his thoughts on it.

"Just imagine, dear reverend sir, how we religious brethren should speak only in our form of the King's English to be good monks, send all people between eighteen and thirty years to England and re-join the tolerant Belfast folk within the British Empire."

I listened as he tittered to himself.

"Dear Brother of the mighty whispering," said I, "you're an assassin of words!"

I spent some of that evening laughing with relief, as I read Myles na gCopaleen's *An Béal Bocht* in my room. I was beginning to enjoy its irreverent honesty. I felt that Malone did not sponsor Counihan to speak to us, who held ideas totally different to what Malone believed. Someone such as Val held such beliefs – he probably sponsored the visits of Counihan.

In November we were sent on 'teaching practice' to schools in Dublin. Instead of three weeks twice in the year we were sent out for only three in all. Whisperer and I went to Synge Street in place of some teacher who was ill. While one of us was teaching, the other sat at the teacher's desk reading. It was all a waste of time. The Professor, who evaluated our performance, awarded each one of us a mark, because we were experienced teachers and not just students. During the lunch hour we sat in the community room. One day I discovered a book of theology by Alphonsus Liguori, founder of the Redemptorist priests. I turned to the chapter on marriage, which was in the original Latin. It contained information which I still do not understand. He said that a person should not make love after a hot bath, and there were other weird insights into sexual activity. I still do not understand why the good man wrote that and what he meant.

I found the boring maleness of that Synge Street house unbearable. One day as I stood by the window watching the depressing rain, I remarked to an old Brother.

"What an awful bloody place this is!"

He mistook me and replied, "Well, we've taken vows and must stay."

I felt within myself, "I damned well won't stay much longer!"

The old man said, "You young fellows have a great time compared to us. Sixty years ago we had meat a few times a week but potatoes every day."

I began to laugh.

"But wasn't that good food?" I asked.

He ignored me.

"Now we live in luxury with meat at meals often twice or three times a day! We were only half-fed then," he went on, "although there was more money than in previous years and young monks often died of TB. Everywhere in Ireland these were hungry days, but nowadays everything is better and you're one of the lucky ones."

Christmas

Christmas was coming and I wished to go back to Tipperary for a few days, but there was no room there and the Superior paid all my expenses in Marino. It began to occur to me that Tipperary was not my home, any more than a barracks is a soldier's, so why spend Christmas there? We had no homes as religious men. There was a small house in Belfast where ten young men were trained to teach in Primary Schools in the Six Counties. They were sent to spend Christmas with us when their classes ended. Ten of us were chosen as 'guardian angels' and I was to be guardian angel to William, who was hardly twenty years old. I was amused that I was considered a reliable person to care for him.

After lunch William came to my bedroom and asked, "Are you going out playing football?"

I looked at him.

"Are you joking? Spend time on the pitch, is it? I'm going out to see my aunt. Coming?"

He seemed to find this funny.

"Can't we leave her awhile? I want to see Dublin City. I've had more than enough of Belfast! Come on!"

My lack of money was a joke to him.

"The boss gave us all a tenner, so I'll pay for bus fares. Are you telling me that you haven't the price of a bus ticket? What lousers the bosses here are!"

He was a boy on holiday, full of more energy than he could use. I was delighted to travel to O'Connell Street with him, and he never stopped talking.

Eventually I said, "By the way, William, this is not the Irish Free State but Éire, the Republic of Ireland!"

He adopted a solemn expression.

"Oh, I thought you were free here, but you're not. What kind of freedom is it without a penny to spend?"

"But we're religious with vows and not meant to be free, are we? That has nothing to do with politics."

William laughed at this. He was five years junior to us.

"We're rid of that rubbish that a Novicemaster dishes up, but we're in the real world in Belfast," he said as a man of the world.

"A real world where's there's no women," I could not resist remarking. "Is that what you're talking about?"

This made him pause but he commented, "Not every man needs a woman. I'm happy without one!"

I said no more on the subject. Apparently he had not reached that point yet.

O'Connell Street was bright and lightsome for the Christmas season. He bought cigarettes and we smoked a few on our way back on the bus to Fairview, which we boarded at O'Connell Bridge after checking whether Malone was there. I was a little worried that I had no toothpaste, to take the whiff of cigarettes from my breath.

"The strongest part of William is his tongue," commented Whisperer to me on the second day, after the three of us returned from a trip to town and rid ourselves of him. "As my grandfather said, 'A cow is caught by her horns but a man by his tongue'. I fear our William has the ways of an all-knowing schoolboy. Ah, he's surely destined for the kingdom of Heaven because, dearest friend, that lad has the mind of an innocent child."

We both laughed and went to the old farm building to smoke cigarettes in peace.

On Christmas Day we had a sumptuous meal at 2pm. When plum

pudding was served, a large jug of sauce was passed around, and half a pint was left after we were all served. A plump monk from Mayo poured this into a glass and became very talkative after drinking the sauce with its good whiskey core.

"Ah," said Whisperer, more to himself than to me, "yonder man from the western reaches of our island has learned to imbibe whiskey and poteen."

"And how do you know?" I asked.

"They drink spirits," Whisperer responded, "to counter the depression bred of bog and rock, which plagues them as it did their ancestors."

We had been told that after Mass we could make our own arrangements about prayers, so Whisperer and I did not bother with them. We made a few trips to the farmyard for a smoke and went for a short walk by Philipsburg Avenue to Fairview. It was dusk and we could see Christmas trees with coloured lights through house windows. There was no one to be seen on the streets, not even a beggar. Whisperer asked me what I did, when beggars asked me for a few pence. He knew that I did not have a halfpenny, and thought that my idea of the vow of poverty was bizarre.

"Here you're short of nothing but cannot give a copper to a poor beggar. It might make sense to Canon Lawyers but not, my dear fellow, to Christian common sense!"

I felt lonely. He stopped and looked at a window bright with Christmas lights.

"Damn this for a story!" he exclaimed, as he gazed at the window.

I said nothing.

"My friend," said he, "Christmas is for a family. Why do we need Christmas? We're the Lord's servants nailed to a holy tree by vows of poverty, chastity and obedience."

I remained silent and then he said, "But, as you well know, we have the grace of God now and eternal salvation in Heaven. The spirit of this Congregation is a spirit of faith, my dear man!"

I heard him utter a few curses and obscenities under his breath.

"They can keep the whole lot if I could be with Elaine."

Elaine again!

"Well, my friend," I commented, "I think that Elaine may be your sister."

He burst out in loud laughter.

"Oh God," he asked, "How did you guess that she was a Sister? How did you ever guess that Elaine was a nun?"

As we can now put it, that really hit me; Whisperer's girl-friend was Sister Elaine, a nun! What a man Whisperer was, to think of skirt-chasing in a nunnery! His face seemed to close in on itself, and I felt that I dared not ask him any further questions just then. I remember that Christmas night at eleven o'clock, long after monastic bedtime, seeing young men sitting on the floor drinking lemonade and others asleep against the wainscoting of the gym wall. What an odd Christmas Day it had been!

I kept thinking about Elaine. On the following evening when we were having a cigarette, I asked Whisperer about her.

"Oh," he answered, "Elaine is it? She's all in the past now."

I persisted in questioning him and he remarked, "Forget about her, will you? I have."

I insisted that he had not forgotten her and that she was haunting him. He was right that he should put her out of mind, because she was a nun and he could destroy her in a special way, said I virtuously. Whisperer became tetchy.

"And who's preaching rubbish now? You're no angel anyway, are you?"

"I never allowed myself to get too close to a woman!"

"And do you think there's anything right about slapping children in school? We're the disgrace of the country for that, aren't we?"

"All the other teachers do it, and the parents. And anyway that's nothing to do with having an affair with a nun and upsetting an innocent girl."

He paused for a while as we walked on and the anger, which had sharpened his voice, subsided. He seemed to brighten up.

"Well now," he said, "and who told you I had an affair with Elaine? Well? Let me tell you I hadn't anything like that with her. The most I did was to kiss her."

He paused and after a moment added, "Two years ago I kissed her, but I never met her alone again. Look here," he continued, "we have better things to talk of, haven't we? I often wonder did Malone ever get his hands on a fair damsel. I bet he didn't know what part of her to kiss!"

He coughed as the cigarette smoke went with his breath.

"Malone is it? As they say at home, that fellow knows damn-all, kiss-me-arse or a ha'p'orth!'"

In the New Year

When we went back to classes after Christmas, it was an anti-climax or, as Whisperer put it, a bump on the hard ground. I was depressed and not depressed, glad to be back to normal business but detesting the unnecessary confinement. William and the others returned to Belfast on 5th January.

"William, that young man," opined Whisperer, "will weary himself of the religious life. Mark my words! He's living in a minefield and doesn't know it."

I laughed at a typical Whisperer fancy, but it was more than that. We heard in June that William had gone off to England with a flighty red-headed girl, who was probably leading him.

"C'est la vie! C'est la vie!" Whisperer noted in a rare linguistic burst. "The sweet girl was just nineteen years old and was employed to help the cook, who was an older woman of mature manner," he narrated with glee. "It took her just a mere month to lure William from chastity with her skilful endeavour. Oh," exclaimed Whisperer in mock-awe as he paused, "I'm much shaken at the innate cleverness of women!"

At this time I began to detest Malone, for no logical reason that I can recall. He never wronged me but I suppose that I, as the victim of my withering religious ideals, now saw him as my gaoler. It is convenient to blame someone else for what is your own fault, and to offload your burdens on another. I began to feel unwell in a general way. There were headaches and loss of appetite, until one morning I fainted for no apparent reason on leaving the oratory. There was then the drama of medical examination and I was sent to the Mater Nursing Home. Whisperer, I heard afterwards, was concerned, but when he called to visit me, he joked about malingering, as it was found that there was nothing much ailing me. I was basically healthy, it was announced, but must be careful.

I was surprised to have a hospital visit from Val Ryan, the Vicar-General of the Brothers, who seemed to know everybody, young and old.

"You look well anyway," he said. "You'll do good work in our Congregation yet. When I was a young monk, medical help was seldom sought, and I knew two young Brothers who died of neglect. Casual neglect of the sick and the ailing was not unknown among us, in the bad old days."

True, I thought, but as he spoke, I began to think of what Albert had not done during Guilfoyle's illness in Tipperary, and of George in Westland Row ignoring O'Neill's serious illness as far as he could. However, they were of the 'old school', were they not? Anyway, they did not have the final word – although they almost had.

Val began chatting about the college and the Brothers' future.

"We'll have to do more abroad, you know," said he.

As Val went on I began to think strongly that I might yet leave them. Why did I not say something about it to him, you may ask? Here is an unusual person who might help me, I thought, and why not tell him? I just could not find what I thought were the correct words to put it gently, so I blurted out:

"I'm a bit worried about myself, sir!"

He glanced at me and as he did so, he seemed to scrutinise me with a puzzled glint in his eye.

"Oh, you're not keeping something about your health secret, are you? You know it's wiser to tell someone here and have it investigated once and for all."

"It's not my health that I'm bothered about, sir," I replied, "but whether I should stay with the Brothers or leave."

He seemed to regain his genial composure once more.

"Oh, young man, you're one of hundreds, not that this is a consolation to a person full of uncertainties. It's natural. Did you speak to Revd Tom Counihan about this?"

I had not and neither had I told anyone else about it, which Val considered unwise. Doubts and uncertainties feed on one another within a person, as he put it. They are more serious the greater a person's reserve about them, he said.

"No wonder you had this odd illness that nobody could diagnose. This probably may have grown out of worry within yourself, which was eating into you."

I felt better after speaking to Val. His parting remark was typical after I spoke to him about a clerical student in a room near me, who had electric shock treatment.

"Oh, my dear man," said he, "the students in that college are badly fed because the Order is French, where young men live on little food. Spare the food on young people and you nourish illness! Religious life is difficult enough for a young person, without restricting his food."

In hospital I heard of the death of the King of England, George VI, in that January 1952, and was surprised at the pro-British attitudes of many people, who regarded him as King of Ireland. To Malone the dead man was a nonentity, *Rí Na Sacsan*, King of the Saxons, as he spat the words out venomously. A few days later I returned to Marino.

One day in March during a History class Johnny mentioned the Mother and Child Bill, which had led to the fall of our coalition government the previous year. The Catholic Church was the supreme authority in our republic, and our rulers admitted that the Church had primacy in such matters. The Church then was at the height of its authority, which lasted for a few more years. Johnny suggested that we should have a public debate on the Bill in April but why he did this, I do not know. I was thinking that holding a debate on this matter was very odd, and was flogging a dead horse. Johnny chose Morrison to speak in favour of the Bill and myself to oppose it. He gave us press clippings and articles to prepare the case. From the outset I wondered why Morrison, who was a musician and not interested in social science, was taking part. After a few days, Johnny made an announcement in class.

"We'll have the Pro-Superior-General present at this debate, so we depend on you to make the Church's case."

As I listened to him, it struck me that this was our version of a trial for treason in the USSR. Our trial was for some political reason, but did Johnny have a personal motive lurking somewhere?

"Could he be so devious?" I asked Whisperer. He considered it as fun.

"Our dear Br John," he noted, "is as cute as the bees with the red arses! My dear sir," as he said, "you're being groomed to be a Superior-General. You'll be the champion of Holy Church in our Brotherhood."

I set to work on Johnny's mound of paper cuttings and pamphlets, but I began to change as I read the material. What was wrong with free medical attention or with nurses of the Health Department caring for mothers before and after child-birth? After all, free medical care was saving the lives of thousands of tubercular patients, and I began to think that the bishops were mistaken in this. Whisperer saw with glee that I was changing course and suggested that I should back Morrison at the debate.

"That will be great fun!" he said. "Oh, just imagine Johnny's annoyance and Malone's anger! It will be the best fun of the year, let me tell you."

He spread the news about my change of opinion, although he had been advising me to keep silent about it.

As it happened, we heard no more about this debate and it was never held. Nothing was said about cancellation and I did not enquire about what happened, but felt that Johnny heard what I had in mind and decided to let the whole matter drop. The saying 'Easiest things are best!' comes to mind. It was at the very least a rather peculiar business. It was the first time that I reached unilaterally an opinion contrary to what the Catholic bishops and the Church proclaimed. It is difficult to realise the power of the bishops and priests at that time. They were as powerful as the army officers in a military dictatorship, so my opposition was hardly fashionable!

Reverend Tom Counihan urged us to use our days in St Joseph's College as a second Novitiate to strengthen our religious convictions. I was forming myself anew not as a Christian Brother but as a free-thinking person, who wished to be himself and go his own way.

A Foreign Mission

About this time Val Ryan invited one of our students, John L. O'Reilly, to visit him. This bothered O'Reilly when he heard of it at first.

"What's going on?" I heard him ask. "Have I said or done something wrong that I must face Val?"

I told him that Val was not just a powerful figure but a gentleman, and surely John must have been keeping company with some woman. He smiled and said nothing. There was a great surprise awaiting him when he met Val. He kept it secret at first. He was chosen to be a member of the first community of Irish Christian Brothers in South America, if he agreed. It was to be founded in Argentina, in Buenos Aires. The Superior was Pop, our Superior during the year in Bray.

O'Reilly had some days to consider the matter, and it was suggested to him that he should consult his parents, so he went home for four or five days. He did not have to consult them because he was over twenty-one years of age, but Val wished that they be consulted. When they raised no objection, Val was glad to send him out. I envied O'Reilly. He had three months to prepare for his adventure and was learning Spanish from a Brother who had lived in Gibraltar. O'Reilly found this very difficult.

"That's the worst of all this," he complained, "learning another language!"

In Ireland we had adopted the British reluctance to learn or speak any language but English. French was taught in convent schools because it was the elegant thing for young ladies to do, but I think that few girls could actually speak French after five years' tuition in a Secondary School. However, we did teach and learn Irish but that was hardly done well either.

I recall what Dr O'Rahilly said about the monks going to a foreign country, and realised that Val thought so too. O'Reilly was excited.

"Would anyone believe where I was today?" he told us one evening. "I was in town being fitted for white suits and neckties to use in Argentina."

As I considered it, I understood that wearing these clothes emphasised his status as a layman, and not as a member of a religious Order.

"You're saying," prompted O'Neill, "that we should all be dressed in tweeds and collar and ties?"

When he agreed, O'Neill remarked, "In that case we'll look like every other man in the country!"

That was it: and I wondered why not? When I said to Whisperer that I envied O'Reilly, he laughed merrily.

"And there you are, good sir, wishing to go where lascivious women may waylay you and bring you to sin and damnation. You're talking one day of leaving us, and now you want to go abroad as a missioner. I doubt if the Holy Ghost has anything to do with your desire to leave our island, but you wish to lust after women in the sun."

When the day came for O'Reilly's departure to Argentina, I began to realise what a break it was with Ireland, and felt that I never wished to leave the country. O'Reilly was pleasant, and I liked him: although he was not as close to me as was the roguish Whisperer, parting with him was not easy.

Malone the Zealot

Malone was sincere and pious, an exemplary religious. To him Irish was our own native language; he considered speaking the Irish language as a religious duty, and playing Gaelic games a special obligation. Once when he was talking about our native language, I asked him this question.

"Isn't it right to say that the native language of practically all the men – including you, sir – is English? It's the childhood language of nearly everybody here."

He gave me a sharp look and spat out, "Don't be talking nonsense!"

I decided to continue.

"This is important, sir. The Irish revival movement was based on what our native language is, as I understood from your talk. Do you agree, sir?"

The room was silent.

"Please sit down, Brother," he said tersely.

It occurred to me that I was sacrificing a normal life for the Irish language and Gaelic games. I became a Brother for religious reasons, but Malone felt that linguistic patriotism was essential to religious life. I remember once I was in a small group with him as he spoke of the tales of Fionn MacCuimhail's [Finn McCool's] men like a child telling fairytales.

"But sir, these are folk tales," I blurted out. "We never had writers like Chaucer or Shakespeare, no novelists and great poets in the Irish language: had we?"

He stared at me and abruptly left us and the others dispersed.

As Morrison put it to me, "No one ever contradicts him or reasons with him in these matters. Everyone listens to Malone, agrees with him to his face and laughs at him behind his back."

It occurred to me that I had noticed that the Brothers accepted him as a stroppy child.

"My dear fellow," Whisperer put it to me one afternoon in his fashion, "you feel that you sought a fish in the religious life and they gave you a frog; you asked for a plum and you got a stone." He laughed. "Oh, leave them at it! We'll go our own way and why should we depend on the likes of Malone?"

Malone was a native of Limerick City, which had the reputation of being a religious place because of the Redemptorists, its moral policemen. Over the years they held a yearly mission to preach three themes. First, there was the sinfulness of sexuality; secondly, the reality of Hell; thirdly the evils of alcoholic drink.

"Ah," Whisperer confided in me, "the Fathers named from the altar a Limerick uncle of mine, when he refused to end his liaison with a niece of one of their friends. They fled to England because it was in the 1930s. What could Irish sinners do without England as a refuge over the years?"

Limerick has changed since then and its fall from Divine Grace was due to Shannon Airport.

As Whisperer saw it, "the Holy Fathers won't have it their own way much longer. At last someone is getting the better of the priests. Limerick," he continued, "is filled with pagan foreigners, especially from the US. Prostitution is becoming a way of life in Holy Limerick now; didn't you know that?"

We said no more after my reply.

"Isn't that how it was always, and still is in cities. Should Limerick be an exception? You're sore over your uncle."

He laughed.

Easter

A new Secondary School managed by nuns named the Sisters of the Cross and Passion was built on the northern boundary of the college grounds.

"Come on!" Whisperer said. "Let's cross over the fence, arouse the passions of the sprightly young ladies attending that school, and follow the desires of Nature."

We learned to look at women without being noticed. Whisperer might say, "A young woman is innocently presenting herself to our gaze!" She unselfconsciously showed her clear leg, which seemed to act as an index to unknown pleasure and delights. As day followed day, I became torn between whether I should leave after the year's study or wait a year and decide before taking final vows. I felt trapped by few choices.

In Easter Week Malone informed us that Valerian Ryan wished to address us one afternoon. We knew him to be pleasant and competent, but also someone who concealed an iron will behind his benevolence. When he decided to do something, it was carefully thought out and those opposed to it agreed with him eventually. Val was unique as an Irish Christian Brother with his fine mind, which saw life through broad lenses. He had never been elected to high office, because none of the religious politicians ever appreciated him. They did not have the least notion of what he could offer and they cared less. Clancy recommended him to the Sacred Congregation of Religious as Vicar-General, when Rome set aside the elected men. He was not one of those whom Guilfoyle identified as a member of the National Church. Everyone liked Val and no one could ignore his clarity and honesty.

When Val began his address to us, he noted that six of us had made final vows.

"You must all realise," he continued, "that you may be tempted to renounce your vocation at any age, and final Profession does not guarantee your perseverance." He detailed the signs that someone was slipping. "If you neglect your prayers, especially the morning meditation, you are in danger of becoming secular in mind. You cannot persevere without prayer; it's as simple as that."

He asked whether we ever heard of *le démon de quarantes*, 'the demon of the forties'. No, we had not.

"My dear men, that is what French religious call the urge to renounce your vocation when you reach middle age, when the desire to marry is nearly always the origin of a wish to leave the Order. We in the General Council notice this in pleas for dispensation from vows from older men. So you're never safe from temptation, but it can become very urgent in middle age to throw your vocation to the winds and renounce your vows."

We had not heard this kind of blunt talk before, apart from Revd Counihan's diatribes against the Irish State. This was practical, unlike the pious verbiage from Malone's pseudo-Gaelic world. Whisperer commented later that he had 'the demon of the forties' tormenting him at twenty-six.

"Oh," he sighed, "what will my forties be like? Should I listen to that little devil who's reminding me of what I'm missing now, and not wait for a more competent devil later?"

Val reminded us that religious life was a never-ending struggle with the temptation to leave.

"No wonder that ancient Irish writers called it 'white martyrdom' compared to 'red martyrdom', which is to suffer death because of your religion. The vow of obedience can be trying also, when you're compelled as an adult to do the bidding of one who seems silly to you. That is the reality of fighting the world, flesh and devil!"

He did not paint a pretty picture of what lay ahead. I just began to try to imagine how at the age of forty I could tolerate someone like the wooden George in Westland Row. This was difficult at the age of twenty, when the temptation to leave had not bothered me and I was living in cloud-cuckoo-land. It was becoming otherwise now.

I was wondering what I should do. How could I ever explain this to my mother? Not only was she bound to be disappointed, but also humiliated if I became a 'spoiled Christian Brother' (and the black sheep of the family, as it happened later on). One of my brothers was a National Teacher and another one, Seán, was a trainee at St Patrick's in Drumcondra. I met Seán once a week during games, when he called to the farmyard where we talked and smoked. I told him of my intention to leave and I was relieved that he understood the situation. In the middle of May I wrote a letter to my father, giving some acceptable reasons why I was leaving and gave it to Seán, which I asked him not to deliver until I made a definite decision. I expected my father to be furious, but thought that my mother could accept it: but she might hardly sympathise with the reasons that caused me to leave.

Towards Year's End

Across the pathway from St Joseph's were the lads in First Year teacher training. They were seventeen or eighteen years old and their lives as regulated as in a religious Artane. None was ever allowed out of the grounds alone or even in a group of three, and they went out on walks in a pack like fifty lambs thrice a week. They had taken yearly vows as most of us in St Joseph's did, but no one in St Mary's trusted them to act correctly except under supervision. They tried to treat us in St Joseph's similarly as much as they dared Johnny, our History teacher, was opposed to this treatment of the younger men.

"Across the road, my dear Brothers," said Johnny, "the young men are treated like prisoners, who will leave the college at the end of August to act as responsible adults overnight. In 1952 this is not thinkable, and I fear for our Congregation! You're treated a little better, but why can't our young men be treated as adults and not potential delinquents?"

We gave him a round of applause and Whisperer beat his desktop with a slipper.

We heard months afterwards that Malone was eavesdropping and heard the sound on the desktop. He suspected that it was Whisperer and as the official word was, he "upbraided" him later and, of course, "admonished" him for his 'disloyalty'.

"You're a finally professed member of our Congregation," he said, "You must give good example, and not act like a badly conducted schoolboy!"

Schoolboy, was it? I think that Malone did not realise that he was treating us that way as much as he dared.

That month of May in 1952 is unforgettable. I longed to be by the river in the Glen of Aherlow between the Galtee Mountains and Slievenamuck. One day Paddy Muldowney brought us to the music room in St Mary's, where there was a record player.

"Well now," said Paddy, "it's time that you heard some good music. You're deep in study and the best break from stress is programme music. May I ask how many have heard Beethoven's 6th Symphony?" He paused. "Just two of you, is that all? Very well, it's high time that you've heard it."

I listened as the first movement was played, which Paddy called "Pleasant thoughts as you arrive in the countryside". As the music filled the silent atmosphere of the room, I could hear the leaves rustling on the trees at Rossadrehid in the Glen of Aherlow and the gushing of the river through the fields. A feeling of frenzied longing for the glen seized me to leave the city of Dublin. We also heard the 2nd and 3rd movements that day and the final two on the day following. Every second day we listened to various pieces. I heard the full William Tell Overture and Beethoven's 5th Symphony and many more, as well as Mozart's *Eine Kleine Nachtmusik*. All these have been favourites of mine ever since.

Muldowney should have been doing research work on Education, but he never had the opportunity because his life was spent teaching and his talents misdirected. A German said to me in the 1980s, "Ireland is a land of wasted talent and opportunity". As I listened I called to mind many people but above all of them was Muldowney. The Brothers spent little time or money on their members' education as if they were in poverty, which they were not in the 1950s. The Irish Christian Brothers in the twentieth century had left the material poverty of the earlier years but they never lost their nineteenth-century poverty of mind. Their members' education was limited to the acquisition of gobbets of knowledge, to regurgitate them on an examination day. Just like Muldowney's generation, mine met with a similar fate. It is clear that in our Ireland talent was not appreciated, and it drove innovative men and women to flee abroad. These people often aroused jealousy instead of encouragement on our island, so they fled to England. Many went there to find work but others went to escape the stifling air of a society dominated by priests, who distrusted and feared independent thought.

One fine afternoon I saw Whistler from my room window, leaving the college and walking to Griffith Avenue. I began to wonder what he was doing, and why he never gave me a hint that he was going out during a time of the day, when it was forbidden. He was not sneaking out, as we did at times, but he told me later that he was going with Malone's permission. I did not know what he had in mind just then. He arrived back in time for tea at 8pm and we went to the farmyard for our smoke.

"And so you were off into the city?"

"How do you know that?"

"Come on now, tell me what you were doing! I saw you going out, and you were not dodging the sentries."

"I was sent to a woman of doubtful virtue in the sinful city, to ask her to return to the path of virtue."

As he spoke, he closed his eyes and cigarette smoke climbed from his nostrils. There was no point in asking anymore at that stage. Some days afterwards he told me what had happened. He wondered whether he should leave the Brothers and he went to the Provincial, Matthew Quinlan, for advice.

"Quinlan," he said, "is not such a bad fellow. I thought he might upbraid me and make me feel small but he didn't. He's a decent skin, when all is said and done."

I was not surprised. We sat silently for a while as I waited for more. At last it came.

"I thought he might have been angry. Not at all! He asked me many questions, such as whether I had thought the matter over carefully. After some while he said that he felt that I was unsure of my position. 'Will you wait and think this out in detail, and then if you still want to leave, come and tell me and I'll request the Vicar General to consider your case.' I was surprised."

Whisperer was silent for a while as he puffed at his cigarette and continued.

"Matt finally said, 'My advice to you at this point is to go back to the college to prepare for your examinations, and postpone a decision until you have thought out the whole matter. Don't forget that in or out of the Congregation you'll need your training as a teacher, so do your examinations and have your Teacher's Certificate'. As I was going out the front door," Whisperer continued, "Matt shook hands with me and remarked, 'Of course, there might be another party involved in this business; am I correct in saying that?' I think I nodded to him but he did not inquire further. Matt only commented, 'Women, my dear Brother, are unknown to us, so we might idealise them. The reality may disillusion us severely later, if a serious decision is made too hastily out of inexperience.' I just thanked him and went away."

He was silent for a while.

"Ah, yes!" he resumed. "'La belle Hélène'! Imagine how Matt Quinlan's decent face might contort in indignation if he knew that I and a holy nun were thick with one another, and were teetering on the edge of the precipice of sinful lust."

"How are you sure that he might take that attitude?" I remarked. "You never expected him to be so calm and kind as he was, before you went to see him, did you?"

The End of that Study Year

The examinations began towards the end of June, and we spent ten days studying before we sat for them. I remember being able to gauge exactly without a timepiece how long I was studying something. We had no watches, which only the finally professed were allowed, such as Whisperer. What a nice touch that was! The examinations took a week and a half of intense concentrated work and I felt fatigued and utterly drained afterwards. In our case we had the same subjects to study, except for the students of Mathematics, who did not take English and vice versa. As a result we spent nearly each examination day from 9am to 6pm in our seats answering questions with a break for lunch and another for afternoon tea. It was one of the most exhausting ordeals of my student life both before this and afterwards. For the first time in my life I found that I needed extra rest when it ended.

We talked about where we might be sent, either as a member of staff or to serve until the holidays. I wished to return to Tipperary. Whistler with great glee suggested that I might be sent to Artane, because he knew how much I hated it. There you were on duty every day of the year and I hated the idea that I might be working as a policeman and an oppressor in that institution. It takes a very good man to do this work as it should be done, and I knew that I was not one of these. I did not want to have anything to do with it. Whistler teased me unceasingly.

"We took our vows 'to teach and instruct the poor without pay or reward from them and their parents', as the rules state," he announced one time. "The boys there are the most miserable of all children. Don't you agree with me, good sir, that caring for them is the real test of our vocation?"

"I don't want to have anything to do with them!" I snapped.

"Look at all these wretched places that we have, where the Department of Education pays hardly anything but peanuts for the work that's done."

"Little we see of the money that we earn anyway!"

"If we weren't there, nobody would do this so we must do it. All we get for it is dog's abuse for our trouble."

"If you refuse to soldier in one of these places," he added piously, "you've betrayed your vocation. Vocation, did I say? Anyway," as he added reflectively, "I wonder at times if I ever had one or have lost it if I had."

He laughed a little but I sensed a touch of sourness in his voice. This caused me to decide that if I was to be sent to an Industrial School, I must write immediately to the Provincial saying that I was leaving the Christian Brothers. There were five Industrial Schools in Ireland, which were situated in Artane and Carriglea Park in Dublin, Glin in Co. Limerick, Letterfrack in Co. Galway and at Salthill in Galway City. Industrial Schools? In British times destitute people were seen as idlers, and the cure for idleness was to force them to work in 'Industrial Schools' or 'workhouses'. This was the Victorian attitude to the poor, who were seen as poor because they did not work. The workhouses were founded originally to force the poor into labour.

Some days after the examinations, Malone at the conclusion of the midday meal read a list of where each one of us was to go. Whisperer looked shocked when he heard he was condemned to go to Letterfrack, and I was relieved that I was to return to Tipperary. I received what I wanted but he did not. Whisperer laughed and swore alternately as he spoke of Letterfrack.

"Just imagine me exiled to that hell-hole among the bogs of Connemara. No one is there but snotty-nosed wretches and bored mad-eyed monks, all expelled from society and the victims of Catholic Ireland. What can I do about it all?"

He was in misery.

"Oh, woe is me that I ever saw Marino or Malone, or had anything to do with the Brothers of the Christian Schools of Ireland!"

He moaned and broke into crazy laughter, until I saw the tears roll down his face as the incongruity of life began to envelop him in a garish form. I was hurt as I witnessed the dilemma of my friend who was trying to decide whether to sever the invisible chains of his religious captivity. He was being transported from Dublin "to the Irish Wild West, which" as he said, "is our native Irish reservation."

"Will you write to Elaine?"

"What's the point? She'll never receive it because they open all her letters. They'd read mine carefully, and she'd never receive any of them. I must ask someone to call to the school where she teaches, and give her a letter from me. Maybe it's better that I see through this business of Letterfrack first, as a final test and maybe I'll get myself out of the monks then."

The evening before most of us left the college we assembled in a little copse near the college with our note-books and burned them on a pyre, while we romped around it. Freedom of a kind from Marino was on its way, although our Roman collars bound us to religious captivity – but within a year, I thought, I may be rid of that. Some of the material contained in the notebooks, which I burned, was what Malone gave us and the others were old copybooks. I kept the good material, which served me well in the years after this act of ritual burning. I still have Johnny's notes as well as Paddy Muldowney's, and also Brendan's History notes from the days in Bray.

Whisperer and I left the college together. There was quite a contrast between this and the day that we met on our way to Marino. Whisperer was depressed and both of us were parting, as events proved, for good. We did not even guess that this was our fate. He was travelling to Letterfrack first by train to Galway City, and I left on the Cork train. While I was delighted at my good fortune, he was upset and looked it. As I shook hands with him in Kingsbridge Station before boarding the train southwards, I felt the finality of the occasion and nearly wept. He looked so unhappy that I wished I could comfort him but how could I? I did not know how in my emotional disability. Before we parted, his face brightened and most solemnly he intoned:

"May the hills of Tipperary greet thee, dear holy sir, and the cows issue welcoming *moos* for thy delight. Amen."

His train was almost ready to go and I saw him walk slowly over to where it stood, with steam building up in the engine for the journey over the midlands to the western seaboard. It moved off slowly, bearing Whisperer out of my life.

At the Road's End

As far as I remember, whenever I went by train to Tipperary town it was always a sunny day. Perhaps this is a pathetic fallacy, because I thought that the sun shone when I travelled there and the skies lowered with sadness when I left it, but it was otherwise, when I left it for the last time.

When I arrived at the monastery, the first person that I met was Austin. He was Principal of the Primary School during the year, and was leaving in September to attend university in Dublin. I was sorry that he was going but he was looking forward to it after his long stint in the town.

"Oh," as Austin put it, "Guilfoyle and I never made any friends outside the walls of the monastery, so they let us stay here for a long time!"

When I climbed the steps leading to the monastery door with him, it seemed for a moment as if I had never left it. There was no one in the house when we went in except Biddy, who told me that I had a different bedroom.

"You're a senior Brother now," she explained.

I smiled to myself as I thought how little like a Senior I felt. In some ways I was still the young fellow, who came from Westland Row and whom Albert overwhelmed with verbose generosity a few years ago. I was older but what was that? Was my age a figure on paper, the impression of other people or the result of a new attitude? I did not know the reality of this and doubt that I know any better since then. Anyway I put my clothes in the wardrobe and drawers, and then looked out towards the blue bulk of Galteemore.

I was at home – but was I? Where was home? Home was no longer where I was born and reared, because my training had estranged me from my background since I left Dungarvan. If Tipperary town was home, then in a year I was leaving that forever also, if I left the Brothers as I had planned. Ah, yes! Home was the object of desire and the illusion of Irish Christian Brothers, but it was an emotional anchor that they had surrendered.

The New and the Old

Since I had gone to Marino, there had been some changes in Tipperary. The Sub-Superior was a little man from Co. Derry, who taught Mathematics in the Secondary School, Albert's precious Abbey. He was known behind his back as the Crab and set to work with grim tenacity, the hallmark of people in that part of Ireland. He had what they called 'plenty of grit', but his pupils liked him. The Crab was so aggressive when he felt challenged, that Bill described him as "a rat with his tail caught in a trap". I always felt that he was a tormented man. I heard that he had an eye for female beauty, but I doubt if he gave any woman the chastest of kisses. His life was pickled with prurience and based on sub-Victorian formalities.

The Crab, with the Brothers and lay teachers of the Abbey, still taught in the old stables and outhouses of the burned school, but plans for a replacement were ready. I heard that the plans for the new building were being finally discussed. There was nothing left of the medieval friary except one gothic-type arch, which stood apart from the ruins of the former Abbey School and is still to be seen. My successor in the Primary School, whom Austin enjoyed greatly, was nicknamed 'Galileo'. He earned this name, as I heard, because he had a keen interest in astronomy at one time, but no one ever heard him speaking on the subject. He had replaced me the previous year but was staying now when I was replacing Austin, who was leaving. Galileo had the face of one who enjoys good wine and food. He was an artist, who produced competent impressions of people and rural scenes in oils and watercolours. He admired Pablo Picasso greatly, I heard, and he understood above all that young monks were artistically ignorant, even more so than their seniors.

It was time for harvesting the strawberries and Austin was busy for some days picking the fruit and preparing the runners for the next year. He acted as if he was staying for many years to cultivate the strawberries, when this was his last crop in Tipperary. He worked hard for little results, but his fruit-growing gave him happy solitude. Austin had the mentality of a hermit in the strawberry patch. The second afternoon after I returned from college, I was surprised when he invited me to work with him.

"We can have a chat," as he put it.

We spoke about the time that I spent in Marino, and he went on to speak of his year as Principal of the school.

"I've had a busy and very fraught year," he began.

"Well!" I remarked. "That was to be expected. As Val Ryan said, 'Uneasy rests the head that wears the crown.' It was after all your first time as Principal."

"Yes, it was."

He was quiet for a while as he grubbed in the earth, and I did not interrupt him. Then, as he pulled out little weeds, he began.

"I discovered that certain boys were interfering with one another in the toilets and so I had to conduct an investigation."

"Interfering? What was that? You don't mean buggery, do you?"

His embarrassment flooded over his face and neck in blushes. He was annoyed.

"Oh, I don't really know!" he snapped abruptly. "How could I? I think that they were just fooling around with one another."

It struck me that Austin was innocent in many ways, probably more innocent than I was.

"You should have a time limit for toilet visits," said I, "but this was a disciplinary matter but hardly of morality."

"I sent for the parents of the four and they were very embarrassed when I told them."

"Yes! There was need for action but not to blow it all out of proportion," said I. "Many young boys fool around with one another innocently, and what a boy has between his legs is not sinful. It is better to keep boys on the move!"

I had forgotten that in his family he was one of two boys. I paused for a moment and added, "Of course, if you had grown boys who were preying on youngsters, you'd have to act otherwise. That's different."

Austin began regaling me with stories of Galileo and seemed to enjoy his antics.

"Our friend is seen regularly in Hegarty's pub every night and doesn't come back for night prayers, but toddles in much later."

Andy was a little younger than he, but I wondered how he accepted this as Superior.

"The boss turns a blind eye to it all, although it seems that Galileo is too friendly with the woman who owns the pub. Maybe he's not, but I suppose he shouldn't give anyone the opportunity for gossip. No one ever knew a monk who gadded about like him, and no one ever saw a monk spending time in a pub."

"So that's that," I remarked, "He's acting like a normal man of his age."

"Hardly like a monk, though!"

He frowned as he reminded me of this. We talked for a while but after a while I excused myself and left. In the community room Guilfoyle was listening to music on the BBC and I heard some excerpts from 'Aïda'. Guilfoyle turned to me.

"So now you're fully interested in good music at last! I can see that you're emerging from the mists that envelop the National Church. Who influenced you in Marino? Hardly Malone, was it?"

I laughed as he mentioned the steely-eyed zealot.

"So 'twas Paddy Muldowney wasn't it? Yes, it thought it was."

I stayed on and we conversed for a while. I began to wonder how he seemed so staunch in his adherence to the Brothers' life in spite of some opinions that he had. On the other hand, I already had considered these, and they were a significant part of what made me leave the Brothers eventually. Oh, yes! His situation was different from mine fundamentally, because he believed in the religious life of a Christian Brother. I had decided that it was not for me and that I must make a final decision to leave my companions for good.

Guilfoyle had a fine resonant singing voice, which was a baritone. Many of his favourite songs were from a book called *Folksongs from Many Lands*, where the airs are borrowed from many European peoples but with English words. In these few weeks before the trip to Kilkee we sat together in the community room at evening and sang. From the songbook I read the words, which Guilfoyle learned over the years. Simple folk tunes from that little book were 'Santa Lucia', 'Fairy Night' and above all, 'My Normandy'. As we sang together these songs which I loved, some thought it odd that we did not go out to enjoy the sunshine instead of singing indoors.

I began to feel that the months of study and thought in Marino had wrought some change in me. I certainly had become a somewhat different person since I had been there, but I had yet to experience fully how extensive that change was. After a week or so I had a letter from Whisperer. He wrote:

"Here am I in the sacred sanctuary of Gaelic Ireland in Connemara, doing what I hate to do. I am a gaoler of small boys who have no one to care for them, so our reverend superiors accepted the chore of confining them, but thick heads like me do the dirty work. No one thanks any of us, especially those who sent us. The streets of the cities and towns are free of naughty boys but we have the burden of repressing the little so-and-sos and making the streets safe."

I felt depressed as I read this. He continued:

"Was it for this I joined the Christian Brothers? Am I fated to be a slave driver? You can ask Reverend Tom Counihan about that matter, because he never calls to places like Letterfrack or speaks about them. I am certain, dear holy sir, that the Devil incarnate in his malice instituted places such as this for eejits like me."

Kilkee

We went to Kilkee on holidays in July. Andy as usual gave me five shillings to buy lunch in Limerick and money for the bus fares from Limerick to Kilkee, instead of hiring Paddy Spring's Bentley as Albert had done when he was the boss. We all travelled together in the bus to Limerick with the exception of Galileo, who arrived late in the evening in Kilkee on the last bus. Austin expressed it in words reminiscent of Whisperer.

"Our reverend astronomer flew to the western seaboard on the slipstream of the Holy Ghost."

I loved County Clare from the first time I was in Kilkee, but it was better travelling through it by bus than car. On the bus we met those not in our religious ghetto and everyone seemed to speak to everyone else, swapping news and stories. When we reached our lodging house on the seafront, I noticed that the landlady had hired a handsome young woman as waitress, who was a university student on holidays, as I was told. She had generous lips and a wary look in her eyes.

"This lady," Whisperer might have remarked, "is careful and cagey in the presence of the overpowering aura of the holy monks."

She seemed to regard us only as mouths to feed as she hovered around serving at table, and doing the housework, and I noticed that she spoke to none of us.

On the first day after we arrived I met a priest from the Holy Ghost Order, who was home on holiday from Nigeria. He seemed to have nothing in common with the other Irish priests, and seemed to be a loner. When I met him, I was on my own and he asked me some question or other so we struck up a conversation. I was not surprised that not only did he not know any African language but had no intention of learning any in the district where he was stationed. However he told me that he had to be de-Africanised when he arrived back in Ireland, "just as all the others have to be". This was last thing I had expected to hear.

"You may wish to ask me why?" he went on. "Little you know of the kind of people that I met in Nigeria. Most were not Christians and the Christians among them still observe many of their old tribal customs. For example, some kept two or three wives, and they wondered why priests did not have even one each. Of course, it was always possible for us to have a temporary wife, if you know what I mean." He smiled as he added, "That also is not unknown out there but let's pass that over just now."

There was a little silence but then he returned to the subject.

"Oh, I mean a priest might always keep a *focaria*," he went on, "as the medieval Latinists called her: a fireside woman to comfort him in bed." He laughed as he said this and went on, "Of course none of us will admit to having had a *focaria*, when we come back to Ireland, let me tell you – or even of thinking of such a lady."

I was going to ask the obvious question but decided not to.

"You know, young man," said he, "I often wonder what we're doing in Nigeria. Are we there to make Europeans of the people or to make them Anglo-African men and women? We certainly seem to be destroying their culture. I often saw little Nigerians doing céilí dances. Imagine that now! That dancing is not even genuine Irish dancing, but is a bogus Irish practice based, as I am told, on the dances of English villagers and brought into our country by Englishmen. Here our nuns are forbidding the Nigerian dances and teaching the other. What a charade!"

He paused a while and then went on.

"Oh yes! Each of us has to be de-paganised when he returns to this Island of Saints and Scholars. Our minds have to be cleansed of the memory of the extraordinary attitudes and beliefs of these people, and of those attractive black ladies who were so forthright sometimes with us. Africa is a place of great mystery, and people of our kind are rather arrogant, when they attempt to impose our weird rules and religion on the African peoples."

"'Weird rules and religion'?" I asked.

"Oh yes," he continued. "Practically all the priests in Nigeria where I was stationed were Irish and so were the nuns, all helping the British to spread their Imperial culture and destroy the African way of life. We're just imperialists, or lackeys of the British Commonwealth as they describe it nowadays."

I was not too surprised to hear this. For the first time in my life I began to realise how arrogant it was to go to another country to campaign against its people's traditions, which sustained their ancestors in the past. Yes! Missionary activity tried to persuade them that their traditions were all completely false. We all contributed pennies to the "foreign missions" when we were children, which were spent in the name of the Gospel to westernise people, who were subject to the British government. Was this the Church of God? As the priest went on and on, it all began to seem very different from what I had been told it was.

"I nearly became one of your people," he said, "but left from Baldoyle."

I looked at him and I realised that he could have been poached for the priesthood as it nearly happened to me in Bray. I thought that I could have been like him, only for that loyalty to our own, which caused me to reject the offer to join his Order of priests.

"Well now, are you glad that you left us to become a missionary?"

He ignored my question but went on.

"You can be sure that you're very fortunate compared to me. Your life is simple and innocent compared to what mine was. I have discovered that there is something wrong with the way of life of the missionary priests, but cannot put my finger on it. Maybe it's probably better if I never discover exactly what that flaw might be."

We met often later in the month but in the company of the other Brothers, so I heard nothing further about Catholic missions in Africa.

On fine sunny days, as we gathered on the rocks at a cove near George's Head, we sang together. The second afternoon that we were at the cove was the first one that I remember clearly from that year. As I approached the cove, I could hear the rousing chorus rising and rolling in the distance. They were singing some boat-song whose title I forget, but I have not forgotten the rhythm of the music and some of the words. Most of the other songs were sung in two parts. All the songs that Guilfoyle and I sang in Tipperary were chorused here also with great gusto. I joined them happily. When my life changed forever a year later, I missed these spontaneous singsongs by the sea during the summer vacations – the only thing I missed, when I left.

In the first week of that holiday someone passed a book on to me.

"Read that, but give it back to me as soon as you can! You have 'til tomorrow at the most, and make sure that Andy and the likes of him don't see you reading it."

I looked at the title, which was *A Moon in my Pocket* and it was being passed around secretly among some of us in Kilkee. Julian Morris [pen-name of Morris L. West], a former Australian Christian Brother wrote it, the author of *The Devil's Advocate* in later years under the name of Maurice West. He described his few years as a Christian Brother in Australia, which was different from ours in many ways. When it was published in 1945 in Melbourne, we heard that some Irish booksellers had ordered large quantities, but the Superior-General bought them all and sent them to feed the central heating furnace in Marino. Not all were burned but a few copies were salvaged from this literary holocaust and passed around secretly. This copy, as I understood, was one of these. The title means 'aspiring to the impossible', it seems, which I understood well by this time. I settled down to read this book during one warm and dry afternoon, when the others were on the beach or at the rocky bathing place.

When the young Australian monk in *A Moon in my Pocket* was on holidays, he never wore black clothes or the Roman collar, which seemed to choke us on warm days. The young Australians apparently lived a less rigorous life than we did. The young man in the book had adventures with his lady friend, which led him to depart from the Christian Brothers and he told his story in loving detail. He described himself out on a lake or a creek boating with this lady, with whom he had an affair. The whole story sounded to me as no more than fantasy and definitely not the factual truth, but it charmed me and I thought I understood how he felt in theory,

at least. It was also quite strange to me, but this Brother's life was outside
Ireland and the background was as much beyond my experience as I could
imagine. I heard that the book reflected exactly the freer life of the young
Australian Brothers. The older hands, who were practically all Irishmen,
had a rigid attitude and were even narrower in mind than the diehards in
Ireland such as George in Westland Row and also Stan and Stick. After all,
I had met one of them in Tipperary.

At the cove the following day I returned the book wrapped in brown
paper to the man who loaned it. He spoke in a lowered voice.

"You wouldn't get away with that kind of thing here! Would you?"

I looked around me as I countered.

"Where on earth could I as an Irish monk find a boat like the Australian
monk did, manage to row it and spend time with a woman? Anyway, we're
hogtied here with our black clothes, but he could not be identified as
a monk from the clothes that he wore on holidays. To tell the truth," I
continued, "that kind of rig-out is what we should be wearing and not
clerical clothes."

A silence hovered between us as I juggled some pebbles in the palm of
my hand.

"They have a good time in Australia, haven't they?" I said.

"It is even funnier," he laughed as he answered, "when you think of
the old lads from Ireland, who come home on holidays from Australia
after thirty years abroad or more. They are from another world and as
unbending as oak trees, and not a bit like this skirt-chaser, are they? The
young Australian monks of our age are a different type to these old hands
from Ireland."

I knew exactly what he meant because of the older Irishman from
Australia, whom I remembered meeting briefly in Tipperary monastery.

He then added, "Isn't it time that we kept pace with them?"

We both smiled in disbelief at that very thought. We agreed that the
Australian had to leave the Christian Brothers because he had been with a
woman.

"You can't survive in this lot after rolling around the blankets or
tumbling in the hay with a woman. I suppose it's easier to leave in that case.
Being with a woman is lubrication against the disgrace that our parents
feel if we leave."

"You know," I said finally, "this country has been closed against the world since long before the war. No breath of air, good or bad, has blown through our little island, and we're living in every sense of the words at the back of beyond."

I felt envious of the Australian, but I kept this to myself in the many discussions of the book that both of us had during these summer weeks in Kilkee.

Something then happened in Kilkee, which turned my life on its head. One evening about eight I went into the kitchen, which I thought was vacant at that time, to pour a drink of water. I was surprised to meet the student who was helping in the kitchen. She was a very reserved girl, as I said, and never spoke to any of us since we arrived for holidays. She filled a glass for me and I stayed standing there while I drank it. As I was supping the water I was very surprised that she talked, while she fussed around making preparations for breakfast. She told me that she was studying History and Irish at University College Galway. I noticed that her jet-black hair was tied in a bun and saw how delicate her thin fingers were. I felt the sharpness of her blue eyes as she worked, and I thought later that her eyes were assessing me in brief glances.

The following evening I went for a drink of water again, and we spoke for quite a while. For the next four or five evenings I found myself looking forward to meeting her, but during the day she always ignored me while she served our meals. One evening when I stayed in the kitchen talking to her, I realised that I should be meeting someone, when she leaned towards me and I kissed her. What an unplanned kiss that was! But then I kissed her again and again. I could not speak. I felt that something had snapped within me, as I looked at her eyes, dark with wordless acts, which flowed around me in warm clouds. It nearly overwhelmed me. I had never felt like this before.

I had a very fitful sleep that night. I awoke often to collect bedclothes from the floor where I had kicked them in sleep. I saw her face in the dark and tried to calm myself but could not. I did not know her name but discovered later that she was Eleanor. We spent five more nights together in the kitchen and she now locked the door to the main body of the house on these occasions. No one knew about our secret meetings until after the eighth night. The owner of the house arrived back, and found the door locked. We did not hear her trying to open it. She made her way into the kitchen from the garden unheard by us. I can picture the scene.

"Eleanor! What are you doing?" The lady paused. "And you, reverend sir," she said, "will you please leave the kitchen and accept my apology on behalf of this witless young woman, who can't conduct herself."

I left like a whipped puppy with his tail between his legs.

Eleanor was not there in the morning because her employer sacked her at once and employed another girl. She never reported the matter to Andy, and no Brother knew anything about it, because I certainly did not tell them. My world had turned upside down. Was this a flash in the pan, a stroke of lightning or a new dawn? Maybe it was a jumble of all three but it marked my entry into the adult world at twenty-four years of age, when I first kissed a woman passionately. With passion, was it? I had not kissed a woman even innocently before this. I never heard of Eleanor again, who entered my life for a few days and then she disappeared from it forever. I wonder what how did she fare?

Back in the Monastic Barracks

After the holidays we had the yearly retreat without a priest to direct it, but Andy read retreat lectures to us three times a day in the oratory. For the first time in years I was spared the usual introspection about the future because I had decided to leave. Changes in the community were generally made before the schools re-opened, and we expected that Galileo might be moved but he stayed.

"He's not being moved," said Bill said with great glee, "but is staying with us to give further holy edification to all."

Sometimes he did not turn up for breakfast with us and was late for school, while his pupils had fun in the classroom until he arrived. They paid for this by being kept in school later, and I could never understand why their parents did not protest at this.

Galileo missed night prayers, because he disliked leaving his friends in the back room of Hegarty's pub. Guilfoyle referred to him as "our dear secular member of the Congregation". I wondered why he had not left years ago. I wondered how Galileo might deal with the eight-day silent retreat. It began at 9pm, but Galileo was in the town 'til midnight. He was not at Mass next morning, but from that onwards he acted the monk and was present "for every Amen", as Whisperer might put it. During the retreat I wondered whether he was using alcohol, and had whiskey in his room to support his unusual solitude. However, he was totally sober and abstemious and I never noticed even the smell of whiskey from him.

The Superior directed everything.

"Did it ever strike you," Guilfoyle once said, "that we should be free to say our prayers and conduct our spiritual life when we wish? The rules smother individualism and as you see, we lead our religious life only in groups."

During the retreat I spent much time in my bedroom, trying to absent myself in spirit from what was happening. I was staying for a year to ensure that I did not act rashly, but later I began to wonder what kind of a fool I was, that I stayed. I took annual vows at the end of the retreat and I stayed for that last year.

Guilfoyle was Principal although he was not the senior, but Galileo was. When Andy offered him the Principalship, he said, "Why do I have to chain myself with that?"

Galileo was honest because a Principal, for example, must come in time for school every morning. Austin and Guilfoyle were separated for the first time since they came to Tipperary. They were both very reserved but friendly with everyone, and they parted on such formal terms that no one could imagine how close they were. Both of them shared a distrust of emotion, which probably shored up their resolution to remain Brothers.

I was glad that Flannery was with us, but in September he was sent to Artane at a day's notice. Someone beat a pupil badly in the school and so the offender was exiled to the West of Ireland, which certainly was not Letterfrack Industrial School. A Belfast man, Canice McShane was sent from Kerry to us, and I went to meet him at Limerick Junction. He was nineteen years of age but looked sixteen. We discovered that he had an outward-looking attitude to everything, knew nothing much about normal life and enjoyed everything. He was an innocuous young boy, who never saw evil anywhere, in anyone or in anything, a grown-up child whose naïve chatter we enjoyed for a while, until he bored us. Above all he irked Guilfoyle to whom he was "our young disciple" at first, but who disregarded his reserve and addressed him as 'Gill', chattering on about every child as if he was his own. He was a good teacher, who did not share our reserve.

"Oh, I do wish he ceased to pester us with his garrulous chatter!" Guilfoyle one afternoon exclaimed when the young lad had talked to him more than he wished to hear. Guilfoyle was finding it unbearable to tolerate "our young disciple".

Often Canice did not return from school for an hour and we were deprived of his presence for a time. One afternoon when I went back to the school at that time, I saw him at the front gate with a young girl whose little brother he was teaching. About a fortnight later Guilfoyle turned to me in the community room.

"I hear that our young disciple is keeping regular company with a young woman."

I told Guilfoyle that I saw him with a young girl one afternoon at the gate and wondered how did Guilfoyle hear about them.

"A former pupil of mine," said Guilfoyle, "told me that he's been meeting her every evening over the last few weeks."

My reply was that they were not sneaking off to hidden corners.

"Ah, my dear fellow, that's the difficulty," retorted Guilfoyle. "He supplies clouds of smoke without a fire and gives needless scandal. One of us should speak to him about it."

I agreed to do it.

Canice was shocked when I told him that he must end these school gate meetings. He had his hands in his soutane pockets, while holding closely a bundle of copybooks under his left arm.

"But I do nothing wrong! Is it against the monks' rules to talk to the older sister of a pupil? Anyway, I'm not a hypocrite!" he exclaimed.

I pointed out to him that appearances mattered.

"You're innocent until you're found out," I said. "Now take her with you up the hills at night and have fun but don't be seen!"

He was taken aback and surprised at my cynicism. I was leaving this divine army and my attitude proves it, I thought, though this was common among religious people.

"Well," Canice said, "it's all right for you and the others. All of you are fully committed for your lives. None of you know how I feel!"

So he was not so innocent as I thought! As for me, Eleanor's constant unseen presence was frustrating and her absence was a blank wall. I thought of her constantly and was obsessed by the need I had of her. It may be asked how Canice fared eventually, who still kept meeting the youngster every afternoon, until Guilfoyle officially reported the matter to Andy. Within three days the young man was transferred to St Patrick's School in Marino. It was normal to transfer someone at once who was on close terms with a woman. The speedy progress of love was well known and the tempted one was moved swiftly from the perfumed path of sin.

Life Moves On

When young Canice was put on the train to Dublin, I waited at the railway station until another train ferried in his successor, Philip who was in the group which succeeded ours in the Novitiate. He had spent nearly two years receiving treatment for tuberculosis. Andy asked me to care for him.

"See that he goes to bed early, eats his food and keep an eye on him. He's a good lad and we don't want to lose him by ill-health."

As Philip's carer I saw to it that he went to bed at 8.30pm and did not arise until before Mass. I watched what he ate and saw to it that he never neglected to take his medicines. As Whisperer might put it, "You're his mother hen, clucking over him from dawn 'til dusk!"

There was a difficulty dealing with Philip. One Saturday when Andy and others were away, I saw Bill washing his cup in the kitchen.

"Don't tell me," I said, "that Biddy left ware unwashed!"

"Cups must be washed," he muttered, "to save us from infection."

Infection, I thought; how could there be infection here? Oh, yes! Did Bill think that Philip was a source of tubercular infection? Did he have to wash his ware before every meal? Biddy confirmed the next day that he did so. All four of us left the refectory later that evening before the next meal with our cups and washed them in the kitchen with laughter and remarks about Philip's harmful presence among us. Bill did his washing more discreetly afterwards.

I had a letter from Whisperer in November. He said he hoped that I was well and that I was looking forward to "the day of your final Profession of vows". He knew that I intended leaving, so I reminded him that I was moving out in the summer. There was a telephone in the house, which we were forbidden to use except for very special reasons. For years I dealt with Whisperer by letter or by rare personal contact, but during this last year I never met him, when we needed each other more than ever. He wrote to me about Maurice, a man who had been with us in Baldoyle, a serious type of man.

"He took final vows three years ago, but sought a dispensation from them lately. He had fallen in love with a damsel, whom he filled with child."

Good Lord, I thought, who could believe that Maurice did that? I thought that the only one that Maurice loved was himself but I could imagine Whisperer's rejoinder, "He procreated a form of himself within the lady and wishes to possess her!"

Whisperer went on to inform me that the good man was impatient waiting for a dispensation, and a fortnight after his application he was transferred suddenly to a Cork monastery. On the journey southwards he left the train to be with his woman, and the two went to London far from the religious influences that had ruled his life. Maurice was now an apostate religious according to Canon Law. There was mini-drama when Maurice did not arrive in Cork. The Provincial phoned the Superior in his hometown, who met his parents. Later they had a letter from England stating that he was there. They were ashamed of his defection with "that little tramp", as his father called his son's future wife and his own first daughter-in-law.

In these years after World War II England was a useful neighbour for many Irish. It was a source of employment for most, a refuge for others who fell foul of the law, and a sanctuary for those fleeing from the might of Catholic bishops, priests and lay zealots. Few people know now how powerful the Irish Catholic church then was. As I was reading Whisperer's letter, I wished that I could walk out, but my case was unlike Maurice's. I was free to go in the summer and not bound by final vows.

Whisperer hated Letterfrack. As I was reading a letter from him, I found it quite morose.

"I get up in the morning at 5.45pm," he wrote, "then swallow a dose of prayers in the chapel and at half-seven the young monk and myself make a loud blast on whistles to get the boys out of bed. The two of us have the rough-and-tumble work to do. The older men go to Galway most Saturdays and Sundays, while we stay with the poor young lads for breakfast, dinner and tea in the weekend. We have lay teachers in the school to take classes, but otherwise the two of us are all alone caring for the young lads. Some boys are orphans, others are children abandoned because they were born on the wrong side of the blanket, and others are here because they were thieving or absent from school. I spent only two days in Galway city since I came here. The young monk is pious, who does his duty for the love of God, but I do it because I have no choice."

Christmas and After

After the main meal at about 2pm on Christmas Day Galileo left the house and went to Hegarty's to celebrate Christmas. When he returned after midnight, we were in bed. Although the monastery was where he slept, it was not his restaurant except for breakfast because "he puts the nose-bag on elsewhere," as Bill put it. Bill became very drunk on Christmas Day. The boss drank a few glasses of wine and others took small amounts. I saw the other young man take sufficient whiskey in lemonade to make him laugh, but it did not seem to inebriate him. Bill was drinking steadily and becoming more talkative and combative. The boss retired about 10pm, as we did on most nights. At about 11.30pm only Bill, another man and I were in the community room surrounded by empty bottles and smudged glasses. I was wondering whether I and the young man with me could bring Bill upstairs to bed, but he was not yet as drunk as he was on former Christmases. I stayed with him until he delivered a final monologue.

"The monks' bosses are no damn good to those who leave the Order!" Bill began.

I felt no surprise at this. It was his Christmas topic, which he mentioned in his cups.

"Bill, how is that anyway?" I asked him. "I hardly believe it."

He pulled himself up in his seat.

"Most of the bosses are as mean as shit!" he announced. "That's why!

There we have a young man who has slaved to earn money for the monks in school, and what does he get if he leaves? Ten quid! Ten lousy green notes! I know of fellows who were sent off with one bad suit of clothes and a few items of clothing. The fellows who treat young men like that are mean rotters, so they are!"

While he was taking a deep slug of porter, I interjected.

"That doesn't happen anymore, Bill. Anyway, why are you going on about fellows leaving?"

Bill wiped his mouth as he preached.

"It's time we told the truth, isn't it? Here's a fourteen-year-old boy who's conned into joining us and they twist him into shape as a teacher. He grows up over the years and if he shows that he feels trapped, they fire him before renewal of annual vows, or maybe he gets out himself. The boss treats him like a traitor, when he decides to leave the monastery. Is that Christian?"

He began repeating himself and lapsed into incoherence. We lifted, carried and dragged him upstairs and dumped him on his bed after taking off his Roman collar, opening his shirt and turning him on his side, as I had learned from Flannery. When I returned to the community room, we talked a while about what he said.

"Bill's brother is still in the Order, isn't he?" asked the other man. "If that's so, he couldn't have a grievance about the treatment of a relative. Anyway," he continued, "I am wondering for the life of me why he began to talk about it tonight."

Bill was in his cups, and who could know why he spoke as he did? Although I thought that this was another bee in his bonnet, it seemed timely for me. I had kept my intentions secret and none except Whisperer knew I was leaving.

The Last Retreat

Before Christmas all of us who were qualified to take final vows were invited to an eight-day retreat in St Joseph's at Marino. There were about forty of us and I wondered should I absent myself because what was the point of going there, when I intended leaving? I decided to say nothing and go to Marino. Many men who sought dispensations in the past stated that they took final vows without realising what it meant. It was decided at the Provincial and General Councils to bring the applicants together to inform them fully what final vows entailed. I heard later that this retreat did not seem to have any significant effect on the numbers leaving after taking final vows, then or in later years. In these eight days there was an opportunity for much thought, but it struck me that it might be a fruitless exercise.

The forty of us had hardly met in Marino for an hour's chat when the retreat silence began. There were a few that had not met for years, and during the retreat they conversed in the farmyard and elsewhere when they could not do so that evening. On the first night I thought the bed was damp and ignored it because I was very tired. I had a cold the following morning and reported it to Malone, who was still the Superior.

"There are no damp beds here!" he snapped back.

I insisted that the bed was damp and he kept on repeating his reply.

"I want a dry bed!" I insisted.

"You can have any bed you like," he hissed, "but there are no damp beds here!"

It struck me afterwards that Malone and I had been on reasonably good terms during the year in Marino, but now I felt neutral towards him at best and antagonistic at worst. He typified much of what had turned me against remaining a Christian Brother.

Malone exiled me upstairs to a dormitory, where I was alone in a small and comfortable cubicle, which had not been dusted for years. I remained happily isolated for the retreat. Malone brought me meals on a tray because he felt that if others did this, they might converse with me. His frosty face almost turned me off food whenever he came but when he went, I was able to eat what he brought. I acted according to the old saying, 'Feed a cold and starve a fever!' I missed half of the retreat. There were books and copies of the *Times Literary Supplement* there, which I read to my heart's content. We were destined for the Irish school system, but these had been there since the missionary college days, when the men were trained differently and attended university before going abroad. Were we ever supplied with the *TLS* or any such publication? Never! There was no attempt at cultivation of any kind, no hint of broadness of vision in our education, and any sophistication in a person was considered a sham. Any person as cultivated as Meares was tolerated patronisingly, but there were few like him.

I left bed to attend the retreat in the four last days, and heard that Revd Br Hanlon was interviewing us. I regarded the Irish Provincial highly, but Hanlon was a newly appointed Consultor, who was writing an Irish Grammar. Later on I never understood how this qualified him to give sensitive direction to any of us.

When I entered the interview room, he asked me, "Do you wish to take final vows or are you leaving us?"

I looked at his closed face.

"I'm leaving."

He paused and said he hoped that I had considered the matter fully.

"Oh, yes, I have thought it over," I said, "for more than three years."

Hanlon remarked that he hoped that I should conduct myself and give no scandal to seculars before I left. What an estimation of my years with his colleagues this was! I looked at him closely with bemusement and thought what a pedant he was.

I stood up saying, "Well, can I presume that our interview is ended and it's time to be going?"

It was indeed time to leave his presence. I was happy that in a few months I was putting an end to any dealings with his type of person, although he was in a minority.

After the retreat the others and I had a short time together to talk and swap gossip. I began to realise what fine decent fellows all my companions were, and knew I should miss them when I left. On the other hand, I knew how crass some men in power such as Hanlon were. Before I left Marino for Tipperary, I met Canice McShane. He said that he intended leaving in August.

"People like you do not understand how it is with me!"

I was amused, so I informed him.

"I'm not taking vows in August. I'm leaving and, let me tell you, I understand your situation all too well!"

He looked puzzled.

"And you were thinking," I went on, "that I was a pillar of the establishment; well I was not and am not. I have feet of clay as you have, but I learned to hide their weaknesses, if you understand me."

It then struck me to tell him not to let anyone else know of my intention to leave. He agreed.

"I don't care who knows about me," he said, "because nobody expects me to stay. My weak point was bad judgment and I suppose that I'm not suitable, if ever I was!"

I could not agree more. He was honest and straightforward and unfitted to be among certain reverend sinners who hid their real and sinful selves for the good of all. I returned to Tipperary from Dublin for the last time dressed in the black uniform of the Catholic Church, and happy to have left St Joseph's for good. I sighed with relief as we approached Limerick Junction on the Dublin-Cork train.

A few days after I returned from the retreat in Marino after Christmas, I received a letter from Whisperer.

He said that I was full of the Holy Ghost after the retreat to carry out the Lord's work, "as long as you are not sent to a place like this to slave for Holy Mother Church and the Department of Justice." He went on, "Anyway, I am tired of the misery of this place and wish I could be out of it. The pious young monk, who was with me, lost his rag and belted a saucy young lad from Dublin. Our higher superiors sent him far from Dublin to spread the word of Christ, who beat the daylights out of the moneychangers in the temple." What a typical Whisperism! "I now have an enthusiastic fellow with me who was found drinking whiskey at the age of twenty-one in Dublin, so he was sent here for punishment. Oh, the disgrace of these young men's conduct, who are discovered emptying whiskey bottles as Albert did! We know that men like Albert are wise in virtue and that they do not sin in spite of all appearances. Oh, yes! Old Carey is also here doing penance for his sins as usual."

Whisperer pointed out the double standards that we saw all around us. I realised that the real error is to be found transgressing. If you ask too much of human nature, it will fail to reach the high standard, so each one must hide his sins. This, of course, was done for the good of all.

We soon learned what Carey's sin was and why he was sent from Limerick to Letterfrack as to a punishment station. There was another retired but active Brother with him in Limerick, whom Carey annoyed. One day they squabbled at table and Carey heard himself described in a loud voice as "the drone of the Congregation". There was silence in the room. Carey took a deep breath and quoted from '*King Lear*': "*You son and heir of a mongrel bitch!*" The young monks roared out laughing. The Provincial sent Hanlon, the flat-faced man to interview everyone in the refectory and decided that the two gave scandal, which was serious because the young monks were witnesses to all that happened. Those innocent lambs! Carey was exiled to the bogs of Letterfrack and the other was sent to Westland Row. Whoever in Booterstown decided where to send the two sinners, probably had a crooked sense of humour. The matter was handled in a silly manner.

I had a letter from Whisperer recording the arrival of Carey in Letterfrack. He wrote, "We have 'the drone of the Congregation' here. He travelled by train to Galway and hired a taxi to Letterfrack over fifty miles away. The taxi-man waited until our boss forked out the fare and he spent the rest of the evening spluttering at old Carey, that charmer, who gives as good a measure of straight talk as he receives. Carey told me that before he came to Baldoyle our boss wet the bed at home, and did not know how to use a knife and fork. What a fine gentleman Carey is, who never piddled in bed and could wield a knife and a fork at two years of age! One of the senior men here calls him a poisonous old reptile."

Tradition of Education

"Isn't it time," I asked Guilfoyle one afternoon, "that the Order should establish a house of studies where research work could be done on Education? After all, we have more money than we need, and why not invest it in research to benefit the Church and the Irish State? We owe them all something."

Guilfoyle thought for a moment.

"To tell the truth," said he, "I never thought of that before." He hesitated a while and smiled. "Can you imagine the old-timers who rule this Order throwing money into something like this? Except for Val Ryan, are there any who'd favour this? Of course, there's Meares, isn't there?"

I began to realise that probably there was no one with the mental competence in authority, who understood as these two did the importance of what I had in mind. How, Guilfoyle wished to know, how should this new house be organised.

"This should be first of all, a house of residence for our university students," I suggested. "Some postgraduate students should be sent there to study new notions of religious teaching, because no one else is doing it, and a study into language teaching should also be undertaken." Guilfoyle sighed as I added, "This is the backwater of Europe since the war and we must go outside Ireland for worthwhile ideas."

He listened but shrugged his shoulders.

Thus we lived in the midst of the Brothers' out-of-date attitudes, which were becoming irrelevant. No assessment of any kind was made, nor thought necessary, to ascertain what they should do in an age utterly different from the era when they were founded. Over the years no basic change ever took place. The Brothers had never left the Victorian Age mentally and were unaware of a new world forming itself after World War II, while its influential men wasted their energies squabbling about who should govern the Order. This led to victory for one side and then to a reversal, when Rome appointed Clancy as Pro-Superior-General. We now know that while they fought their own barren feuds, the Congregation was gradually drifting into the shadows but it was never apparent to any of them.

"Why," I often asked myself, "should I remain an Irish Christian Brother?"

I saw the sacrifice of normal urges as a waste of my life under such circumstances. It struck me that the Catholic Church taught that when a man married, he received a sacrament that is central to Christian living, but yet the Profession of vows was presented to us as superior to this sacrament. As monks we were urged to glory in our religious Profession as if it was superior to a sacrament, which it was not. When I had spoken at length over weeks to Guilfoyle about this, he finally smiled wearily.

"Why bother your head about all that? We're here 'to do and teach' according to our emblem, and not to be intellectuals. If we become irrelevant in spite of what we do, our Congregation won't survive."

This fatalistic answer surprised me.

"Why don't we emulate the Jesuits, who formulated Catholic education in the sixteenth and seventeenth centuries?" I asked him at this stage.

Guilfoyle simply said, "Let's allow our bosses to decide that for us. And anyway," he added, "the Roman authorities suppressed the Jesuits for some years. They educate their members with great thoroughness, and they were the only ones, who survived that suppression as a religious Order."

Yes, I thought to myself, but why should I sail on a ship on its way to becoming a wreck because it was neglecting what it was founded to achieve? Why should I sacrifice the life of a lay man for this destructive outcome?

Practical Teaching

We had to deal with the Primary School Inspectors, who came on official visits and on casual sorties. We regarded them as 'visitors'. They never worried us, but I discovered afterwards that sometimes Inspectors bullied young teachers in National Schools, many of whom lived in fear of them. They never tried to bully Christian Brothers because we dressed like the ruling class of free Ireland, the Catholic priests. The Inspectors were recruited from the ranks of National Teachers. I remember once asking a young man why he became an Inspector.

"Every morning I cycled to my school half a mile away and often in the rain. One day I thought, 'Must I do this for the rest of my life?' Then I knew that I must get a Degree and become an Inspector."

That year a School Inspector called to assess me for the National Teacher's Diploma. In the first two years after leaving the college the teaching of National Teachers was inspected, but we Brothers faced them in our sixth and seventh years because we did not complete the full training college course earlier. Obviously the children had to be taught well and regularly, but there was more to do. A yearly scheme of teaching was drawn up, teaching notes were written each weekend and a progress report kept. The Inspector sent written notice of his visit and spent the day examining the children, which was not done in Secondary Schools. We Primary Schools teachers were treated by the Department of Education as the skivvies of the teaching profession. As Brothers we knew that we were the heirs of those who pioneered Catholic Elementary Education in urban areas, and the National Teachers did this in the rural schools and in small towns and villages. That has never been acknowledged as it should have been.

The Last Act

In the month of May I asked my brother to give the prepared letter to our father to inform him that I was leaving. From my father I expected Olympian anger but he replied stating that my mother and he completely agreed with me. He asked whether I needed money until I had secured a teaching post. I was very surprised, I must admit. My mother wrote to me every month since 1942 except during the Novitiate year and I was surprised when she stopped, knowing that I was leaving. She never wrote to me until long after I left, and when I had no letters to acknowledge, I never wrote to her. The news shocked her. I heard she had said that she hoped I did not "hang about the place" when I left, which ex-clerical students did. She forgot that I did not need to seek refuge at home, but was a professional teacher who could earn a salary. I expected my mother to understand what I was doing, but she did not. Years later I realised that I should have hinted to her that I was unsettled. Just as a priest in Ireland was "his mother's priest", I was filling that role as a Brother – but I learned too late, what I knew in theory.

As the months went on, I felt ill at ease and suffered from vague illnesses, which might be described as psychosomatic. I seldom arose for morning prayers. In May the Superior, Andy, called me into his room for what he said were 'a few words'.

"I have to remind you," he began, "that you are due to take final vows in August and you know that we senior men will be writing about your suitability." He appeared embarrassed as he continued, "What I must remind you is that you should attend morning prayers and meditation from now on. If you do not, I and the other seniors will have to report it, and you know what the consequences will be."

I began to realise that I had never even hinted my intentions to him before this day, and neither did the Provincial in Booterstown know what I planned since Christmas or even before it. So I blurted out what I intended doing.

"I'm sorry that I didn't tell you: I have no intention of taking vows."

As I spoke to him I saw a look of dismay in his face.

"I never knew a thing!" he muttered. "I'm sorry to hear this but it's your life after all, I suppose, and I wish you the best for the future."

And that was the end of the 'few words'. I felt sorry that I hurt him needlessly.

I went to Bill's bedroom. He was surprised to see me walk in without knocking at the door, because we felt strongly about our privacy in our bedrooms. Bill started thanking me with mock pomposity about the whiskey, which I gave him. I told him that I was leaving the Order. He stopped talking but then – much moved – he took me by the hand.

"Here's wishing you all the best when you leave!" he said. "I hope that Andy treats you right, when you're going. I suppose you'll go on teaching, will you?"

"Of course!"

"If you want a reference, I'll give you one. Remember now," Bill went on, "it's no disgrace to leave – because some mothers consider it a crime if their sons do. Don't ever let that bother you but go your own way."

Bill was often rude to people but there was a gentleman hidden in him somewhere.

I never said a word about the matter to Guilfoyle but decided to tell Galileo. When he was not gadding about town or holding court in the backroom of Hegarty's house, he spent his time painting in his classroom. I went in there after speaking to Bill and Andy, and noticed that he was preparing a palette.

"Will you recommend me for final vows," I asked, "when you're asked for your opinions about my fitness?"

He laughed and said, "Well, I will but amn't I an odd person to be recommending anyone? Am I anyone's notion of a good monk?"

I was touched by his frankness.

"Well now," I said, "Let me tell you, I won't need any recommendation. I might as well tell you straight that I'm leaving."

He stopped what he was doing and muttered, "Are you now?" There was a slight pause as he absorbed what I told him and added, "I wish you the very best whenever you go."

I pursued him with the question, "Aren't you sorry now that you did not go when you had the chance at my age?"

The question startled him and he shrugged his shoulders, laid down the canvas and began fiddling with the palette. He never replied to me. It was clear that I embarrassed him, so I went quickly from the room.

A few days later I heard that an ex-pupil of mine from Westland Row was a postulant in Baldoyle, whom I encouraged to join the Brothers. I recalled the words in Paul in an epistle, "Having preached to others, I myself have become a castaway!"

Preparing to Go

I began to consider my future. First of all, I must secure a teaching position. I was due to leave about ten days before 15th August but if I left on the last day of June, I might secure a post for the fortnight before the holidays and collect holiday salary. I needed to be financially independent, because I could not return home, and I was not likely to receive any worthwhile money from Andy when I left. I thought that I might receive leave of absence from Rome for the six weeks if I requested it, though I never heard of this being done in these circumstances.

There was no difficulty. A week before I left, I received leave of absence from the Vatican through Val Ryan, and Andy received a copy for the house files. I applied too late for a teacher's post for 1st July, so I decided to stay at an aunt's house near Cappoquin. I needed to have references as a teacher. Andy gave me one but I was surprised when the Provincial and the Vicar General sent me farewell letters, which were so laudatory that I blushed and I used them as references later.

I was lonely to be leaving my companions, but our objectives in life were diverging so significantly and I should have to go eventually. It was better to do it now. Five days before I left, I overheard Andy talking about some monk who had just walked out without leave.

"Oh, that man is crazy," he said. "Why did he do it? He shouldn't have been admitted to final vows!"

Later on Bill asked me, "You must know that crazy man, who was in Letterfrack?!"

"Oh, don't say it's Whisperer, is it?" I muttered.

"That man walked out without even a permit or a by-your-leave," Bill said simply. I was astonished at first, but disappointed that he had not told me that he was going. Little did I think that Whisperer might leave so dramatically before I did, but I should have guessed he might do so. A few days later I had a short note from him:

"Dear friend," it began, "you may have heard that I have fled the coop. I have no job and am basking in the warmth of parental domesticity. My father laughed when I arrived and my mother said, 'It's about time you left that lot!' All the best to you when you are granted gaol release and just indict some lines of prose to me. You are discharging yourself according to the rules; I acted the maverick, which suits my kind of spirit."

I knew what happened in such cases. The 'apostate religious', as Canon Law described him, was ordered to return. If he did so, he was granted a dispensation but had to spend a night in Marino, a few hours in some room before leaving. I heard that Whisperer arrived in Marino at about midnight three years later, spent the night in a room and left at five in the morning with his dispensation in his pocket.

The evening before I left, we heard that someone was coming by train to replace me. Andy sent a taxi for him and after tea we went out to await the newcomer. When he arrived, I saw it was Paul, who was in the Marino group after me. Everyone shook hands with him and welcomed him. When I approached him, he turned his back on me and made me feel like a deserter. The others smiled and Bill whispered, "What an almighty bloody clown he is!"

The next morning Andy and I travelled by bus to Limerick. Before we left the monastery, he handed me £20 note.

"This is what I've been ordered to give you." He took out another £20 and said, "And this is from myself!"

I heard later that a National Teacher's basic salary for a month had risen to £25 then. I pocketed the money with a brief word of thanks.

Later

I came to Limerick dressed as a Christian Brother and now reverted to being Patrick Power as my parents named me at birth. I walked up William Street to the railway station to take a train for Mallow Junction and travel to my aunt's house outside Cappoquin, my refuge from family embarrassment, where I could lie low for a while.

This was my day of freedom but I was completely unprepared for it. I was unable to handle money and also did not know how to act in a hotel or how to buy clothes, nor did I know what to do if I went to a pub for a drink. Some of my fellow Christian Brothers did not have these drawbacks, but I had them because I had kept the rules of the Order, which socially disabled me over the previous eleven years.

As I went along William Street towards the railway station I noticed that no one saluted me. It struck me at last that I did not wear a Roman collar, which attracted salutes from people in these days. As Flannery might express it, I was now an ordinary Joe Soap.

The train brought me to Limerick Junction and here I took another one for Mallow. I felt completely alone as I stood on the train platform, where I boarded yet another train for Cappoquin. In Mallow I was alone for more than an hour because it did not strike me to go for a cup of tea or a drink or any kind of food.

Ten days after leaving, I secured a position as Principal Teacher in a hillside school on the border between Counties Limerick and Cork. It was a two-teacher school, different from anywhere that I had served or experienced up to that time. I taught for one day before the summer holidays began – this qualified me for holiday pay. I did not receive a penny until 10th October – after I returned in September and taught more than a full month there. The Department of Education acted this way towards people like me in case I pocketed the holiday money and did not hold my position after the holidays.

Some three weeks after leaving I had a letter from Whisperer, who informed me that he was teaching also. He intended doing this to provide himself with money, but was leaving the classroom as soon as possible.

"The blackboard and clouds of chalk dust," as he put it, "are not for me anymore!"

I was formally a member of the Irish Christian Brothers until 15th August. On the morning of that day I met my successor in Tipperary, Paul, but he was not in clerical clothes on the streets of Cappoquin.

"Paul," I asked, "where's the uniform?"

He replied bitterly that he had been rejected for final vows. I enjoyed this enormously. He then began to blame a monk for his dismissal.

"That Cullen fellow reported that I was difficult to live with! I appealed to the Vicar-General, Val Ryan, and when we met, he angered me so much that I lost my temper. I shouted that Cullen was a hound and a blackguard to tell the truth, and never a word of a lie. Val looked at me in that sneaky way that he has and said nothing.

"When I finished, Val said 'I believe that you have not made a case against your dismissal. I regret to tell you that you must go.'

"I was shocked. How could they do this to a loyal member of the Order? I can't understand it all. An appeal did I say? I was tried in Val's kangaroo court!"

Val had to dismiss him because Paul was, as the regulations called his type, 'of a quarrelsome and litigious disposition and a person not amenable to religious control'. He proved this by his attitude when he claimed that his dismissal was not fair. He was, therefore, considered unfit to take final vows. I was amused to note that he had forgotten how he treated me that evening when he came to Tipperary. As I consoled him, I laughed to myself at his lack of any sense of humour.

"Remember now, Paul," I advised him, "telling the truth is a bad business and you should always avoid it when [the truth] is inconvenient!"

He never noticed the sarcasm of my remark. I must say that Cullen was a strict old-timer but was fair to everyone that he met. To hear Cullen described as 'a hound' and 'a blackguard' must have impressed Val badly, because he was not either of these.

Former Companions and Acquaintances

O'Neill lived a healthy and normal life after being discharged from the sanatorium, and he taught full time without a relapse until his sixties. I was very surprised when I read in a newspaper one Sunday morning that he had died suddenly at a Co. Meath monastery in the 1990s. He died of cardiac failure.

Our Superior in Bray, Pop Lawlor, who founded the house and school in Argentina, was in Buenos Aires during the *coup d'état* of 1955, which toppled General Perón from power. Pop returned home afterwards a very sick man suffering, as I heard, from a rare tropical disease. He died some years later, when he had reached his sixties. I can recall the shock that swept over me as I read his death notice in the newspaper.

I never heard any more about Tony since those days – he and his wife probably stayed in England. He was one man whom I cannot forget although I have never met him since that time.

I heard that some years after Austin went to Dublin from Tipperary he suddenly left and married, after being Superior in the Training College at St Joseph's. I was amazed at the news. I never heard any details, such as how he met his wife or if he left with a dispensation from vows, or if he walked out as 'an apostate religious'.

In 1973 I met a Brother who had been with me in Marino. It was 20th August and I asked him how many had been finally professed on 15th August.

"Oh," he said, "we had only one this year."

I could not help recalling to him that the year that I left, I was the only one of the profession group of about forty who left voluntarily. The twelve others who left had been rejected for vows and were 'dismissed' as the phrase was.

"If all of them came back now," said he, "and even if we could persuade you to come, we'd welcome all of you with open arms. The top men never appreciated the qualities of people that they were stupid enough to fire."

There were well over 1,500 members of the Order in Ireland in the 1950s, but there were only a few hundred in 2000AD all mostly over fifty years of age.

We stood there on the street in Clonmel talking.

"I still cannot understand," I said, "why twelve of the thirteen men in 1953 were rejected. Didn't they include men like Morrison, and Paul the pianist? Weren't they all talented and worthwhile just as so many others were?"

My informant agreed that they were.

"Of course," he added, "young men were expendable in these times. There were plenty of them available but still – to fire that number of them was a shocking waste."

I never heard any satisfactory explanation for these dismissals but it should be said that they were not unique in those times.

Since the 1980s most Christian Brothers' schools have been taken into the care of laymen, and many monasteries were closed because few people joined. The recruiting of young lads of fourteen, which proved to be so injudicious, was discontinued after the Vatican Council (from 1966). Depriving young lads of a normal life in their early teenage years had not worked to any good conclusion. The idea that it was good to take them young was expressed in a saying about the use of alcohol, which I found in an old catechism: 'They will never long for what they have never known.' Oh, I wonder! You may baulk, delay and frustrate the urges of Nature but these urges will out eventually.

How Others Fared

Cal, teacher of Mathematics in Baldoyle, remained hale and hearty until his death in old age. On his last birthday he went swimming near Sutton in calm summer weather, but his body was discovered that afternoon edging out to sea on a gentle summer tide. I do not know when and where his bully-boy brother Colman died, and I was never interested in what happened to him.

Meares suffered from narcolepsy and spent his final years in St Patrick's, Baldoyle, where I visited him.

"It is interesting," said he, "how the Vatican Council did so much good for the Church and relieved people of some silly notions. Can we forget the poor Brother who attended twenty Masses in the morning in Kilkee expecting to accumulate grace twenty-fold from them like a greedy shopkeeper? Oh, the simplicity of some errors!"

He was alert for nearly half an hour and then suddenly sunk into deep slumber and I left him quietly. He was the only sick monk that I ever visited after I had left.

Galileo quitted the Order in his late forties and married, as I heard, but I had no further news of him. I think he went home to Donegal and was one of the few men from that part of Ireland in the Christian Brothers, whom I knew or of whom I heard.

For three years after we left, I had regular correspondence with Whisperer. He had gone to England, where he studied while he held a teaching position until he became a qualified chartered accountant. I heard less and less of him as our letters became fewer, when we were being absorbed into our different backgrounds. We simply ceased to exist for one another. This other living form of me began to fade from daily reality and we lost contact. I was deeply shocked, when I heard in 1985 that he died from cancer in Wales. He was now definitely gone from me forever.

Patrick Muldowney, one of the most intelligent men that I ever met, taught in Secondary Schools until he retired and died at St Patrick's, Baldoyle. I remember this brilliant man as someone whose talents were misdirected and wasted by the Christian Brothers, and there were some others like him.

As for me, I began teaching as soon as I could find a position, ten days after leaving Tipperary town. This was the job I was trained for, this was my calling in life and it remained that way until I retired.

There were limits as to where former members of the Irish Christian Brothers might teach. To return to teach where we served as monks was discouraged. We were blocked where our former lords and masters could do so, and that was in urban areas in Ireland. I heard that some brethren regarded us as letting them down. Need I say that we were barred from teaching in Christian Brothers' schools above all?

In my new life as a teacher my bosses were the local parish priests. Although I found some to be good Christian men, very many were not. They seemed to regard teachers as rivals or something of that nature, especially those who were former Brothers.

I knew that the Brothers' chief men never allowed injustice towards anyone to go unresolved. Among the Catholic clergy it was often otherwise, and some parish priests seemed to do as they liked and were immune from their bishops' intervention. I heard that this had to do with the parish priests' 'apostolic succession' from the apostles. I wondered sometimes did some inherit it from Judas.

A Final Leave Taking

A meeting of members and former members of the Christian Brothers took place in Belfield on 2nd August 1994, the first and last time that such an assembly was held. Some months beforehand all former members of the Brothers were invited to this reunion with those who had stayed. A small number accepted this and afterwards I heard that some Brothers refused to attend this meeting, where we were recognised at last as friends and colleagues and not as traitors or the like.

When we arrived at Belfield, we all met informally in a great hall. I noticed that most of my contemporaries no longer dressed as we had done but were attired in non-religious dress, rather tastelessly in some cases. Many of these Christian Brothers did not seem to know how to dress correctly as lay people.

We attended a Mass that afternoon, which lasted three hours. I was amazed that not one of the former Brothers, who had been ordained priests after they left, was asked to celebrate this Mass, but a priest of the Holy Ghost Fathers did so. Just imagine, one of that priestly Order who tried to poach us in Bray was given this honour, and our priestly ex-members who were there, ignored as if they were not real priests.

"Will anything change?" I thought. I was disgusted by this attitude to our own.

I should not have forgotten to mention one Brother who stayed in the Congregation until he retired from teaching. A parish priest with more ambition to recruit priests than to exercise common sense then persuaded him to become a priest. As a priest he was unhappy and treated badly by his new young colleagues from the farming and business classes in the diocese. He was seen as a second class priest and 'not one of us', but a mere former Christian Brother.

I should have been bored and restless at the three hours spent at this Mass, but I was not. I perceived among the monks a sense of spirituality and even of mysticism, which I did not remember from the days when I was one of them. Was it something that I missed when I was with them, or the result of what they endured over the years from their enemies?

At the Offertory seven people addressed us. One was a priest, formerly a Brother, another was still a Brother, three were former Brothers and finally two were former Brothers' wives. The monk spoke of his change of attitude towards us. He had seen us as having "let the Order down by leaving," he said, but regarded us now as newly respectable Christian human beings.

"Oh!" I thought to myself. "How very nice of you indeed! You're being Christian, though you rejected me years ago as a person because I dared to think for myself and saved you bother, when I could have plagued you with thoughts and ideas."

As I recorded it in my diary at the time, this Mass was "a huge outpouring of emotion from deep spirituality," and no longer from the cold rock of discipline, as it had been in the common experience of all of us as one of them in my time.

We had dinner in the restaurant afterwards. As we sat at table, the conversation turned to hurling and football. The staple subjects of conversation among the Brothers were still the same since I had left them forty years before. At least this much had not changed, I thought.

After the lengthy time in the dining hall I decided to go to bed. I felt exhausted and wondered what ailed my left foot. Philip, whom I had cared for during my last year in Tipperary town, accompanied me although we were in different houses.

When I reached my room, I began to shiver and decided to have a hot shower but then I began sweating. The alternate sweating and shivering continued until I calmed a little and slept for a few hours. When I awoke in the morning, I was no longer lame and felt fine. What on earth had happened to me and why did it happen?

I was delighted to meet Brendan Donovan and John Campion during that summer meeting at Belfield. Both of them looked much the same as they did in 1943-52. Although each was now over eighty years of age, nevertheless it was amazing how spruce they looked after all that time. These two men and a few more were smartly turned out in the old clerical dress, and were in complete contrast to many of the younger ones.

I had breakfast with Brendan and Johnny before I left. I had forgotten about Johnny's penchant for gossip, when he leaned towards me.

"The young priests," he half-whispered, "are not like their older colleagues."

He paused a little for effect.

"Did you hear," he continued, "about the priest in your diocese, who left for a month's holiday last year without making any arrangements for a priest to visit the sick and dying?"

I had not.

"Well, I can assure you that this happened," he said. "What on earth are these modern priests coming to at all? That could never have happened in the olden days."

Alas! Neither of these two men had discovered the secret of immortality and they died a few years later. As I spoke with both of them, I never felt as if we had been separated for over forty years. What they represented was true Christianity.

The Brothers were founding prayer groups and recruiting former members to join them. All those monks, who in former days avoided us as if we were lepers and traitors, needed us when their Congregation was facing extinction. I refused to join any of them.

"I couldn't do that!" I said to one man. "Why do you think I left you? Couldn't we meet to socialise together or isn't that enough?" Then I added as an afterthought, "Couldn't we meet and celebrate by eating bread and drinking wine, but with no talk of someone who faced the contemporary gallows in Jerusalem?"

"You're the same rebel that you always were!" he said, smiling.

It struck me that socialising might lead to an exchange of opinions, but the recitation of prayer formulae was quite safe. The dangerous practice of thinking for oneself can be avoided in that kind of group. Oh, yes! I had enough of that, I told myself.

I left next morning very happy about one aspect of my life. I was as certain as anyone could be that I had done the right thing to leave the

Congregation, and I had not wasted my life when I moved away from them in 1953.

I met one former monk who still dressed in a black suit and wore a black hat, which gave me the feeling that he regretted ever leaving.

"Are you married?" I asked him.

"I am!" said he.

"Oh," thought I to myself, "Just pity his wife! That woman married an unrepentant Christian Brother!"

What did I miss, when I left in 1953? I missed the great all-enveloping cloak that we wore in winter and often during morning prayers in spring and autumn. I also missed the singsongs by the seaside during the holidays.

For about seven years afterwards I had the same recurring nightmare, when I felt myself locked within the junior Brother's bedroom in Tipperary over the hall door, screaming for release. After that I found relief from this nightmare when I did university studies, which finally freed my mind, and I had some books published.

Those Christian Brothers who are still in the Congregation have to live with the frequent public criticism, which is often their lot in modern Ireland. It is so odd to recall that some of those remaining are now standing alone, overwhelmed at times by the accusations poured over them from television, radio and some newspapers.

Oh, yes! Some of them had resented those of us who left, as if we betrayed them – but not any more. Scripture says somewhere in the Psalms:

"Those that drink wine have made me their song."

We, who left them, must admit that we are invisibly bound to them. I remember a conversation with another former member when I first left.

"Don't ever try to explain to anyone what it was like to be a monk," he said. "Not one person apart from us will ever be able to understand anything that you have to say about your experiences!"

I wonder was he right?